URBAN GOVERNANCE IN INDIA

URBAN GOVERNANCE IN INDIA

C. Nagaraja Rao

KALPAZ

ISBN: 978-93-5128-183-2

Price: ₹ 890

First Published, 2016

Published by

Kalpaz Publications
C-30, Satyawati Nagar,
Delhi – 110052
E-mail: kalpaz@hotmail.com
Ph.: 9212142040

Printed at: G. Print Process, Delhi

Cataloging in Publication Data—DK
Courtesy: D.K. Agencies (P) Ltd. <docinfo@dkagencies.com>

Nagaraja Rao, C., 1954- author.
Urban governance in India / C. Nagaraja Rao.
pages cm
Includes bibliographical references.
ISBN 9789351281740

1. Municipal government—India. 2. Urbanisation—India. 3. Urban policy—India. 4. Infrastructure (Economics)—India. I. Title.

JS7011.N34 2016 DDC 320.850954 23

Dedicated to my parents

Chaganti (Ryali) Janaki
Chaganti Mrutyumjaya Sarma

Contents

Acknowledgement

It is my pleasure and privilege to place on record with grateful thanks the invaluable support and inspiration I received from Dr Prasanna Kumar Mohanty, I.A.S. (Retd), former Chief Secretary to Government of Andhra Pradesh, Hyderabad, in updating the doctoral thesis and for his valuable Preface to my book. I am thankful to Mr. G. Sai Prasad, I.A.S., Principal Secretary to Government of A.P. for encouraging me to take up this study.

I acknowledge with grateful thanks the invaluable guidance, support and constructive comments of Dr M.A. Hussain, my Research Supervisor and Professor, Department of Political Science & Public Administration, S.V. University, Tirupati, without which the dissertation would not have been possible. I am equally grateful to Mr D.V. Rao, Consultant, Centre for Good Governance, Hyderabad for editing the proof.

I express my profound sense of gratitude to the following academics for their cooperation and valuable suggestions:

Professor Ivaturi Ramabrahmam, Central University, Hyderabad

Professor G. Gurappa Naidu, S.V. University, Tirupati.

Professor C.Venkata Subba Reddy, S.V. University, Tirupati

Professor V.C. M. Rao, S.V. University, Tirupati

Professor B. Krishna Prasad, Andhra University, Visakhapatnam

Professor Bhupati Rau, Director, RCUES, Osmania University, Hyderabad.

Professor U.B. Singh, Director, RCUES, Lucknow University, Lucknow

I sincerely thank Mr Clay Wirt, President, International City Managers' Association, New York, U.S.A. for his useful correspondence which enlightened me on certain important issues relating to urban life, Mrs Cynthia Seelhammer, Town Manager and Mr Tom Condit, Town Engineer, Queencreek, State of Arizona, U.S.A. for providing valuable information on funding of urban services in Queen Creek.

I am grateful to the authorities of the following institutions and libraries for having kindly permitted me to collect material from the respective institutions and libraries during the course of my research work:

- S.V. University Library, Tirupati.
- Regional Centres for Urban and Environmental Sciences, Osmania University, Hyderabad and Luknow University, Luknow.
- University of Hyderabad, Hyderabad.
- Office of the Mission for Elimination of Poverty in Municipal Areas, Hyderabad.
- Human Settlement Management Institute, HUDCO House, Lodhi Road, New Delhi.

I am thankful to Mr Mohammad Humayun for typing the thesis with utmost care and Mr Mohammad Iqbal Hussain for his role throughout the preparation of the dissertation. Finally I am thankful to my publishers for their unfailing cooperation.

Hyderabad-500032, **C. Nagaraja Rao**

Date: November 9, 2015

Preface

Urban growth in India during the last few decades has posed several new challenges to policy-makers, planners and civic administrators. While coping with the concentration of large numbers in cities, the urban local bodies (ULBs)must ensure that the positive effects of urbanisation are not overshadowed by its negative consequences. Cities throughout the world have driven growth and structural transformation during their periods of urban transition; the Indian story is no different. Contributing 62-63 per cent of GDP, Indian cities are expected to increase their contribution to 75 per cent of GDP in the next two decades. However, economic growth in cities is accompanied by many critical problems such as over-crowding, shortage of housing and basic civic amenities, pollution, congestion, environmental degradation, slums, poverty, violence, crime and social unrest. Decades of implementation of programmes of integrated development in rural areas have not been able to stop rural poverty-push and urban prosperity-pull migration to cities. In the absence of proper policies by cities to accommodate migrants and the urban poor, the result has been the mushrooming of slums. Even posh localities in certain metropolitan cities wear a squalid look due to the haphazard growth of informal settlements around them. Until the launch of national urban missions in recent years, urban areas in India were not paid the attention they deserved, keeping in view their contribution to GDP.

The increase in urban population from 286 million in 2001 to 377 million in 2011, along with increase in the number of cities and towns from 5,161 to 7,935 over the same period, has created a tremendous pressure on urban infrastructure. The existing systems are crumbling due to decades of under-investment and neglect. This is associated with weak urban planning, financing and governance. As a result, essential services like drinking water supply, sewerage, drainage, solid waste management, street lighting, public transport, etc. are under severe strain. The urban poor and marginalised sections of the urban society suffer the most in the present state of urban affairs.They are required to meet huge coping costs, including those relating to adverse health consequences due to non-provision of "lifeline" services by authorities. Apart from meeting the backlog and current needs, Indian cities must position themselves to address the growth needs of urbanisation with adequate attention paid to problems of slums and urbanisation of poverty associated with migration and annexation of rural areas to cities. These problems are gigantic as it is projected that India's urban population will increase from 377 million in 2011 to 814 million in 2050.

Inclusive and sustainable development of cities is a huge challenge that calls for concerted reforms in the way Indian cities are governed. Good urban governance is the key to the efficient and effective delivery of civic services to the masses. Inclusion does not occur automatically in the process of economic growth; deliberate policies are required on the part of central, state and local governments to address the problems of the slum-dwellers and the urban poor, including women, children, differently-abled and vulnerable occupational groups like street vendors. Sustainability calls for balancing the interests of the present and future generations, especially with regard the use of scarce environmental resources. Sustainable development is a continuous process that aims at meeting the needs and aspirations of the people, taking into account their social, cultural, political and economic contexts and constraints. It calls for the empowerment of the people with improved and equitable access to resources and services.The urban local bodies have to aim at providing adequate shelter and basic minimum amenities to all the urban residents, especially the poor with focus on land tenure, affordable housing, water, sanitation, education, health, social security and livelihoods development.

Though there are several books written on urban governance, most of them have dealt with a few particular aspects. However, the present book tries to address all key urbanisation and urban governance-related issues comprehensively, with municipalities placed at the centre of discussion. It covers varied aspects of urban governance such as organisation of municipal government; powers, functions and responsibilities of ULBs in the changing urban scenario; interactions between deliberative and executive wings in municipalities; urban finance and resource mobilisation; issues of urban infrastructure; accountability, transparency and grievances redressal in the delivery of civic services; urban poverty alleviation; and training for capacity building. This volume is expected to not only meet the needs of undergraduate and post graduate students of universities that have included Urban Governance as part of Public Administration or Public Policy programmes but also serve as a guide to municipal functionaries in the country in their day-to-day functioning.

The views presented in this book draw from the doctoral thesis and practical experiences of the author who held several important offices in the Department of Municipal Administration and Urban Development, Government of Andhra Pradesh. The author has combined practical experiences with good theoretical understanding on urban issues, and thereby attempted to contribute to the pool of policy-relevant knowledge to address the urban problems faced by the country. Besides dealing with the various aspects of urban governance the author rightly stresses the need for the Governments at all levels - Central and State and Local- to recognise the importance of the urban sector for the economy and to plan cities and towns in such a way that urban areas effectively discharge their role as locomotive of economic growth and socio-economic transformation. Cities must occupy a central place in the strategy of development of the country in view of the multiplier effects they generate for growth. The author rightly suggests that governments at various levels should partner in the implementation of urban infrastructure development plans with focus on sustainable outcomes and enhancement of services to the urbanites, especially the poor and the slum dwellers.

Capacity building and reforms in urban governance are important aspects of urban governance as the effective preparation and implementation of urban infrastructure development plans and projects are not possible without adequate capacity and skills at the local government level. Unless urban local governments are geared up to boldly face the colossal challenges of urbanisation, with state-of-the-art skills, tools, techniques and capacity for people-centric programmes founded on the principles good governance, the positive contribution of Urban India to the country's socio-economic progress cannot be sustained. Reforms in governance must go hand in hand with the implementation of urban infrastructure projects. Transparency, accountability, participation and responsiveness in service delivery are key criteria that need to be integrated to all policies, plans and programmes concerning cities. The ULBs will need to concentrate on meticulous urban planning, development of core infrastructure to meet the backlog, current and growth needs of urbanisation, mobilisation of resources and delivery of good governance. The present volume running through 11 chapters suggests measures to address these issues. I hope this book will be of value to students, researchers, teachers, planners, policy-makers, administrators and the general readers.

Dr. P. K. Mohanty

Formerly Chief Secretary to Government of Andhra Pradesh and Mission Director, Jawaharlal Nehru National Urban Renewal Mission

Abbreviations

A.P. : Andhra Pradesh
A.P.M.Act : Andhra Pradesh Municipalities Act
ADS : Area Development Society
AIF : American Indian Foundation
AMRUT : Atal Mission for Rejuvenation and Urban Transformation and Medium Towns
APURMS : Andhra Pradesh Urban Reforms and Municipal Services
APUSP : Andhra Pradesh Urban Services for the Poor
BPL : Below Poverty Line
CAA : Constitution Amendment Act
CBO : Community Based Organisation
CDP : City Development Plan
CDS : Community Development Society
CEA : Chief Executive Authority
CENA : Capacity Enhancement Needs Assessment
CGGH : Centre for Good Governance, Hyderabad
CHV : Community Health Volunteer
CIAL : Cochin International Airport Authority
CPHEO : Central Public Health Engineering Organisation
D.P.H. : Diploma in Public Health
DFID : Department for International Development
DPC : District Planning Committee
DRF : Dr Reddy Foundation
DWCUA : Development of Women and Children in Urban Areas
EGCIP : Expert Group on Commercialisation of Infrastructure

EMI : Equated Monthly Instalment
GHMC : Greater Hyderabad Municipal Corporation
HPEC : High Powered Expert Committee
HUDCO : Housing and Urban Development Corporation
I.A.S. : Indian Administrative Service
IDSMT : Integrated Development for Small and Medium Towns
IHSDP : Integrated Housing and Slum Development Programme
IIFC : Indian Infrastructure Finance Corporation
IIR : Indian Infrastructure Report
IKP : Indira Kranti Padham
IUDP : Integrated Urban Development Programme
JNNURM : Jawaharlal Nehru National Urban Renewal Mission
LIC : Life Insurance Corporation of India
MAPPR : Municipal Action Plan for Poverty Reduction
MCP : Metropolitan Planning Committee
MDG : Millennium Development Goals
MEPMA : Mission for Eradication of Poverty in Municipal Areas
MGI : McKinsey Global Institute
MSW : Municipal Solid Waste
NABARD : National Bank for Reconstruction and Development
NAC : National Academy of Construction
NCEUS : National Commission for Enterprises in the Unorganised Sector
NHC : Neighbourhood Committee
NHG : Neighbourhood Group
NIUM : National Institute of Urban Management
NSDP : National Slum Development Scheme
NSS : National Sample Survey
NSSO : National Sample Survey Organisation
O&M : Operation and Maintenance
PMS : Performance Management System
PMSDIP : Public Management and Service Delivery Improvement Projects

RCA	: Rapid City Assessment
RITES	: Rail India Technical and Economical Services
RTI	: Right to Information
SHG	: Self Help Group
SJSRY	: Swarna Jayanti Shahari Rozgar Yojana
SSA	: Sarva Siksha Abhiyan
T&C	: Thrift and Credit
UCD	: Urban Community Development
UDA	: Urban Development Authority
UIDSSMT	: Urban Infrastructure Development Scheme for Small
ULB	: Urban Local Body
ULG	: Urban Local Government
UN	: United Nations
UPA	: Urban Poverty Alleviation
UPADHI	: Urban Programme for Advancement of Household Income
USEP	: Urban Self Employment Programme
UWEP	: Urban Wage Employment Programme

1

Introduction

Urban Governance has come to be recognised as a separate intellectual discipline, an important social science of study not only in view of the quick pace of urbanisation but also because of the special impetus that urban India needs to be given in the fast changing urban scenario. Urban governance which was a part of public administration has become a specialisation of its own and needs a special treatment, encompassing all issues relating to urban administration: management of urban development like urban crisis, accelerated urbanisation, the ideologies of the environment, the intervention of the state, urban planning, popular revolts, urban politics, urban infrastructure, growth of unorganised sector in urban areas etc. This necessitates the establishment of an efficient, effective and accountable urban local administration in the country.

The Constitution (74th Amendment) Act, 1992 accords the status of a "third tier government" to municipalities and prescribes an institutional framework for good urban governance. Though the Constitution (74th Amendment) Act, 1992 aimed at widening the functional arena of the ULGs by transferring 18 subjects as belonging to their exclusive domain and guaranteeing their fiscal health, the practical result is not much and effective as expected. After the amendment has come into force, several state legislatures have incorporated these provisions in their respective local government acts but could not implement democratic decentralisation and improved governance at local level that ensure inclusive development and better delivery of civic service.

Importance of Urban Governance

The importance of urban local governance is due to its proximity to the people and their problems. Urban areas have the capacity to shape and reshape the economy of the country through markets, jobs, transplants, technology, and capital, through which ULGs can strive to build a self-generating economy to keep pace with growing requirements of finance. Hence, urban governance needs a special focus and a firm place in the national agenda.

Urban population has touched 35 per cent of India's total population as per the last census (2011). This figure is likely to touch 50 per cent in another two decades. Hence, urban administration is now concerned with two fifths of the country's population. Administration in the modern sense is not merely maintenance of law and order and revenue administration but it has a wider meaning. To describe it simply, administration is the regulation of life in modern society, ensuring civic welfare by providing all necessities to the city dwellers to their best satisfaction. Governance in the modern sense requires that the initiatives and potential of all sections of society are allowed to fructify and maximise without any hindrance. It should provide a strong relationship between the governors and the governed. Citizen is the most important subject for good governance.

The passage of Indian economy from agriculture to industry has led to large scale rural-urban migration in search of better living conditions, employment, education, medical facilities etc. This has resulted in villages becoming towns, and towns becoming cities during the last two decades. This fact discloses the importance of urban administration and the special attention it needs on par with rural administration. The one time popular adage that "India lives in its villages" is now no longer valid in the changed national scenario. India has now begun to live in its towns and cities only, as indicated by the enormous growth of urban population. Added to it, the inclusion of several subjects like welfare, traffic management, health, education, poverty alleviation, employment, security measures etc. in urban administration, underlines the importance of urban local governance.

Urban Local Governments (ULGs) in the past were mere conservancy boards but in the modern context they are entrusted with specific responsibilities to fulfil, exclusive of the control or supervision of the state government or central government. The ULGs in modern sense are not merely providers of services but facilitators and catalysts of growth and development. Since urban areas are the engines of economic growth, ULGs should exploit the potential to the fullest extent and the opportunities created by global trends. In the context of the Constitution (74th) Amendment Act, 1992, Urban Local Governments are expected to function as full-fledged Local Self-Government units, which are the foundations of democracy, providing for citizens' participation in decision-making. "There must be a felt-need for public safety, health and willingness to organise collective efforts to achieve civic services required for a healthy and bright life."[1]

According to W.E. Jackson 'Local Governance' implies that it is concerned with localities. The term further implies "some jurisdiction or activity of public nature, it implies also the existence of authorities empowered to exercise that jurisdiction and activity."[2] A Local government in the modern sense can be defined as the "administration of a locality by a body representing local inhabitants, possessing a fairly large amount of autonomy, raising at least a part of its revenue through local taxation and spending its income on services which are regarded as local and, therefore, distinct from state and central services."[3] "Local Government is a public organisation" authorised to decide and administer a large range of public policies within a relatively small territory…"Health, happiness and progress towards ideal goodness depend on the efficiency of local administration."[4] The essential attributes of local governance, according to S.R. Maheswari are: its statutory status, its power to raise finance by taxation in the area under its jurisdiction; participation of the local community in it in decision-making in specified subjects and their administration; the freedom to act independently of central control and its general purpose in contrast to single purpose character.[5]

Lord Ripon, the founding father of the ULG devised the concept of municipal authorities as units of self-government. His resolution of 18th May 1882 dealt with the constitution of local bodies, their functions, finances and powers and laid the foundation of local self-government in India.[6] The structure of ULGs in India by and large have remained the same since then, but the number of urban areas and their problems increased from year to year and have become even more complex.

Governance at the grass-roots level is instrumental to promote people's participation which is essential for decentralised planning.[7] People's participation, involvement and control in local level planning must be the objective in the evolution of planning methodology.[8]

The ULGS in India at present are not structurally, functionally and financially equipped to achieve the goal of creating conditions for healthy city life to urban dwellers by providing adequate civic and welfare services. It is, therefore, pertinent to study the present functioning of the ULGs, measures required to improve their functioning through extending administrative, financial and technical support to them. Cities need improved governance in view of the growing importance of urban areas for the country's economy.

The growing pace of urbanisation which is an inevitable consequence of technological revolution in industry and agriculture has given rise to unprecedented urban problems. Mass illiteracy, growing unemployment, poor levels of health, housing and sanitation, inadequate urban services and other essential amenities are the common civic problems which pose great challenges to all urban managers.[9] Besides, there are other urban problems in general like haphazard growth, sprawl, inadequate housing and work places, especially for the poor, insufficient land for public amenities, traffic congestion, and lack of resources to finance urban infrastructure. That is why P.K. Mohanty says that "India needs to invest in resource-generating cities, to propel a self-financed process of economic growth, powered by the forces of externalities,"[10] since "Agglomeration externalities, in conjunction with knowledge externalities, established the pivotal importance of cities in the structural transformation of nations."[11]

Cities play a dynamic role in the country's socio-economic development and as such urban administration assumes greater significance. Urban areas are not only the promoters of growth but they are also the centres of socio-political, administrative and cultural activities. Cities and towns have played a significant role in the social and political life of the people throughout the history of India. They have developed a thorough-going system which reconciles the principle of democracy with big territorial expanses. Hence, Urban Local Governments have to play a significant role in the life of the local population as well as the nation. As remarked by De Tocdquelli, local institutions constitute the strength of a free nation. A nation may establish a free government but without municipal institutions it cannot have the spirit of liberty. No national democracy can have a sound footing without local institutions which are actually grassroots democracies. They form an integral part of the democratic system and actively reinforce the general tenor of a country's political liberalism.[12] The everyday well-being of people depends on the quality of the services rendered by local authorities.[13] Local Government creates consciousness of the principles of management of administrative affairs and a sense of responsibility among people. "It is in the area of local politics that people most easily learn their first lesson in the act of governing themselves."[14]

According to James Bryce, the best school of democracy and the best guarantee for its success is the practice of local self-government.[15] "Local Bodies are important to help and to achieve the decentralisation of political power and promotion of democratic values. They are also an indispensable part of governmental machinery contributing to the efficiency at the higher echelons of government by relieving them of purely local tasks. Local Bodies are the media through which functional compartmentalisation can be canalised into a coordinated plan of all round development at the community level."[16]

Municipal Administration in its present form of democratic urban local government was introduced in India by the British during the British rule to suit their requirements. They created the local institutions after the known models. The local self-government, created by the British, was undoubtedly a bold step taken by the British rulers.[17] According to K.M. Panikkar, the British created civil government in this country under municipal authorities.[18] Every ULG has to function through the mechanism that constitutes the structure of the system which is subject to the input-output process by which it receives demands from the environment and responds to the demands through its output transactions.

The functions of Urban Local Governments created under the Act of 1850 were limited to the provision of street lighting, sanitation, streets and drainage maintenance and prevention of public nuisance.[19] But gradually more and more subjects relating to urban development, urban development management, health activities including preventative medicines etc. were added to the subjects to be dealt with by Urban Local Governments that enhances the importance of urban local governance.

The Rural-Urban Relationship Committee set up by Government of India in 1963 pointed out that local government should play a role in the promotion of social and economic development of the local communities and be an integral part of the National Government. The Constitution (74th) Amendment Act, 1992 has fulfilled this objective, duly providing clear delineation of powers and functions. The amendment aims at making Urban Local Governments as Local Self Government units with constitutional status. The amendment has high potential to transform the society from the feudal to the democratic mode and alters the character of democracy from representative to participative. The amendment is an important initiative of the Government of India that provides a basis for State Legislatures to guide the state governments in the assignment of various responsibilities to ULGs and in strengthening municipal governance. Accordingly certain state governments including Andhra Pradesh have amended their municipal laws in order to bring them in conformity with the constitutional provisions. The CAA evinced extraordinary interest in the role of municipal governments in financing urban infrastructure and services and enhancing the quality of India's socio-economic ethos.[20] The amendment also enables people's participation in the development process at ward, municipal, district, metropolitan and regional levels. By the CAA, the ULGs have become an integral part of the national government structure, the level of government closest to the citizens and in the best position both to involve them in the decision-making process to improve their living conditions and to make use of their knowledge and capabilities in achieving all round development. Article 243W allocates to the ULGs the function of preparation of plans for economic development and social justice, apart from the traditional municipal functions of being providers of civic amenities. The Twelfth Schedule includes urban poverty alleviation as a municipal responsibility. The CAA thus takes the ULGs to a much wider area of action encompassing economic and social planning.

The Urban Local Governments in India have been rather sluggish in their performance owing to various reasons. It is necessary to study urban administration in a wider perspective taking into consideration their assigned role in the changed urban scenario with added responsibilities, burgeoning urban population and expanding boundaries, all of which call for fresh and vital study of urban administration in the modern context. Most of the urban problems are the result of urban poverty and the inability of national, state and urban local governments to create institutions to provide sustainable solutions to poverty. But the ULGs in India have not so far addressed this important issue. Cities and towns are emerging as centres of domestic and international investment. Within this framework, urban development calls for an approach that aims to optimise the productive advantages of cities and towns, while at the same time minimise or mitigate the negative impact of urbanisation.[21] ULGs have, therefore, to take up planning to attract domestic and foreign investment which would help to bring about the development needed for expanding cities and towns.

In order to have a well-planned, economically productive, socially just, environmentally sustainable, culturally vibrant, citizen-friendly and safe urban areas, States will have to ensure balanced development commensurate with the requirements of urbanites by promoting alternative urban centres as counter magnates; improve urban infrastructure through integrated planning; improve the quality of municipal services through strengthening citizen charter at affordable costs; local services are to be run through local management and control; ensure provision of adequate shelter and basic services for all urban dwellers.[22]

The Complexities of Urban Local Governance

Urban India faces daunting challenges, the most important of them being:

- Environmental deterioration
- Population growth due to accelerating rural urban-migration
- Growing rural push and urban pull in search of employment in the unorganised sector

- Rising unemployment
- Economic deprivation, the low quality of life of slum dwellers and isolation of persons of ill-health
- Inaccessibility to improved services

The most important felt needs of the urban areas in the country are:

(1) Provision of safe drinking water, extension of distribution lines to unserved areas and replacement of faulty water supply distribution lines;

(2) Slum networking to improve civic amenities in all urban slums;

(3) Widening of all thoroughfares and providing traffic dividers with central lighting for efficient traffic management;

(4) New shopping complexes to meet the requirements of ever-increasing trade and commerce as well as providing petty shops to small traders to remove hawkers and encroachers of road margins; and

(5) Protection of environment by effective control of pollution.

Urban administration today has grown, more than ever before, very big and complex requiring particular measures to enforce greater accountability to make their functioning more effective. It ignores accountability at its peril. In the light of the changing urban scenario and increased functions of the ULGs, new paths in search for better accountability of urban local administration should be explored which includes providing right leadership and drive. An integral view of accountability should be formulated and put into application. It includes the provision of necessary policy inputs by the elected body in respect of the areas of operation, gearing up official machinery to ensure the effective implementation of its decisions and instilling a sense of efficiency, purpose and economy in the functioning of the ULG.

Management covers the whole complex of actions involved in planning, programming, budgeting, development, operation and maintenance. Efficient management of an urban area not only improves living conditions but also enhances productive capacities through the provision of basic services and the establishment of functional linkage. Thus, urban management has a direct role in achieving national economic objectives. Urban management encompasses local goals of economic growth which means local development plan including employment generation.

Urban Local Bodies must have a mandate to take decisions to raise revenues, to deploy human resources and to deal as an equal partner with other governmental agencies if they have to carry out their tasks in achieving the set goals of urban development. These tasks are:

- Forward-planning of the over-all structure of the city/town duly anticipating development trends into workable physical patterns;
- Integrating the programming of infrastructure, so as to support development and guide into the expected patterns;
- Generation of revenue for the installation and operation of infrastructure and for the provision of services;
- Operation, maintenance, rehabilitation and the upgrading of physical infrastructure and facilities of the city; and
- Assurance of health, safety and welfare of urban residents through the application of appropriate and affordable regulatory measures.

Urban Local Governments have to undertake the above core tasks so that the urban areas function in a workable manner.

The classical tools of effective management of the ULGs like inspection, visit, control and supervision by higher authorities have fallen into disuse or are perfunctorily undertaken. Besides activating these tools, the inefficient performance of the public functionaries must be penalised and punished and efficient performance rewarded so that all those who are accountable become more sensitive to these measures. Drastic simplification of rules and procedures expedites disposal of work and removes confusion in the public about them so that they will become well aware of the way to approach the local government to get their things done. Despite certain measures taken in certain states to ensure accountability and transparency, there is a wide gap between the normative principles and actual manifestation of accountability. Accountability in urban local governance is undermined by ineffective and unenlightened local political representatives and untrained official machinery, hierarchical social environment and low citizens' participation.[23] While accountability of public representatives is an essential component, this function cannot be taken for granted. There are no specific institutions or well-defined law to ensure the accountability of public representatives. It is not wrong to say that many of them presume to be a law unto themselves. Accountability implies the responsibility of Urban Local Governments to communicate to the urbanites the activities that they carry out in their capacity as local government officials and that they are also answerable to the urbanites for their actions. Responsiveness involves representing the interests of the urbanites and acting towards improving their welfare.

Kerala state enabled transparency and accountability through a vision document on decentralisation of power in the state, and through incorporating measures within the functioning of the local government units. Although Karnataka state made efforts for greater changes in the political sphere, it could not achieve the same in the administrative and fiscal areas.[24]

An organised system of Urban Local Government was designed for the first time in 1882 with the principle objective of providing a forum of political awareness and popular education. But the avowed objective was not fulfilled owing to several reasons. Urban Local Governments have to act as instruments of economic activity and engines of economic development, besides providing a democratic way of life at the grass-roots level to bring about the required socio-economic change for a better quality of life for all urban dwellers. They are expected to initiate strategic planning by investing human and material resources in a planned manner so that they contribute to the over-all development of the towns and cities, provide the needed civic amenities to the people and create adequate employment to the unemployed urban poor, besides indirectly helping the urban informal (unorganised private) sector. But the Urban Local Governments have failed in the objective set for due to:

(1) Organisational incapacity of the local bodies in the face of severe service deficit;

(2) Haphazard and irregular peripheral growth of towns and cities bringing with them several problems of infrastructure; and

(3) Lack of motivation on the part of Municipal Governments to face the challenges of growing urbanisation.

The key issues involved in accountable, transparent and good governance are decentralisation, integration of the poor and the marginalised, environmental sustainability, mobilisation of municipal finance, civic involvement in urban affairs for better urban management and capacity building for efficient urban service delivery. The added responsibilities and functions within the domain of ULGs call for their greater accountability to urbanites (These details are dealt in greater detail in chapter on Good Urban Governance-Issues and Reforms).

Urban Local Governments (Municipalities and Municipal Corporations), a part and parcel of the three-tier system of government in the country and which are now given a constitutional status under the Constitution (74th Amendment) Act, 1992 as full-fledged local self-government units, have to perform eighteen specific functions contained in the XII schedule to the Constitution apart from their earlier role of merely providing civic amenities. The role of the ULGs in organising and regulating urban life, therefore, has now become more dynamic and responsible one than before. The question before the stakeholders of urban management is as to how far the ULGs in India are able to fulfil their constitutional obligations to the best satisfaction of urbanites in the light of their changed role.

Civic engagement in urban affairs provides for transparency, accountability, equity and a more mature and wholesome city functioning. In recent times several civic society organisations have risen with an urge to increasingly participate in the affairs of the city. This is a welcome development in urban life since it further promotes transparency and accountability in urban local administration, resource allocation, service delivery and monitoring, civic education and poverty alleviation. Civic engagement builds consensus and strengthens true democracy at the city level of administration.

Reforms in Urban Governance

Although the ULGs are local self-government units, the state governments exercise control over them which are legislative, administrative and financial in nature.

(1) Legislative Control

The legislative control is exercised by enacting laws; amending the statutes relating to urban local administration through putting questions; and by issuing ordinances.

(2) Administrative Control

The State Government has the power to constitute, supersede and abolish a municipal council or corporation. It has the power to fix the strength of the elected body including reservation of seats to the Scheduled Castes, Scheduled Tribes, Backward Classes and Women; it appoints the officers of the ULG and transfers them at its will; it has the power to depute officers to supervise and to conduct annual inspection of the ULGs; it modifies, suspends or cancels the resolutions of the ULGs; it can remove the Mayor, Chairperson or any elected member of the ULG for specific reasons; it has the power to approve the bye-laws passed by the urban local bodies; it can direct the ULGs as to any specific works to be executed in preference to others in public interest-this power is often exercised through the head of the district administration.

(3) Financial Control

The Government exercises financial control chiefly under three heads: Sanction of municipal budget and approval of proposals for new taxes and rates; determination of criteria for release of grants; and audit of municipal accounts through the Local Fund Audit Departments of the State Governments.

It is clear from the above that although the municipal bodies are autonomous, the state government has a good deal of administrative control over them. It is, however, desirable that the state government exercises limited control over the ULGs to ensure that their autonomy is not affected.

Accountability and transparency must be given adequate emphasis in the Acts governing urban areas. The village committees constituted in Karnataka in the 1983 Act were intended to be a forum where accountability could be manifested. The concept of Village Committee (*Gram Sabha*) was expected to function quite effectively in transparency, accountability and participation, which enabled the citizens to ventilate their preferences and needs on development activities and the activities of the local bodies. They are the only channel for the citizens to communicate with elected members and officials. The accountability level depends on the measures employed to ensure it since there is a correlation between the institutional measures and accountability of representatives and officials in governance. Political orientation and social awareness among citizens contribute to the demand for accountability. People's active participation in local governance naturally enhances accountability in governance.

In order to bring about reforms in the functioning of Urban Local Governments to enforce an accountable administration, the Government of India has approved the National e-Governance Action Plan. The objectives of the plan are to keep the citizens informed of the local developments and provide basic municipal services such as registration and issue of birth & death certificates, payment of property tax etc. electronically and so on. The key objectives of the e-Governance initiatives include:

- Provision of single window services to urbanites;
- Enhancement of the efficiency and productivity of Urban Local Governments;
- Development of a single and integrated view of ULG information system across all the ULGs in the state;
- Provision of information management system relating to the municipal functions and plan schemes to enable effective decision-making etc.[25]

The Ministry of Urban Development, Government of India finalised a Model Municipal Law (MML) of India in October 2003 with the primary objective of implementing in totality the provisions of the Constitution (74th Amendment) Act, 1992 for empowerment of the Urban Local Governments and provide the legislative framework for implementing the Ministry's urban sector reform agenda. This initiative is expected to enhance the capacities of the ULGs to leverage public funds for development of urban areas as well as create an environment in which the ULGs can play their role more effectively with improved efficiency duly ensuring better service delivery.[26]

Objectives of the Study

The primary objective of this study is to examine the functioning of the Urban Local Governments at present in India, the reasons for their inability to come up to the expectations of the citizens, the changing role of Urban Local Governments in the present urban scenario and to study the measures to improve their performance so that a better deal for the urban dwellers could be ensured keeping pace with the requirements of fast urbanisation. The main thrust of the study is to examine the responsibilities of Urban Local Governments in their everchanging role and the measures needed to enable them to fulfil their constitutional obligations.

In this study an attempt is also made to study the functioning of Urban Local Governments in India in the light of the new responsibilities added to the urban agenda, measures required for generation of additional revenues, and the method of achieving transparency and accountability through active citizen participation in the administration of Urban Local Governments, and suggest remedies for the sluggish functioning of Urban Local Governments.

The study becomes relevant, particularly in the light of the ideals spelt out in the Constitution (74th Amendment) Act, 1992 which aims at making the Urban Local Governments perform perfectly eighteen specific functions which belong to the exclusive domain of the municipalities/municipal corporations. The emphasis is laid mainly on the study of the requirements of urban local governments for better performance, planning for urban development, citizen-participation in the decision-making, augmentation of municipal finances through generation of local revenues and devolution of funds from higher levels of government for improving urban infrastructure to keep pace with fast urbanisation and finally to enforce efficient urban local governance to ensure the best satisfaction of citizens.

Limitations of the Study

The research study is mainly concerned about measures to revamp municipal administration to suit the present needs; measures required to enable urban areas continue their positive contribution to national product; the way the ULGs have to cope with the fast urbanisation instead of making efforts to prevent urban pull and rural push through lop-sided rural development.

Methodology

The data for the study has been collected from both the primary and secondary sources and also through administering a questionnaire. The data has also been collected from the available literature: books, pamphlets, magazines, newspaper clippings, government orders, circulars as well as from the opinions of political leaders and officials dealing with urban administration.

The methodology adopted includes a review of relevant literature on urban administration, practical study of the functioning of certain municipal corporation in Andhra Pradesh, a questionnaire on the citizens'satisfaction or otherwise with the services rendered by the Urban Local Government and deficits in urban basic services etc. The study is conducted through participant observation. On the basis of the close observations of the present functioning of the ULGs the researcher, as one connected with municipal administration, has formulated the objective of the study, besides quantifying the data on the basis of the categories framed for this purpose. Both qualitative and quantitative analyses have been adopted for study.

The study confines itself to select Municipal Corporation in Andhra Pradesh mainly because the issues raised, problems encountered, challenges faced, and the solutions sought after are likely to be applicable to other similar corporations and municipalities in the country. In this sense, this study is likely to be fairly representative.

The present study also analyses the strengths and weaknesses of the ULGs, the opportunities they have and the threats they face and the measures required to be taken so as to ensure better performance of the ULGs. Only a few select states have been chosen for the study since there is a well-defined and well-established municipal law in these states and there are several welcoming developments in these states which can be emulated by other states. The study also endeavours to find out the lacunae in the municipal laws that have led to the miserable failure of Urban Local Governments in certain areas in delivering goods to urban dwellers.

This study is necessitated by the fact that although several books have been written on urban governance most of them have dealt with only certain aspects of urban administration but did not cover a comprehensive view of urban governance and they pay only scant attention to the accountability of ULGs to civic welfare. Urban governance and accountability have not received adequate attention of researchers. The works on the ULGs published so far have not dealt with the civic actors and the factors responsible for the poor performance of Urban Local Governments and the measures to be contemplated to improve their performance to fulfil their constitutional obligations.

The Urban Local Governments in India should be so organised as to enable the beneficiaries of urban development contribute their share to the smooth and efficient conduct of local administration through their active participation in local affairs and in decision-making. This aspect has been dealt with in detail in the present study.

Urban Administration was not regarded as important a subject as Rural Administration in India till the 'seventies' of the last century since the pace of urbanisation was not so rapid till then. But during the 'eighties' and 'nineties'there was rapid urbanisation due to large scale migration of people to select urban areas and forming settlements in search, particularly, of employment in the unorganised sector and perhaps a better quality of life. This rapid urbanisation has brought with it several new challenges to urban areas necessitating a better deal for urban dwellers and accountable administration in all urban areas of the country. After the enactment of the Constitution (74th Amendment) Act, 1992 (CAA), the ULGs have become State Governments writ small. In the light of the above scenario the present study examines:

- Urbanisation in the Country and the effects of urbanisation;
- Urban Challenges and Urban Governance in general in India;

- Urban Infrastructure needs for fast expanding urban areas;
- The Management of Urban Development, Role of different stakeholders and Public-Private partnership in the management of urban development;
- Resources Mobilisation, Revenue Enhancement and Property Tax Administration;
- Measures to ensure transparency and citizen participation in decision-making and administration of Urban Local Governments and effective service delivery;
- Urban Poverty and Poverty Alleviation programmes;
- Training of municipal functionaries for capacity enhancement for better performance of their tasks;
- Structure of Urban Local Governments and the Department of Municipal Administration and Urban Development; Urban Affairs; and
- New Urban Agenda in the light of the Constitution (74th Amendment), Act, 1992.

Urban Local Governments have to cope with greater numbers, plan to provide basic services needed for a fast growing urban population, find resources to meet the cost of required urban development and maintenance of urban services, improve infrastructure, respond to urbanisation of poverty, protect and preserve urban environment and retain their competitive edge. Cities have to prepare themselves to face these enormously complex challenges systematically, effectively and efficiently. The search for additional resources of revenue to meet the ever-increasing urban challenges is, therefore, of paramount importance.

References

1. Rajendra Prasad, K., *Municipal Administration in Andhra Pradesh: A Case Study of Nellore Municipality* 1965—85, Doctoral Thesis, S.V. University, Tirupathi, December, 1990, p.1.
2. Jackson, W.E. *The Structure of Local Government in England and Wales*, Macmillan & Co., London, 1959, p.1.
3. Venkatarangaiah M. and Pattabhiram M., *Local Government in India: Selected Readings,* Allied Publishers, Bombay, 1969, p.1.

4. Duane Lock Word, *International Encyclopaedia of Social Sciences,* Vol. ix, 1968 p. 451.
5. Maheswari S.R., *Local Government in India,* Lakshmi Narayana Agrawal, Agra, 1993, p. 3.
6. David Savage and Shubhagato Dasgupta, *Governance Framework for Delivery of Urban Services* in India Infrastructure report 2006, Oxford University Press, New Delhi, 2006, p.41.
7. G.V. Joshi, *Local Governance and People's Participation in Decentralised Planning for Rural Development,* Local Government Quarterly, Vol. LXXIX, No. 2, April-June, 2009, p. 53.
8. M.L. Dantwala, *Rationale and Limitation of Decentralised Planning* in M.L. Dantwala and others(ed) Asian Seminar on Rural Development, Oxford and I.B.H., New Delhi, 1986, quoted by G.V. Joshi, *ibid*, p. 54.
9. S.N. Seth, *Foreword to Urban Government and Administration in India,* Anu Books, Meerut-India, 1986, p. xvi.
10. Mohanty, P.K., in Preface to *Cities and Public Policy*, p. xv.
11. *ibid*, p. xv.
12. Maheswari S.R., *Local Government in India,* Lakshmi Narayana Agrawal, Agra, 1993, p. 5.
13. Venkata Rao V., *A Hundred years of Local self-government in the Andhra and Madras States*, Local Self-government India Bombay, 1960, p.10, quoted by Y. Adilakshmi in her doctoral thesis entitled "*A Study of the* Organisation and Working of Proddatur Municipality in the Cuddaph *District of Andhra Pradesh*, S.V. University, Tirupati, p. 4.
14. Munro W.B. and Anerist Morely, *The Government of Europe,* 1950, p. 272.
15. Bryce James, *Modern Democracies*, Max Millan, New York, 1962, p.133.
16. *Report of the Rural-Urban Relationship Committee, Volume I, Government of India, Ministry of Health and Family Planning, New Delhi*, 1966, p.16.
17. Bhattacharya Mohit, *Management of Urban Government in India,* Uppal Publishing Company, New Delhi, 1976, p. 3.
18. Quoted by Amareswar Mishra in *Urban Government and Administration in India,* Anu Books, Meerut-India, 1986, p.18.
19. Ratna Swamy, *Some Influences that made British Administrative Systems in India,* Madras, 1956, p.161.
20. Om Prakash Mathur, *Urban Finance* in urban Infrastructure Report 2006, O.U.P., New Delhi, 2006, p. 82.
21. *Indian Urban Sector Profile*, National Institute of Urban Affairs, New Delhi, 1998: xiii.
22. Sriram Maheshwari, *Accountability in Public Administration: Towards a Conceptual Framework,* paper presented to the Seminar-*cum*-Workshop

on Developments in Public Administration, April 18-20, 1999, Indian Institute of Public Administration, New Delhi.

23. V. Vijaya Lakshmi, *Transparency, Accountability and Governance in Local Governance in India* edited by Niraja Gopal Jayal, Oxford University Press, New Delhi, 2006, p. 385.
24. *Ibid*, op. cited, p. 391.
25. Hitesh Vidya & Mukesh Mathur, Implementation of e-Governance in Municipalities in *India Infrastructure Report* 2006, Oxford University Press, New Delhi, p.18.
26. Chetan Vaidya and Hitesh Vaidya, Model Municipal Law to Enable Urban Reforms, in *India Infrastructure Report* 2006, Oxford University Press, New Delhi., 2006, p. 19.

2

The Concept of Urbanisation

The definition of urbanisation differs from country to country. In India, urbanisation is defined as the growth of cities in population. There are two significant features of urbanisation in India: one, there has been massive growth of urban population as indicated by the absolute number of people living in urban areas; two, there has been an increasing concentration of population in Class I towns, that is, towns and cities with more than one lakh population. Urbanisation is the inevitable consequence of the socio-economic changes taking place in the country. The accelerating rural-urban migration in search of better living conditions, education of children, employment in the unorganised sector, medical aid etc. have led to enormous urbanisation, particularly during the last two decades. This quick pace of urbanisation has a positive role to play since it is highly beneficial to the country's economy as a whole but at the same time creates several problems like infrastructure deficiencies, poor quality of urban basic services, growth of overcrowded slums etc. which, if not properly and promptly addressed by the ULGs, will retard or diminish the positive role of urban India. That is why urban policies are to be viewed in the light of broader economic and social policy environment for national development.

India is emerging as one of the fastest urbanising courtiers in the world with an already staggeringly large urban population and the growth of metropolitan cities from 35 in 1981 to 53 in 2011. India is very likely to become more urban than rural by the middle of the twenty-first century or even earlier. The economic base has already shifted from rural to urban centres which indicates that the future of India is inescapably urban. There has been an unprecedented shift of human settlements to select urban areas in search of better living conditions in the entire country as indicated by the steep increase of urban population from 286 million out a total population of 1029 million (27.81 per cent) in 2001 to 377.1 million out of a total population of 1210.2 million (31.16 per cent) in 2011, a net addition of 91.0 million, an increase of 3.35 per cent in proportion of urban population in the country during 2001–2011. The growth rate of population in urban areas was 31.8 per cent. There was a phenomenal growth of urban areas from 85 in 1981 to 2774 in 2011[1] (Census of India 2011, Urban Growth).

Urbanisation has become the defining trend all over the world. While in 1947 India has only four cities with a population of one million and more, it has increased to 35 in 1981 and 53 in 2011.

Urbanisation involves concentration of people in high density population areas; large scale rural-urban migration of people for various reasons; shift from agricultural to non-agricultural occupations and change of land use from agricultural to non-agricultural purposes. The contribution of urban India to GDP is as follows: 1950-51: 29 per cent; 1980-81: 47 per cent; 2007: 63 per cent. This figure is likely to rise to 75 per cent by 2021, which clearly establishes the fact that cities are the places of innovation and improvement which enhance productivity and growth. While urban areas contribute 66 per cent to GDP currently, it is expected to increase to 75 per cent by 2021 which clearly indicates that India will be at the epicentre of urbanisation in the coming decades. This trend indicates that a great number of cities in India have become the centres of great human enterprise and cultural activity. Cities and towns in India are centres of cultural diversity and varied opportunities.

Most of the Indian cities are over-urbanised. Rural migrants seek jobs either in industry or eke out livelihood in the unorganised sector in cities who find shelter in slums, since there is nothing for these rural migrants to do in rural areas. The rural poverty thus contributes to urban misery. Government of India has for several decades after independence concentrated mostly on rural development since Indian economy was predominantly agricultural. But the lopsided rural development with scant attention to urban growth and development could not prevent the rural push and urban pull during the last three decades as indicated by the massive urbanisation. Many developing countries had concentrated on rural development to control migration to larger cities but in vain. Urbanisation is not only inevitable and unavoidable but is a resource. Policy-makers in India for a long time did not recognise urbanisation as a resource. If the positive aspects of urbanisation are carefully exploited it enables urban areas enhance economic growth and improves the quality of lives of millions of poor people. Rural-urban migration is not only for earnings or for better living conditions or facilities but also in response to expected earnings rather than actual earnings.

The views expressed by policy-makers, planners and political leaders perpetrated a negative view of urbanisation and developed an anti-urban mindset among the people. They ignored the fact that sustainable rural development and poverty reduction crucially depend on growth-augmenting and resource generating cities. Urban areas in India, as elsewhere, provide adequate opportunities for accelerating economic growth and poverty reduction which should not be missed. Thus, urbanisation is a positive force in the growth of national income and urban challenges are economic opportunities.

Table 2.1 discloses the growth of urban population in India and urban growth. And further indicates that India is becoming predominantly urban and the near future is expected to see an unprecedented scale of urban growth. There has been significant amalgamation of rural pockets into the urban areas contiguous with them and thus the urban areas have naturally extended beyond their signified boundaries. For example, Visakhapatnam city in Andhra Pradesh has extended up to Gajuwaka, while nine big towns contiguous with Hyderabad city in Telangana were merged into Hyderabad Municipal Corporation, renaming both cities as Greater Visakhapatnam Municipal Corporation and Greater Hyderabad Municipal Corporation respectively. The same is the case with most other cities in the country. These urban trends in the country put greater stress on urban administration in regard to the provision of urban basic services commensurate with the increasing requirements of the fast growing urban areas besides enforcing an efficient local administration which attends to local call.

Table: 2.1 Urban Population of India: 1901 – 2011

Year	*Urban population (million)*	*Percentage of Urban to total population*	*Decadal growth rate (per cent)*
1901	29.9	10.8	-
1911	25.9	10.3	0.4
1921	28.1	11.2	18.3
1931	33.5	12.0	19.1
1941	44.2	13.9	32.0
1951	62.4	17.3	41.4
1961	78.9	18.0	26.4
1971	109.1	19.9	38.2
1981	159.5	23.3	46.1
1991	217.6	25.7	36.4
2001	306.9	30.5	41.0
2011	377.1	31.16	22.87

Source: Ministry of Urban Affairs, New Delhi.

Table 2.2: Urban Population of India

Population 2011 (in millions)		*Per cent of Urban to Total Population*			
Total	**Urban**	**1981**	**1991**	**2001**	**2011**
1210.2	377.1	23.3	25.7	30.16	31.16

Source: Census of India, New Delhi, 2011.

An important feature of urbanisation in India is that urbanisation in class-I towns is growing, that is, the process of urbanisation in the country has been large city oriented as indicated by the massive increase in the percentage share of urban population in class-I cities from 26.0 in 1901 to 68.7 in 2001. But at the same time the number of class-I cities has also increased over the decades-there were only 24 class-I cities in 1901 whereas the number increased to 393 in 2001. The future of India is, therefore, inevitably and unavoidably urban which contributes to economic growth and social justice. The unprecedented growth of towns and cities in India set new trends-social, political, cultural and environmental-in the country. Historically cities have been the driving forces in economic and social development. Thus, sustainable urbanisation is the most pressing challenge facing the nation in our times. Therefore, governments' focus should shift from rural to urban India. The recently introduced centrally sponsored urban development schemes like *Jawaharlal Nehru National Urban Renewal Mission, Urban Infrastructure Development Scheme for Small and Medium Towns, Integrated Housing and Slum Development Programme,* AMRUT etc. are some of the appropriate steps in this direction which will enable the needed urban development to keep pace with the increasing demands of the fast expanding urban areas and burgeoning urban population.

Rapid industrialisation and the growing tempo of modernisation lead to large influx of rural migrants to towns and cities creating problems of social maladjustments. Since the exponential increase of urban population cannot be controlled, the social and environmental challenges of urbanisation have to be addressed properly to cope with fast urbanisation.[2]

Cities provide many opportunities for social advancement and economic development under favourable conditions. India's National Commission on Urbanisation Report (1988) stressed the role of cities as engines of economic growth, reservoirs of capital and skill, centres of knowledge and innovation, sources of formal and informal sector employment, generators of public financial resources for development, and hopes of millions of rural migrants.[3] The Rural-urban Relationship Committee in its Report describes the role of ULGs thus:

(a) to function as local units of self-government;
(b) to provide local public services and convenience for healthy living, work and play;
(c) to ensure planned and regulated development of urban areas;
(d) to mobilise local resources and utilise them to the maximum good of the community; and

(e) to promote social, economic and cultural development in an integrated manner.[4]

It should be the endeavour of the governments-central and state-to strengthen the ULGs by all means to achieve the above goals.

Over the years "The big cities attained inordinately large population size leading to virtual collapse in the urban scenario and followed by basic problems in the field of housing, slum, water, infrastructure, quality of life etc."[5]

Table: 2.3 Distribution of Urban Population by Size Class of Towns

Class	*Population Range*	*No. of Towns*	*Share of Urban Population*
I.	1, 00,000 & above	300	65.20 per cent
II.	50,000 to 99,999	345	10.95 per cent
III.	20,000 to 49,999	947	13.19 per cent
IV.	10,000 to 19,999	1,167	7.77 per cent
V.	5,000 to 9,999	740	2.60 per cent
VI.	Less than 5,000	197	0.29 per cent
	All Classes	3,696	100 per cent

Source: Ministry of Urban Affairs, New Delhi.

Basic Features and Pattern of India's Urbanisation

The basic features of urbanisation in India can be highlighted as the following:

- Lopsided urbanisation has induced the growth of class-I cities.
- Urbanisation has occurred without industrialisation and a strong economic base.
- Urbanisation has been mainly a product of demographic explosion and poverty induced rural-urban migration.
- Rapid urbanisation has led to a massive growth of slums followed by misery, poverty, unemployment, exploitation, inequalities, degradation in the quality of urban life.
- Urbanisation has occurred not due to urban pull but due to rural push.

Problems and Challenges of Urbanisation

Urbanisation in India is on the quick pace sans industrialisation, infrastructure and urban services leading to serious problems of services, housing and environment. The level of civic services in urban India is amongst the lowest in the world. Inappropriate technologies, outdated and outmoded regulatory measures, lack of foresight and comprehensive perspective of development, conservation of indigenous resources, ecological imbalance and destruction of nature pose a serious threat to sustainable urban development. The exponential population growth in most of the urban areas in the country has disrupted the quality of life, livelihood and local markets, posing a challenge to ULGs to comply with several requirements to sustain the quality of urban life.

The pattern of urbanisation in India is characterised by continuous concentration of population and activities in large cities.[6] Urbanisation is associated with higher incomes, improved health, higher literacy, improved quality of life and other benefits. Yet, along with the benefits of urbanisation have come environmental and social ills. Urbanisation affects the environment in three major ways: implication due to urban poverty which is a result of migration, stressed infrastructure and management systems and finally increasing consumerism. Urbanisation in India is followed by some persistent basic problems: inadequate housing, mushroom growth of slums, poor transportation, water supply and sanitation, water pollution, sound pollution and air pollution, inadequate provision for social infrastructure (school, hospital etc.). Class-I cities such as Kolkata, Mumbai, Delhi, Chennai etc. have reached the saturation level of employment generating capacity. Since these cities are suffering from urban poverty, urban unemployment, housing shortage, and crisis in urban infrastructural services, they cannot absorb any more distressed rural migrants. Mega cities grow in urban population but not in urban prosperity and culture. Hence, it is urbanisation without functional characteristics. Urbanisation causes degeneration in social and economic equalities leading to social conflicts, crimes and anti-social activities. All these put together lead to degradation in the quality of urban life. Hence, the accelerating rural-urban migration makes the urban crisis more acute. Urban managers have, therefore, to address these issues and tackle the problems created by urbanisation effectively.

Urban areas today represent high levels of social and economic inequalities and significant concentration of poverty. Thus, the current global trends in urbanisation imply nothing less than the urbanisation of poverty and social exclusion. The efforts made by governments so far to arrest urban poverty have not yielded satisfactory and expected results, and as a consequence the widening gulf between the rich and poor continues as before. If anything, it has only widened further. Now, the responsibilities of both Central and State Governments is "a rights-based and need-based approach to development" which is important for both distributing development gains and ensuring equal participation of all stakeholders in the development process in order to make urban areas better dwelling places. Such an approach means continuously endeavouring to provide basic amenities, safe drinking water and sanitation for all citizens, facilities for education and healthcare, land and housing and create income generating opportunities. In short life must be made liveable.

Incorporating these rights in national policies and state legislation is critical in bringing about a fundamental change in our approach to sustainable urban development. A rights-based approach enables the generation of the political will and creation of culture of resource allocation that places the interest of the downtrodden on par with that of the upper strata of society. Different Governments have proposed different initiatives to achieve this objective. The role of urban local governments in implementing these initiatives is more important than that of the State Governments and Central Governments whose business is only to initiate and propose schemes for urban development encompassing urban poverty alleviation.

The importance of Urban governance should be recognised since urbanisation is a process that supports growth, and in order to increase and improve the positive contribution of urban areas of the country, since the structural transformation of the Indian economy, from agricultural to industrial and in sustaining high rates of economic growth, matures into a modern sector-dominated developed economy and since cities are not only the centres of growth and economic activity but also the centres of knowledge and innovation and the preferred destination of foreign direct investment and business process outsourcing. It should, therefore, be government's endeavour to promote healthy and orderly urban growth.

ULGs have, therefore, to facilitate urbanisation in order to sustain India's economic growth momentum. ULGs have to address the challenges of urbanisation through measures like increased investment in infrastructure development, strengthening the governance framework and capacity enhancement of both ULGs and functionaries. In order to further cope with the trends of urbanisation ULGs have to initiate planned development action with concerted efforts of land acquisition, its development, slum clearance and rehabilitation of inhabitants, provision of social and economic infrastructure to provide a quality of working and living environment in the entire urban area so that urban areas provide the best opportunities to urbanites to bring in their local knowledge and enthusiasm to bear on their local problems.

Need Based vs. Right-based Approach to Urban Development

All Urban Local Governments in India do take up urban developmental works as per the felt needs of the urban areas. But their approaches to meet the 'needs' are wanting in the correct perspective. There is a dire need to shift from the need-based approach to rights-based approach in the prevailing circumstances. The States and Nation have recognised the rights affirmed in the "Universal Declaration of Human Rights" and have tried to put them into effect. Several socio-economic, political and territorial changes have taken place during the past six decades, but the promotion and protection of human rights-civil, cultural, economic, political and social-continue to be the challenges to face. The rights included in the Universal Declaration are expected to be more elaborate. This includes the right to development, the right to safe drinking water, the right to a clean environment, and the "Right to the City". The "Right to the City" concept encompasses direct participation of city dwellers in the decision-making process of Urban Local Governments, the right of city dwellers to enjoy urban life fully with all the services and advantages that the ULGs provide. This right directly relates to social inclusiveness in human settlements and their sustainable development. Certain current initiatives implemented by the Government of India through the ULGs have contributed to some extent to reducing exclusion and increasing social cohesion as well as inclusiveness in urban areas. Examples include Urban Self-Employment Programme (USEP), Development of Women and Children in Urban Areas (DWCUA) and Thrift & Credit Societies components of the Swarna Jayanti Shahari Rojgar Yojana (SJSRY) scheme and other Urban Poverty Alleviation schemes. The innovative urban policies and programmes and the efforts to promote legal reforms towards increasing democratic urban governance and expanding citizens' rights fulfil the objective of "The Right to the City" to some extent.

"The Right to the City" is a new concept to India since urban development in India has so far been through need-based approach rather than rights-based approach. An urban area in the modern sense is one in which the solidarity of citizens is established and which provides a multi-cultural atmosphere, enables humanisation of urban environment and makes urban dwellers aware of their rights. The urban areas have to formulate and implement new urban policies taking into account the felt needs as well as the recognised rights of the citizens. Sustainable urban development is possible through production and enhancement of human and natural resources. The need of the present times is to plan and develop urban areas in accordance with sound economic, social, cultural and environmental principles.

There are substantial national and international initiatives for a consolidated approach to inclusive urban legislation and improved urban governance. These approaches are yet to be conceptualised. As a first step in this direction the Indian Parliament enacted the 74th Constitution Amendment Act, 1992, giving Urban Local Bodies a constitutional status to function as full-fledged local self government units. Administrators and experts from different regions and various fields of competence who include academicians, researchers, and city professionals from local governments, civil servants from urban local bodies and the State and Central Governments have spent sufficient energies on innovating new urban policies to be implemented to bring about efficacy of urban development commensurate with the demands of the current age. The major issues identified by experts at various international fora include respect for Human Dignity, Equality, Tolerance and Justice, Law and Urban Planning, Urban Governance and Democracy, Civil Cosmopolitanism, Urban Law promoting Institutions, Social Cohesion and Competitiveness, Rights and Responsibilities of both Municipalities and Urban Dwellers, and Solidarity among Urban Dwellers.

Though the above ideals are valuable, they have mostly remained on paper as far as Urban India is concerned. Research institutes on urban policies and citizenship could only analyse the existing normative tools and initiatives, provide training and conduct workshops for city managers and provide a platform for transfer of knowledge and exchange of information for researchers and decision-makers on urban policies and citizenship, but have not provided any practicable solutions to urban problems and challenges. The stake holders of urban development are quite unaware of their duties and responsibilities but are overconscious of their rights and privileges. Power and authority at the municipal level provide the required ground for improving political career to politicians, but have not served as a training ground for them in urban policies and urban governance.

During the recent years several new issues have been added to the urban agenda. Local community concerns are to be given their due place in the national urban agenda and the critical importance of inclusiveness is to be highlighted. These ideals include active role of the public, private and civil society sectors in local governance which is necessary to enable the civil society to develop a sense of belonging in providing and improving urban infrastructure. An innovative approach is required to address the urban challenges and to find practical solutions to urban problems. The private sector shares the insights and experiences of urban planners on what would improve the quality of life in the country's growing cities. Some of the ideas expressed by the stakeholders of urban development in this direction are:

- There is the need for all stakeholders of urban development- citizens, local governments, state and central governments, private sector and civil society organisations- to prepare a common urban agenda and play their part effectively without transferring their responsibility to others.

- Risk-taking and pursuit of innovation must characterise municipal leadership if urban areas are to achieve sustainable development.
- Appropriate engagements, partnerships and relationships need to be built up in an inclusive manner to understand the urban challenges better and develop practical solutions to urban problems.
- The importance of transparency and accountably should be recognised. Citizens should be made aware of the urban challenges and the steps that are being taken by Central, State and Local Governments to address them.

The Emerging Urban Issues

Urban issues have become a major challenge of our time. The fast expanding urban areas are putting an increasing number of poor people at risk of natural disorders and diseases. Urban slums are rapidly increasing on the outskirts of all major towns and cities of India which pose a serious threat to healthy living urban environment. Certain cities and towns sit on the high flood risk zones. The fast growth of urban areas also brings with it several problems like disease, crime, pollution, poverty and social unrest. Another serious problem of urban areas is that more than 50 per cent of the population live in slums that have little or no access to basic amenities like shelter, safe drinking water, sanitation, education and health services. Yet another serious challenge before the urban managers is environmental deterioration as a result of multiplication of population and generation of waste and non-ecological use of resources fuelled by commerce and industry. Besides, the thoughtless and even callous discharge of industrial and household effluents into water bodies has emerged as another major hazard. The growth of informal settlements with heavy human concentration and scant urban infrastructure has added to the dangers of disease and epidemics, particularly in vulnerable areas. The unbridled rise of automobiles rendering the air unfit for inhaling leading to respiratory diseases has added to the already present health hazard. The increasing use of non-degradable material by the majority of population has resulted in solid waste management becoming pathetic, even desperate day by day in many cities. The lack of adequate sanitary dumping and recycling facilities has further aggravated the problem. Thus, urban environmental care has become another important challenge the ULGs have to face.

While at the global level 30 per cent of all urban dwellers live in slums creating several infrastructure problems, the magnitude of the problems has increased substantially during the last decade and an half: 283 million more slum dwellers have joined the global urban population. At the national level 55 per cent of urban population live in slums. While the annual growth rate of urban population is 3 per cent, the growth rate of slum population is 2 per cent (as per 2001 estimates). Besides, the slums are overcrowded and have become poverty-stricken corners of a geopolitical chess board fraught with problems with thousands of poor joining them everyday, adding to the already existing problems like inadequate shelter, sanitation, electricity and other services which are essential for an acceptable standard of living. The biggest problem arguably, confronting humanity during the twenty-first Century is *'how to manage the situation?'* The responsibility of urban planners and stakeholders of urban development is not only to plan for urban development to keep pace with the increasing demands of rapidly increasing urban population, but also to contrive measures for rural development to minimise the accelerating rural push and urban pull. The national, provincial as well as local governments have, therefore, to muster and energise all their strength as never before in the quest for sustainable urbanisation. The role of governments, the ULGs and the civil society partners therefore, in *making a difference for the better* is clearly underlined. "One of the most crucial challenges facing developing countries over the decade will be meeting the growing demand for basic social services, infrastructure and public facilities in cities."[7] These negative aspects of urbanisation are to be effectively dealt with by appropriate policies to minimise the adverse effects of urbanisation. The solution for all the negative aspects of urbanisation is sound management of urban areas and the areas contiguous with them.

The urban local governments in our country should address the new urban challenges created by fast urbanisation efficiently and effectively to make urban life meaningful and comfortable. It requires the planning, financing and servicing of the equivalent of a new urban area of equal population to the existing town/city over a period of a decade. The investment required to plan for and provide basic services including shelter in urban areas should be viewed as a major impetus for socio-economic development. Some of the measures for addressing these urban challenges are:

- All stakeholders of urban development should show a willingness to build effective coalitions to address the needs of the urban poor. There should be firm decisions and commitment of Central, State and local authorities to improve the quality of urban life. The stakeholders of urban development should be actively engaged with civil society organisations and their representatives in supporting their initiatives that improve their housing and access to basic services. They should realise the need to engage with and support community initiatives to improve the living conditions of the poorest of the poor and the most vulnerable groups and to improve the urban environment.
- The Central and the State governments should meet the challenges of slum upgradation through sustainable infrastructure development. They should take all steps to attain the slum upgrading targets. The urban challenge is a shift from relying on international development finance to tapping local capital markets. The national and state (provincial) governments should play a catalytic role in building the capacity and improving the credit worthiness of cities and towns. A separate fund must be created to provide financial assistance for investments in pro-poor housing and urban infrastructure.
- Urban development schemes like housing for urban slum dwellers, infrastructure in urban slums etc. should be implemented through meticulous planning and careful execution for sustainable urban development and environmental protection. Urban development planning is not simply the role of government officials and urban planners but of the civil society which is the ultimate beneficiary of urban development. Urban planning should be inclusive,

transparent and ethical encompassing the divergent points of views of the urban planners as well as stakeholders of urban planning in order that it is sustainable. Sustainability is the backbone of new forms of planning.

Some of the observations of urban planners at certain international fora may be summed up as follows:

- The commitments made by certain national and provincial governments for urban development and their poverty reduction strategies have not yielded the expected results in improving the living conditions of the urban poor. In several states there is a wide gap between the objectives set and the actual achievements. The discrepancy needs to be addressed if sustainable urban development is to be achieved.
- Sustainability and poverty are unavoidably linked. Sustainability is a major challenge facing all urban areas in the country, though towns and cities in different states may face challenges pertaining to them that can be addressed by a more systematic exchange of best practices and good urban polices among all stakeholders of urban development at the national, state and local levels.
- The youth represent a considerable proportion of people living in cities and their active participation in urban planning, and urban development would go a long way in setting up the right goals. Youth, women and the vulnerable groups in urban areas could play a decisive role in the decision-making process and, therefore, they should be involved in decisions that affect their lives since they can adopt strategies, bearing their specific needs in mind. The ongoing poverty-reduction schemes meant for urban poor women would considerably contribute to the sustainability of cities and communities.
- As urban areas are largely the product of private investment, the strong presence of the private sector in urban development is underscored by towns and cities. Private sector participation in urban development supplements the state-sponsored schemes and expedites progress.

- Recognition of local needs (which differ from city to city) and decentralised planning, empowerment of local authorities, active participation of civic society, the private sector and other stakeholders go a long way in transforming towns and cities to become better places of living.
- Different departments of the governments need to prioritise the items of the urban agenda in their respective plans and policies.

The items of urban development may be classified into six categories:

(1) Slum Upgrading and Affordable Housing for all
(2) Public Involvement: The Inclusive Approach
(3) Urban Finance
(4) Urban Safety and Security
(5) Urban Planning and Management
(6) Assets-based Development of Towns/Cities.

In response to the fast urbanisation and shelter crisis the governments and urban local bodies should take up a full-fledged programme taking into consideration the dynamics of urban problems, guided by experts, academics, urban planners, stakeholders of urban development and finally those who are in need of basic services. Policy-makers and local communities must come to grips with the urban problems and find workable and lasting solutions. The ultimate objective of all urban development programmes is "Cities without Slums." A four-point strategy is suggested for attaining this goal: advocacy of global norms, analysis of information, field-testing of solution and financing. These core functions consist of monitoring and research, policy development, capacity building and financing for housing and urban development.

The United Nations millennium declaration recognises the dire circumstances of the urban poor and articulates the commitment of the member states to improve the lives of at least 100 million slum dwellers by the year 2020 (Millennium Development Goal No.7). This is, however, only 10 per cent of the world slum population, which, if left unchecked, is expected to multiply threefold to 3 billion by 2050. India has, therefore, to contribute its best to tackle this appalling issue within its boundaries. This should be commenced with reduction by half of the number without sustainable access to safe drinking water. This would be possible through the collective efforts of government, regional and local authorities, civil society and the private sector.

Campaign for Housing and Secure Tenure

Urban slum dwellers beyond count are homeless and women and children among them are the first victims of violence, crime, over-crowding, and all the health hazards associated with inhuman and dangerous living conditions in our rapidly growing towns and cities. It is among the slum dwellers that epidemics take the heaviest toll. Women are the most affected in forced evictions, resettlement schemes, slum clearance, domestic violence, civil conflict, discriminatory inheritance laws and practices, development projects and globalisation policies. A well-planned land management and tenure system, well-defined policies and legislation help achieve adequate shelter, security of tenure and equal access to economic resources for all with a specific focus on gender equality. It is, therefore, necessary to take up a campaign for secure tenure that promotes adequate shelter for all by providing sustainable housing and land policy, particularly for women. This programme enables slum upgradation and the prevention of evictions. The successful programmes in one city can glean the best practices from another city. The two main components of secure tenure campaign are: (1) Implementation of land, housing and property rights and secure tenure for women; and (2) Housing Policy and Development Section, which component focuses on building standards and technologies and work to ensure a rights-based approach to housing policies. Urban development programmes should concentrate particularly on women and child development since they are more prone to the problem of insecurity.

The poorest people in over-crowded cities, especially women and children, often have no rights to safeguard their legitimate interests in the face of evictions or harassment by authorities. Governments–national, provincial and local–should, therefore, launch a Housing Rights programme as a joint initiative with the primary objective of helping stakeholders of urban development in the successful implementation of the urban housing programme and to ensure the full realisation of the right to adequate housing to all houseless urban dwellers. Employment opportunities in the unorganised or informal sector run the risk of disruption and uprooting. The city planners have to go beyond spatial concepts and look at the social-economic realities in the entire planned process. As part of the anticipated expansion of urban population comes from immigration, the Constitutional rights of these migrants are to be protected against exclusion from older city dwellers. Supporting cosmopolitan development that promotes multi-cultural and multi-ethnic neighbourhood, therefore, is vital for peace, law and order and safety in cities.

Water, Sanitation and Other Infrastructure

There has been acute scarcity of water in most of the towns and cities in the country. The rapid and reckless growth of urban areas during the last three decades has led to fast depletion of previously bountiful fresh water sources. The urban water challenge is taking an ominous dimension in a large number of towns and cities of India. In order to ensure that water is not wasted or contaminated an integrated approach to urban water management is essential for the social, economic and environmental sustainability of urban areas. Water scarcity in urban areas is the most potential source of social conflicts and political rivalries. It is not fanciful to surmise that water wars may, in the near future, substitute political wars and economic wars.

Water, sanitation and infrastructure have now been the areas of concentration for most of the urban local governments. ULGs have to build capacity for augmentation and distribution of adequate safe drinking water, proper maintenance of sanitation and provision of infrastructure commensurate with the increasing needs and demands of the fast growing towns and cities. Governments should take up a well-coordinated fast track approach working with urban local governments enabling them to reach out to the poorest of the poor. This approach includes water demand management, values-based water education, improved sanitation for the urban poor, urban catchment management, and advocacy, awareness-raising and information exchange. Any urban development programme should focus on urban poverty alleviation through community-based urban water services, urban environmental sanitation and improving urban water governance.

The other contributory factors for the deterioration of living conditions in urban areas are rapid motorisation, imperfect urban transport planning and deficient traffic management which have been the cause of a number of road accidents, needless deaths and injuries every year, that ultimately result, among other things, in lost economic productivity and environmental pollution. It is, therefore, imperative to find ways to promote urban productivity and improved living and working conditions for urban population by appropriately meeting transport needs in a manner economically efficient and socially sustainable. This would be possible through a service of strategic programmes that would make life in cities and towns safer. This includes sustainable cities and good urban governance.

References

1. Arabi, U., *Recent Urbanisation Trends: Their Impact on the Poor in the Developing World,* Local Government Quarterly, Vol. LXXIX, No.2, April-June, 1999, p. 5.
2. Amareswar Mishra, *Urban Government and Administration in India*, Anu Books, Meerut, India, 1986, p. 4
3. Arabi, U., op. cited, p. 8.
4. Government of India, *Report of the Rural-Urban Relationship Committee*, 1966, Vol. I, p.6, quoted by Amareswar Mishra, op. cited, p. 4
5. Pranati Datta, *Urbanisation in India,* Indian Statistical Institute, 203 B.T. Road, Kolkata June, 2006) p. 1.
6. *Ibid*, p.12.
7. Dennis A. Rondinelli, *Extending Urban Services in Developing Countries: Policy Options and Organisational Choices,* Syracuse, New York, 1986, p.1.

3

Good Urban Governance: Issues and Reforms

Governance is to work around the needs and aspirations of the people. Good urban governance is the efficient and excellent management and handling of urban affairs and the promotion of values such as integrity and honesty. As Hayden says, "Governance refers to the formation and stewardship of the formal and informal rules that regulate the public realm, the arena in which state as well as economic and societal actors interact to make decisions."[1] Urban management covers the entire gamut of administrative functions that make for efficiency and excellence in handling city organisations. The UNDP (1997) defined eight principles as associated with the concept of good governance which are widely accepted by all. They are: (1) Participation; (2) Rule of Law; (3) Transparency; (4) Responsiveness; (5) Consensus Orientation; (6) Equity, Efficiency and Effectiveness; (7) Accountability; and (8) Strategic Vision. The four key aspects of good urban governance, according to Constitution (74th Amendment) Act, 1992 are: democracy and representation; effective civic service delivery; transparency and accountability; and civic engagement and participation. Good urban governance also encompasses decentralisation, integration of the poor and marginalised, environmental sustainability, mobilisation of municipal finance, transparency and civic engagement, better municipal management and capacity building.[2]

Good urban governance is a dynamic concept and has no permanent definition that can be applied to all ULGs and for all times, since it has to encompass the quick pace of socio-economic and socio-political changes in their administrative jurisdiction. Empowering people for active and meaningful participation in the development process must be one of the key interventions of governance at all levels, particularly at urban local government level, in their attempt to usher in sustainable urban development. Good governance is responsive, citizen-friendly, ethical and excellent and is an essential ingredient for socio-economic development of the country. The survival of governments depends on providing strong and effective governance.

Governance relates to interactions between stakeholders with different degrees of power and responsibility, duly ensuring the quality and prompt delivery of service. Governance refers to the functioning of an institution or authority as per the rule of law. Good urban governance is the exclusive activity of an ULG with political, administrative and legal framework. The conventional form of governance was top down, unilateral, authoritative and controlled which has resulted in inefficiency, poor quality and low accountability. But in modern sense efficient urban governance is bottom up, inclusive, transparent, service-oriented, accountable and citizen-friendly. It involves a shift from the present "top-down" approach to development to a "bottom-up" approach which takes decentralisation of power away from the upper tier to grassroots level. The traditional and conventional forms of urban governance are being gradually replaced by a new system of good urban governance which ensures efficiency and accountability. Urban governance in India is experiencing a change over the last two decades with the efforts to develop and implement systems of good and efficient urban governance.

Good urban governance, in the modern sense, is not merely a conventional law-enforcing, service providing local government institution but it implies a process of development through active participation of citizens in the governance and takes into consideration the interests of all stakeholder groups in the society. It is a process that encourages sustainable urban development, provision of improved quality of services and promotes socio-economic, human and cultural development of all citizens in its jurisdiction. Efficient urban governance has three distinct aspects:

- the establishment of a well-organised local government for every urban area with well-defined functions, duties, responsibilities and powers;
- the efficient management of national level, sate level and local level economic and social resources;
- capacity of ULGs to design, formulate and implement plans and policies for the best benefit of the denizens.

Good urban governance aims at eradicating poverty and promoting development, creating and sustaining an urban environment which fosters strong and equitable development which is an essential complement to sound economic policies. According to World Bank's ideal, "good governance fosters strong state capable of sustained economic and social development and institutional growth."[3] It is built on the rule of law which helps to protect governance against erratic and uneven enforcement of law and the whims of public officials and hold them accountable to people for their actions. The principle objectives of good urban governance are:

- To encourage efficient and dynamic political leadership that reflects and promotes ideals of good citizenship.
- Bring about administrative reforms, restructuring of procedures to suit the current times,
- Decentralisation of powers,
- Transparency and accountability in service delivery mechanisms; and
- E-governance initiatives.

Good governance simply is least government and maximum governance. It works towards the accomplishment of better outcomes by setting performance benchmarks as tools. It aims at creating an urban environment in which all citizens can get their grievances redressed and have access to all services and in which all citizens, irrespective of other considerations, can develop to their full potential.

Good urban governance envisages improving the quality of life in cities through improved local governance by reinventing a city as an inclusive city, which provides space and voice to all its stakeholders through inclusive decision-making. It affords adequate opportunity to women's thoughts and initiatives since women are the biggest levers of positive change in society. Governance is the manner in which power is exercised in the management of a country's economic and social resources for development. It is the manner in which public officials and institutions acquire and exercise the authority to shape public policy and provide public goods and services.[4]

Good and efficient urban governance is achievable through well developed institutional framework, well-structured organisation of the local government and human resource management. It includes strategies of enabling, participation and capacity-building. Political empowerment of ULGs and professionalisation of urban management improve municipal organisation and urban institutional performance.

The Global Campaign on Good Urban Government suggests certain norms for good urban governance which include:

i. Sustainability through the balancing of environmental, social, and economic needs of present and future generations;
ii. Subsidiarity of authority and resources to the closest appropriate level;
iii. Efficiency in delivery of civic services and in local economic development;
iv. Equity in access to basic civic necessities and decision-making processes;
v. Transparency in local government operations with information disclosure on all aspects of local government functioning;
vi. Accountability for actions to the public at large;
vii. Civic engagement and citizenship development; and
viii. Security to individuals and their living environments.

ULGs have to cope with the pressures of urbanisation, the increasing financial constraints and fragmented responsibilities that inevitably necessitate initiatives towards better governance. Efficient urban governance is concerned with a network of systems of governance in which all stakeholders of urban governance (public, private and social organisations) play their role efficiently in decision-making process. Efficient city governance is the result of a dynamic interaction among these major stakeholders and the external agencies operating outside the city.

Certain structural changes and innovations are required in the ULGs of India to improve city governance through reforms and innovations in order to attract investment, create competitiveness and improve service delivery keeping pace with the changing requirements of the cities. The World Bank and other funding agencies have considerably influenced the governance reforms which aimed at improving service delivery besides changes in the institutional framework.

The quick pace of urbanisation in the country necessitates strengthening of urban governance through a unified and efficient administrative framework with clear accountability to citizens. Good urban governance has emerged as a broad reform strategy through a set of initiatives to strengthen the functioning of the ULGs. The edifice of good urban governance rests on ethos, ethics, equity and efficiency.

The role of ULGs has changed from mere service providers to facilitators which suggests the need for enhanced participation of different stakeholders who include state, private sector and civil society, in the development process. The Urban Local Governments should create local administrative machinery which moves forward with dedication and commitment to civic welfare and which is always alive to public expectations and which will establish a lasting partnership between the people and the local administration in the endeavour to provide a citizen-friendly administration responsive to civic call. It involves the active role of non-state actors to take on their part what used to be core governmental tasks. In good urban governance beneficiaries of urban development and urban services are "makers and shapers" of policies and programmes, and "users and choosers" of services. Governance is a multi-stakeholder process with different actors, who, through mutual cooperation, solve collective problems through framing the policies, plans, programmes and practices that seek to ensure the development of basic infrastructure, shelter, and employment commensurate with the population growth.

Urban Local Governments have, *inter alia*, wide ranging functions to perform in the present urban scenario which are: (i) Regulatory functions; (ii) Services; and (iii) Environmental protection which include efficient financial management and resource mobilisation; improvement of urban infrastructure commensurate with burgeoning urban population and expanding urban areas which is essential to the efficient operation of the city; improved quality of essential services; urban poverty alleviation; housing, particularly weaker section housing; upgradation of slums; efficient solid waste management; provision of services that develop human resources, improve productivity and raise the standard of living of the urbanites; regulation of private activities that affect community welfare and the health and safety of the urbanites; provision of services and facilities that support productive activities and allow private sector participation to operate efficiently in urban areas, the development and promotion of appropriate policies and tools for municipal finance and administration, land management, organisation of municipal institutions to promote greater efficiency and responsiveness in urban service delivery. In order to perform these functions efficiently and effectively urban governance has to:

- Invite active participation of individuals as well as societies in public service delivery;
- Ensure enduring relationship between the actors regarding public service provision;
- Ensure that each actor invests in concrete activities materially and immaterially; and
- Ensure better cooperation rather than conflict in civic affairs.

In the light of the above ideal consensus is essential for efficient governance since a decision is binding on all concerned, and the civil society owns the programme initiated and implemented with consensus. Consensus allows the civil society an opportunity of increasing role in the decision-making process.

Indicators of Good Governance

- The chief administrative authority is a servant of the people who functions as per "the likes of his subjects" with "no personal likes;"
- The heads of both deliberative wing and executive wing will not be absolute, arbitrary or authoritarian-they function as per the collectively agreed upon goals and execute them in time;
- The administration is carried on with people's welfare as the broader goal of achievement;
- The heads of both the deliberative wing and executive wing should lead a rigorously disciplined life observing an elaborate code of conduct since their code of conduct and behaviour would become a model for all urbanites to emulate;
- The elected members as well as the executive wing should observe strict economy in expenditure;
- Provision of civic amenities, redressal of public grievances as per the time frame fixed in the Citizen Charter and ensuring the safety and security of people should be the primary responsibility of both wings of the ULG;
- The ULGs should procure highly talented and well capacitated personnel for service in the ULG;
- Both wings should perform their functions with a sense of commitment and dedication and be accountable to the people and should be removable and recallable for non-fulfilment of their legitimate duties ordained by law.

This means that good governance is the promotion of social will, duly replacing individual will and promotion of moral power. A moral political wing and a moral executive committed to the welfare of the people will enable the emergence of a local democratic government to propel good urban governance.

Salient Features of Good Urban Governance

1. **Decentralisation**: Decentralisation signifies the devolution of certain powers and responsibilities from a higher authority

to the lower ones. Decentralisation has three tiers: (a) Functional and financial decentralisation from State to ULGs; (b) Decentralisation within the council from City centre to Wards; and (c) Involvement of civil society in decision-making and implementation.

Decentralisation takes decision-making close to the scene of action and promotes democracy at grassroots level since it allows direct and more meaningful participation of citizens in the urban governance and brings governance closer to the people, enhancing 'proximity' so that the chances of local bodies delivering better services on the actual needs of local citizens will increase. The participatory process of urban development as well as management enhances the commitment of citizens to the civic cause. The Constitution (74th Amendment, Act, 1992 had enjoined upon the State legislatures to "by law, endow the ULGs with such powers and authority as may be necessary to enable them to function as institutions of self-government and such law may contain provisions for the devolution of powers and responsibilities upon the ULGs at the appropriate level." Decentralisation in the ULG's sense is administrative decentralisation but not democratic decentralisation.

The unique advantages of decentralisation are that—

- it expedites action at the local level;
- it helps increase people's understanding and enable them to contribute to their own activities, social, political and economic;
- development programmes at the local level become more realistic and result-oriented;
- it trains people in the art of self-government;
- it helps increase popular capacity to ensure responsibility and accountability;
- it improves delivery of services by keeping in view the local needs, and creating conditions for innovations;
- it makes local development plan more responsive to local conditions and enables its implementation by facilitating local resources mobilisation;
- it quickens the process of decision-making.

2. **Integration of the Poor and the Marginalised**: It signifies "making services work for the poor, in which user services and their relations with service providers have to receive more attention than earlier." More importance is given to the role of citizens and their social networks and civil society organisations as important players. Effective implementation of poverty alleviation programmes to meet the needs of the urban poor and initiation of steps to promote their access to shelter and basic services are of paramount importance in order to make urban life meaningful and purposeful. In order to improve the lot of the urban poor the ULGs have to: (i) Build organisations of the poor; (ii) Provide Bank credit at subsidised interest; (iii) Provide weaker section housing; (iv) Provide basic services in slum areas; and (v) Provide skill up-gradation training and employment opportunities.
3. **Environmental Sustainability**: Environmental protection through public service provision and the regulation of the private sector is an equally important aspect of good urban governance, particularly in view of the environmental deterioration of urban areas arising out of large-scale rural-urban migration, growth of urban slums, the ever-increasing rural push and urban pull in search of employment in the unorganised sector, increasing vehicular traffic, release of industrial effluents etc.
4. **Municipal Finance & Resource Mobilisation**: The main challenge the ULGs in the country are facing is that fiscal pressures have persisted in most of the Urban Local Governments and have mixed with the new demands on local communities. The problem of urban finance is that the fiscal role of the ULGs in India's economic framework has never been systematically assessed with the result that the finances of the ULGs have always been in doldrums. The situation necessitates the search for additional resources to meet the ever-increasing daunting urban challenges.

The Constitution (74th Amendment) Act, 1992 points towards a larger role for the ULGs in the country's development affairs and suggests a larger fiscal space for them. Urban Local Governments should, therefore, make every effort to ensure that urban areas deliver a quality life that would enable them to become national assets and engines of economic growth. ULGs have to improve their finance base by exploiting all the sources of revenue to the fullest extent besides seeking additional sources.

There should be a resource sharing mechanism, which lays emphasis on the urban local government's maintaining better financial discipline and ensuring better realisation of its revenues. In order to achieve this goal,

- The ULGs should be empowered to make all municipal services cost-effective.
- Where the income from the services rendered is less than the cost of the services, the deficit should be filled by grants from the State.
- Resources raised by the ULGs should be utilised exclusively for maintenance of services.
- All capital works, developmental works, recreation facilities should be financed by the Central and State governments in the form of grants.
- The ULGs should have an effective machinery to realise their revenues and should be empowered by law to disconnect essential services like electricity, water supply, drainage etc. for tax defaulters and tax evaders in order to ensure cent per cent realisation of local revenues.

5. **Transparency and Civic Engagement**: Transparency means the conduct of public business affording wide accessibility to stakeholders in decision-making process. It assumes added significance in the context of enforcing efficient urban governance. Since it is possible to establish close relations among various civic actors in an urban area, transparency has enormous potential in effective decision-making and proper implementation of the collective decisions. Transparency

ensures greater accountability and integrity on the part of the official machinery in the performance of public duty and service delivery. The ULGs through appropriate mechanism must report to the citizens their performance as against the targets fixed, and the beneficiaries or citizens will analyse and assess the performance, and accountability can be ensured. Performance evaluation must be done by the public.

While transparency is the core principle of good urban governance, citizen welfare is the centre of all activities of good urban governance. While Government are the controller of the economy in ordinary governance, its role is transformed to be a facilitator and promoter of economic growth in good urban governance. Transparency also includes dissemination of information which is crucial to good urban governance since it reflects and captures the activities and processes of urban local government. Citizens should have access to information about the activities of the ULG consistent with public interest, so that they can actively participate in the local governance process. Updated information empowers the people to exert demand for better services and empowers the service providers to make efforts for improving the quality of services.

Active civic engagement in public affairs and in decision-making, planning and implementation of various welfare schemes holds greatest promise in increasing accountability and builds up and deepens the spirit of a true democracy and contributes to the common good and translates the concept of sovereignty of the people into reality, when the government is not a regulator, funder and service provider but an equal partner with the citizens. The ULGs, through a legal framework and appropriate mechanisms, processes and procedures, must enable the widest possible participation of all the stakeholders and citizen groups who are the ultimate beneficiaries of urban development.

Democratic governance is more representative than participatory in which citizens have no role to play except in elections. Representative democracy is an old concept while participatory democracy is a modern one. The reinvention of the citizen is a decisive factor in urban local governance. Citizens in the modern society must be not merely taxpayers but active participants in ULGs' governance, its decisions and their implementation, evolving policies and plans as well as monitoring the performance of the government. The Constitution (74th) Amendment Act envisages the active involvement of citizens in the vital areas of governance, economic development and welfare.

Active citizen governance enables the successful functioning of democracy at grassroots level since it:

- is value based and removes the barriers that separate the bureaucracy of the ULGs and the citizens;
- gives tangible benefit to the society from the governance;
- enables citizens to act as vision builders and advisors and frame issues of concern for communities to guide planning and action to achieve a community vision;
- helps strategic planning and its effective implementation, leading to desired results duly ensuring public services to meet the concerns of citizens, local government machinery perform their duties fairly with ethical accountability, preventing the squandering of public money without giving value to it.

The ULG should create avenues for active participation of citizens in governance and social audit of public works; stimulate involvement of citizens in governance to the extent that it produces desired goals so that citizen governance becomes a continuous process; encourage the involvement of community-based organisations in order to build a collaborative community culture.

Furthermore, citizen governance

- Enables quick response to people's needs and demands, in which people can identify their felt needs and demands and design policies and programmes to meet them in a highly transparent way;

- Is a means of achieving improved and efficient governance?
- Promotes problem identification, problem analysis, monitoring, evaluation and further follow up action;
- Develops a governance model that is sensitive to the felt needs of the citizens that provides efficient leadership and seeks support from the private sector.
- People-centred approach to development enables people to own the development through sharing the cost of development works;
- People review and audit their own expenditure;
- People own community assets created and manage their own institutions.

ULGs have to adopt new systems and methods of governing cities that are inclusive, since participatory approach in urban governance ensures effective decision-making and implementation to the best satisfaction of the urbanites. The Government of A.P. had implemented an innovative partnership programme called the "Andhra Pradesh Urban Services for the Poor" (APUSP) in 42 class-I, towns during 2000-2008 funded by the Department for International Development, Government of U.K. The active civic involvement in the entire process made the programme a great success and enabled the improvement of municipal functioning, provided civic infrastructure and strengthened the local community based organisations.

6. **Better Municipal Management and Capacity Building:** There is the need to enhance the capacities of the ULGs as well as the municipal functionaries to enable them to play their role efficiently in delivering essential services to the urbanites. Capacity development is a continuous process to build or enhance the capabilities of individuals, organisations, societies and groups in order to enable them to understand

and deal with the development needs, priorities and problems of ULGs; formulate and implement various policies, programmes and projects and to perform their core functions and solve all local problems.

Urban governance in the modern sense includes several subjects within the purview of urban local governance which calls for a fresh urgency to study urban local governance in a new light. Good urban governance is possible by substantially and systematically enhancing the existing capacity of the ULGs.

Capacity building is required to establish an effective partnership with national, regional, global networks and external support agencies, and to promote and encourage dissemination of information and emulation of best practices and promising options. Capacity building is required for efficient infrastructure management, improvement of municipal finance, and institutional administration. For this purpose, urban management experts are to be invited to provide the structure needed to institutionalise the capacity building objective over a long term. Efficient urban management helps Urban Local Governments to strengthen their contribution towards economic growth, social development, and alleviation of poverty.

Measures for Improvement of Urban Governance

Political Trust: Political trust is an important measure of political legitimacy embodying citizens' support to ULGs since it is the tie between individual citizen and the ULG. This trust is absolutely necessary to build a harmonious society and to fulfil the strategic aim of efficient urban governance. Besides the provision of infrastructure and basic services ULGs in the modern times are concerned with investment of human and material resources in the areas of education, health, social security and other aspects of social welfare. In view of this need, political trust assumes greater significance.

Effective Public Service Delivery: Effective public service delivery is a crucial challenge for ULGs in India due to: (i) inadequate finances given for service delivery; (ii) incapacity of the service delivery staff to perform the tasks effectively and efficiently; and (iii) lack of accountability for results. The ULGs have to develop an appropriate institutional mechanism that strengthens the capacity of the civil service for effective public service. Since autonomy and accountability are necessary for strengthening the capacity of the civil service for effective public service delivery, the following steps are required for improvement of public service delivery:

- Improve accountability;
- Give autonomy to the service providers to pursue clearly articulated goals with adequate resources;
- Delegate responsibilities for outputs and outcomes; and
- Have enforceability with teeth so that the non-performers are punished and the effective performers are rewarded.

Reforms in Urban Local Government

The CAA provides an important leverage to the state governments to involve urban local governments in the implementation of welfare programmes oriented towards the urban poor. The Act was a major policy directive. This harbinger effort is a turning point in the life and functioning of urban local governments in the country. This historic amendment provides for people's empowerment, democratic, decentralised and participative civic governance duly recognising municipalities as constitutional bodies forming the third-tier of the federal polity of India. The CAA aims at altering the governance structure of the country. The principal object of the Act is to refurbish the entire system of urban local governance by restructuring the municipal authorities with devolution of additional functions, planning responsibilities and a new system of fiscal transfers. The amendment seeks to provide the much-needed institutional capability to improve urban governance with the impulses of urbanisation and urban growth. The Act further seeks to provide a framework for political, functional and fiscal improvement of Urban Local Governments for good governance. It also provides for the constitution of Ward Committees in municipalities/corporations with a population of more than 3 lakhs, Metropolitan Planning Committees and District Planning Committees for preparation of plans of spatial, economic and social development.

The Act aims at decentralisation initiatives to undertake municipal reforms in financing urban infrastructure. These measures include: clear distinction of functional responsibilities among various levels of government; devolution of adequate revenues to Urban Local Governments commensurate with their functions; and ensure citizen-friendly urban local governance.

These measures enable towns and cities to become credit-worthy entities to attract the finances needed for infrastructure development in urban areas.

The new role assigned to the ULGs through the Constitution (74th Amendment) Act necessitate drastic administrative as well reforms in the organisation and procedures of administration to meet the ever-increasing demands and needs of urbanisation. In view of the transfer of several subjects to the exclusive domain of the ULGs they have become responsible to protect life and property of the citizens and to provide for their overall progress, growth and welfare, delivering goods and services to meet the requirements of the urbanites from time to time to their best satisfaction. There is a marked dissatisfaction among the urbanites in most of the urban areas in India with the quality and quantity of services provided by the ULGs. Though the Constitution (74th Amendment) Act aims at proper devolution of powers and functions to the ULGs to enable them to function as full-fledged local self government units, the absence of political and bureaucratic will on the part of the States has failed to give efficacy to the desired objective. The amendment has given the ULGs an honour and a constitutional status but not adequate strength and vitality to function as institutions of self-government. Besides, the CAA is recommendatory but not mandatory on the States which is also responsible for the slackness in bringing about the changes required in the functioning of the ULGs. There is, therefore, the need to overcome the weaknesses and short-comings of the system now in vogue and bring about necessary reforms in the organisation and structure of ULGs, in the administrative machinery, processes and procedures for the better. Urban governance structure should be completely revamped through reforms so that the nation can fully exploit the positive contribution of urbanisation. There should be a foolproof urban policy which could be implemented *in toto* in all ULGs in the country. These include

Administrative Reforms; Structural Reforms; and Capacity Enhancement.

The Urban Local Governments can address the growing urban challenges efficiently by:

- Collaborating with other agencies in policy making and implementation, involving private agencies and voluntary organisations.
- The engagement of all stakeholders of urban management in issues like local strategy, planning and resource mobilisation and in service delivery.
- The intensive and widely spread knowledge management for creating awareness in the stakeholders of urban management.

The performance of the ULGs is critical to the effective management of urban life. The ULGs as well as the private sector have to take special initiatives in improving the structure, process and resources of the ULGs to meet the ever-increasing urban challenges, since they are themselves the contributory factors to effectiveness. The ULGs perform better if the decentralisation of administration is accompanied by devolution of powers, functions and finances commensurate with the responsibilities of the ULGs so as to enable them to achieve economic development and ensure social justice.

Improvement of urban governance in India is likely to be a long drawn struggle. It has greater chance of success if an integrated approach is adopted along with making the necessary changes in the enabling environment. The ULGs have to adopt the following measures to improve urban governance:

- The political management in local authorities should be restructured so that decision-making is more transparent to local communities.
- Adaptation of the best practices for continuous improvement of services, in relation to the achievement of economy, efficiency and effectiveness.
- An efficient community leadership is required to make local government authorities responsible for taking the lead in

formulating community strategies which will be used to deliver a better quality of life for all urban dwellers.

- Undertaking a much wider range of economic, social and environmental improvement initiatives agreeable to local communities for ensuring community well-being.
- A prescribed standard of conduct of officials and local politicians.
- Increased financial discretion for executive and engineering authorities of Urban Local Governments for expediting decisions and their implementations.
- Public consultation, public involvement, user involvement and citizen engagement in the affairs of the local authority.
- To provide user and citizen feedback in relation to service and financial planning.
- Simplification of procedures and techniques in order not to overload the capacity of managers.
- Preparation of inventories of infrastructure to be maintained and services to be delivered;
- Prescription of service delivery standards and indicators;
- Specification of service maintenance tasks and frequency;
- Prescription of indicators of service efficiency in cost output terms with year-to-year comparison at constant prices;
- Short-term work planning, organising, resource planning and control;
- Productivity improvement measures, incentives and trainings.

Modern urban governance has several stakeholders who include, besides elected public representatives and officials, trade unions, government departments, ratepayers' associations, resident welfare groups, Chamber of Commerce, business associations, non-governmental organisations, self-help groups, professional organisations etc. The interactions among these and many other stakeholders are to be managed effectively to enforce efficient urban governance. The CAA aims at ushering in strong grass roots level democracy through the establishment of institutions. This will be possible only through the creation of strong urban institutions that play a decisive role in guiding the ULGs in the performance of their legal duties and to the best satisfaction of the citizens. Their finances, internal organisations and operating procedures must be clearly defined in the local urban governance laws.

Reforms in Rules and Procedures: This is one of the most important features of good urban governance. The existing municipal laws and procedures are most cumbersome and lengthy resulting in inordinate delay in the delivery of service and they very often lead to red-tapism, delay and corruption. There is, therefore, the dire need to simplify the procedures dealing with the delivery of various services like approval of building plans and layouts, issue of birth and death certificates, sanction of water tap connections, assessment, levy and collection of property tax, trade licence fee etc. It is imperative to build a service-oriented local government which is indispensible to promote socio-economic development and to improve the quality of urban life. There is the need to enhance governance performance in the ULGs so that they function to the best satisfaction of the citizens. The ULGs have, therefore, to pay special attention to certain key issues of urban governance.

Municipal level reforms under JNNURM: Introduction of accrual based accounting system, reform of the property tax by using GIS information, levying user charges to recover 100 per cent of operation and maintenance charges, provision of basic services to urban poor, and internal earmarking of budgets for this purpose.

State level reforms under JNNURM: enactment of public disclosure law, full implementation of the provision of Constitutional 74th Amendment Act including the setting up of DPCs and MPCs, enactment of community laws, associating elected representatives in city planning, repeal urban land ceiling act, reform of rent control act, and rationalisation of stamp duty.

Urban Local Governance should be responsive to the needs arising out of urban growth and to keep development on pace with demand. Mediation of different interests of the society enables the ULGs to reach a broad consensus on what is best for the whole community and how to achieve it. Since ULG is located closest to the citizens, it will have firsthand knowledge of the local problems and as such it has to serve as a forum for the locals to deliberate on their problems and contrive solutions in conformity with the local prevailing situation.

All plans for urban development must be inclusive so that all citizens will have opportunities for their improvement and maintaining their well-being. A society's well-being depends on ensuring that all its members feel that they have a stake in it.

References

1. Hayden, (Quoted by I.S.A.Band in *New Forms of Urban Governance in India,* New Delhi, 2008, p. 6.
2. Centre for Good Governance, *Recommendations for National Action Plan for Good Urban Governance,* published by Hyderabad, 2007 p. 3.
3. World Development Report, 2004.
4. Dr A. Gunasekharan *Good Governance in Poverty Reduction,* 2008, Chennai University, p. 278.

4

Organisation of Urban Local Government

The Department of Municipal Administration and Urban Development (M.A. & U.D), or Urban Affairs Department as is called in some states, in most of the Indian states consists of three main wings, namely the Administrative wing headed by the Commissioner and Director of Municipal Administration, who is always a senior officer of the Indian Administrative service; the Public Health Engineering wing, headed by an Engineer-in-Chief; and the Town Planning wing, headed by the Director of Town Planning. All the three heads function under the overall supervision and control of the M.A.&U.D. Department in the Government (Secretariat) headed by the Principal Secretary to Government who is one of the senior most I.A.S. officers in the State.

The Department of Municipal Administration and Urban Development handles planning and development in urban areas. The development is achieved through Master Plans prepared for urban centres and rural areas.

The main functions of the Department, besides directing the ULGs in routine administrative matters, are to:

- Assist the government and ULGs in town planning matters.
- Coordinate with various departments involved in development schemes like A.P. Housing Board, A.P. State Housing and Urban Development Corporations, A.P. Industrial and infrastructure Corporation, Industries Department, Urban Development Authorities and others.

- Offer technical recommendations to the government in matters like change of land use proposals, alienation of lands and relaxation of rules.
- Suggest and implement layouts and regulate the development of industries and other buildings as per suggested norms.
- Suggest and implement various Environmental Improvement Schemes, Remunerative Schemes and Road Widening Schemes.

Urban Local Governments in India

"Local self-government is that part of the government of a nation or state which deals mainly with such matters as concern the inhabitants of the particular district or place, together with those matters which, parliament has deemed it desirable, should be administered by local authorities, subordinate to the central government."[1] Local government institutions existed in India right from the Vedic times. The Rig Veda reveals that the ancient Hindus led a corporate life. According to K.P. Jayaswal, "the national life and activities in the earliest times on record was expressed through popular assemblies and institutions."[2] Kautilya refers to those institutions. Urban administration in ancient India was not only advanced but was also well-organised as is evident from historical documents.

Megasthenes gives a description of the administration of a large Hindu town in the third century before Christ. The city consisted of six bodies each one to look after industrial arts, entertainment of foreigners, birth and deaths, trade and commerce, manufactured articles, and tax collection.[3] Although local government existed in India since time immemorial, the ULGs in their present form and style of functioning owe their existence to the British rule in India.[4] "The two dominant considerations that led the British to establish local government institutions in India were the administrative problems due to the large size of the country and the paucity of the finances of the imperial power. The earliest steps towards the setting up of the local authorities in urban areas were motivated by the need of mobilising local fiscal resources for roads, public works, education, health and the like which were regarded as matters concerning the local people."[5]

While the first municipality was established in Surat in Gujarat, the second municipality in the country and the first municipality in Andhra Pradesh, India was established in the year 1861 in Bheemunipatnam when the Dutch started their shipping activity there.

The word Municipality derives its name from the Roman word *'municipium'* a free town possessing the right of Roman Citizenship but governed by its own laws.

The Municipal Office or Urban Local Government has two wings: the deliberative wing called the municipal council or the municipal corporation and the performance wing called the executive wing. The executive wing is headed by a Commissioner, or Chief Officer or Secretary to the council who is the Chief Executive Authority (CEA) of the Urban Local Government who coordinates the services of an Engineer, a Town Planning Officer a Municipal Health Officer, a Revenue Officer and a Manager. The elected wing consists of elected representatives (Ward Members) headed by the Chairperson in case of municipalities or Mayor in case of municipal corporations. Though the Commissioner is not a direct subordinate to the Chairperson, he is under the administrative control of the elected civic chief as prescribed by local law. The Municipal Authorities entrusted with the implementation of Municipal law are:

In respect of Municipality:

- Council, consisting of elected ward members;
- Elected Chairperson.
- Commissioner appointed by the Government; and
- Wards Committees;

In respect of Municipal Corporation:

- Corporation consisting of elected Ward Members;
- Standing Committee;
- Commissioner appointed by the Government; and
- Wards Committees.

Urban Local Governments can be broadly divided into three categories viz., *Nagar* (Town) *Panchayat*, Municipality and Municipal

Corporation. The population and income criteria for constitution of Urban Local Governments are as follows:

1. Nagar Panchayats

Major *Gram Panchayats* with urban characters whose population exceeds 25,000 and is below 40,000 with an annual income of Rs 40.00 lakhs and above and in which employment in non-agricultural income is 50 per cent or above shall be constituted into a *Nagar Panchayat* which is a transitional area between a *Gram Panchayat* and a Municipality. There is not much difference between a Third Grade Municipality and a *Nagar Panchayat* in regard to the staff pattern or functioning. They both work under the same Act with the same powers and functions. The different nomenclature is only to signify the fact that it is gradually switching over from rural to urban area.

2. Municipalities

There are different Grades of Municipalities with the following income criteria:

Table 4.1 Grades of Municipalities

Sl. No.	*Grade of the Municipality*	*Income (Rs. in Lakhs)*
1.	Grade – III	100.00 or less
2.	Grade - II	100.00 to 200.00
3.	Grade - I	200.00 to 300.00
4.	Special Grade	300.00 to 400.00
5.	Selection Grade	400.00 and above

Source: Certain Urban Local Government Acts.

The number of grades of municipalities differs from one state to another state.

There is no population criteria prescribed for the grading of municipalities.

3. Municipal Corporations or Large Urban Area

An Urban area with a population exceeding 3, 00,000 and having potentialities for international trade and commerce can be constituted into a Municipal Corporation (This criteria differs from state to state).

In the light of the vast experience gained over several decades of the functioning of the elected local authorities what can be suggested is that there should be clear demarcation of responsibilities rather than powers among different political and administrative authorities of Urban Local Government in order to ensure greater accountability of the ULGs to the citizens.

Andhra Pradesh and Tamil Nadu are among the well-organised States in enforcing an efficient urban administration in the States, despite the poor financial position of certain Urban Local Governments. Each higher grade Municipality is organised in such a way that it functions like a State Government writ small, since it encompasses all the subjects of the State Government and even more.

In the year 1965, the Government thought it desirable to enforce a uniform system of administration in the entire state duly enacting a common law. Thus, the Andhra Pradesh Municipalities Act, 1965 (A.P.M. Act, 1965) was enacted which came into force on April 1, 1965 in order to securing uniformity in the laws prevailing in both the regions, and with a view to providing more scope for the elected representatives on the Municipal Councils to have greater voice and control in administration and also to minimise the control of the Government over the Municipal Bodies to the extent possible.

The enactment of APM Act, 1965 brought with it several problems and administration of Municipalities in the State had almost come to a stand-still for 4 years due to innumerable lacunae in the law. Most of the powers of the Commissioner, who is the chief executive authority of the municipal council, were transferred to the Chairperson and the Commissioner was reduced to a stooge simply to nod his head to the tune of the elected Chairperson. Owing to various reasons the Chairperson did not pay proper attention to the administration of the Municipality with the result that the official machinery was baffled and was quite unable to deliver the goods. An accountable and service-minded administration had gone out of the reach of urban dwellers, necessitating urgent amendment to the A.P.M. Act, 1965. The amendment transferred certain powers to the Commissioner. In the year 1971, a comprehensive legislation was made clearly defining the functions, powers and responsibilities of the Commissioner. The Act was further amended in 1993 in order to set things right in the light of the working of the Act for over 28 years. In Tamil Nadu the District Municipalities Act, 1920 governs the functioning of the ULBs in the state. In other states, the ULBs function according to the local state acts.

Structural Organisation of Urban Local Governments

The ULGs in most of the states in India have a similar official structure with six (6) main sections each performing a specific function: (1) Establishment Section; (2) Accounts Section; (3) Revenue Section; (4) Engineering Section; (5) Town Planning Section; and (6) Health Section. After Poverty All eviation hass been added to the essential functions of the ULG, a separate section colled Urban Poverty Alleviation Cell is established in all ULGs which is called by different names in different staes, like MEPMA in A.P., Kudumbasri in Kerela soon. Each Section is headed by an officer and the entire official machinery functions under the overall administrative control and supervision of the Commissioner or Chief Officer of the Municipality or Municipal Corporation. The appointment of the officers heading each section is as follows:

- *Commissioner or Chief Officer*: He is the Chief Executive Authority (CEA) of the ULB (Urban Local Body). He is appointed by Government mostly on the recommendation of the Commissioner and Director of Municipal Administration.
- *Manager*: He is a member of the State Municipal Ministerial Service. He is appointed by the Commissioner & Director of Municipal Administration. He heads the Establishment Section of the ULG.
- *Municipal Engineer*: He is appointed by the Engineer-in-Chief (Public health) in respect of lower grades and the Government in respect of higher grade engineers. He heads the engineering section of the ULG.

- *Accountant*: He is a member of the State Accounts Officers cadre. He is appointed by the Director of Local Fund Audit in certain states and the Commissioner & Director of Municipal Administration in other states. He heads the accounts section of the ULG.
- *Revenue Section*: He is a member of the State Municipal Ministerial Service. He is appointed by the Head of the Department of Municipal Administration. He heads the Revenue Section of the ULG.
- *Town Planning Officer*: He is called as Chief City Planner or City Planner or TPO based on his cadre and the grade of the ULG. He is appointed by Government on the proposal of the Director of Town Planning. In respect of ULGs of lower grade there are only Town Planning Supervisors or Town Planning Building Overseers who are appointed by the Director of Planning.
- *Municipal Health Officer*: He is a Civil Assistant Surgeon with a Diploma in Public Health (D.P.H.) who is deputed by the Director of Health but the Director of Health is, however, not within the purview of the Municipal Administration Department. He heads the health section of the ULG. In certain states there is no Municipal Health Officer and the Public Health wing is headed by a Sanitary Officer.

The Functions of Each Section

It is an established fact that most of the Urban Local Governments are only perfunctorily, but not perfectly, performing their functions. The reasons are not far to search. It is, therefore, necessary to probe into the reasons for the dismal performance of the Urban Local Governments so that the deficits can be identified and the measures to tone up the functioning of the Urban Local Governments can be arrived at in order to ensure cent per cent accountability of the ULGs to the urban dwellers.

1. Establishment Section

The establishment section mainly deals with the service matters of the office staff and organisation of the municipal office. In each

ULG office there will be an office order clearly specifying the functions assigned to each designated official in the Municipal Office Manual. The functions assigned to the Commissioner of a ULG may be performed by his subordinate officers or the Heads of the Sections as per the delegation of powers given by the C.E.A. The efficient functioning of the establishment section depends on the thorough knowledge of the establishment staff relating to the section. Every member of the establishment must make himself thoroughly conversant with the Act, rules, regulations, bye-laws and executive instructions issued by the competent authority from time to time. If the establishment section is to be made accountable for the due discharge of its duties efficiently, the plea of ignorance of the staff dealing with the section should never be accepted as an excuse for their inefficient role in the management of the section. But, owing to the heavy financial deficit in budget allocation to the department of municipal administration, the governments of certain states have almost stopped fresh recruitment of staff to the vacancies caused due to the retirement, death or resignation of working staff. And whatever recruitment there was for over a decade and an half was limited only to the appointment, on compassionate grounds, of the dependents of employees deceased in harness, their appointment being based on a legal provision but not on merit. Thus, ignorance was substituted for intelligence and intellectual calibre. The stoppage of fresh recruitment of staff to the municipalities is also aimed at reducing expenditure on establishment. The steep reduction of efficient hands in the establishment section has adversely affected the efficient functioning of the section.

Adding insult to injury the undue interference of the local politicians in the administration of the ULG prevents the staff from discharging their duties impartially and as per law, resulting in growing indiscipline and irresponsible attitude of the municipal staff, thus failing in their accountability to the public. The first step to efficiently organise the ULG, therefore, is to "divide the office into convenient sections, and to draw up a clear distribution list, showing the subjects dealt with by each clerk."[6] The establishment section is headed by the Manager (in respect of Municipalities and *Nagar Panchayats* and the Superintendent in case of Municipal Corporations) who supervises the despatch of business of the section and its discipline. This section mainly deals with correspondence which includes opening, registering, indexing the papers received daily, fair-copying and despatching, the transfer of papers to the record room, their number-wise and chronological arrangement, their issue from the record room when required for reference and such other matters. The establishment section is responsible for prompt disposal of business. But inordinate delay is experienced in the section owing to incapacitated staff, inadequate infrastructure needed for quick disposal of work commensurate with the demands of the current age, political interference, absence of regular recruitment to various cadres of posts in the office, improper maintenance of registers etc, all of which will result in poor accountability of the section. The poor accountability of establishment section leads to over all inefficiency or poor performance of the administrative system of the ULG. The staff of the ULGs must be made to develop work culture and each public servant must realise that human life becomes more meaningful and fruitful with fulfilment through work.[7] A public servant, through his total commitment and dedication to work, fulfils his accountability to the public. All of man's life and achievements have always had a relevance to committed work. This dedication and commitment would be possible through developing a keen interest in the task given under the statute. Even during the Vedic times, the Indian *Hindu* society was divided into four *Varnas* (categories or communities) based on the functions they had to perform. The whole community, divided into four compartments, was supposed to perform all the society's work and cater to its needs.[8] In an exactly similar manner, the public servant or a government official has to perform his tasks strictly according to law, to fulfil his legal obligations to his employer, that is, the local self-government. Nowadays, although work is a professional exercise for earning a living, it does not seem to represent a centrallife interest unlike a few decades ago when work was pleasure and public servants regarded sincere discharge of their official duties as primary and all other activities as secondary to them. Nowadays there is a wide-spread and just feeling among citizens that there is a serious slackness of interest, concern, sense of duty and responsibility among a majority of municipal employees. The environment in which they work encourages these tendencies among them. They owe it to themselves, the institutions in which they work, and the society they belong to. They should realise that they have to discharge their assigned duties sincerely, promptly and responsibly.

The municipal staff, both technical and non-technical, lack capacity for planning, realistic budgeting, preparation, implementation and management of projects and social mobilisation. The sooner they realise this wisdom, the better it is for them. The development of work-culture is, therefore, of paramount importance in order that the public servants perform their functions to the best satisfaction of the citizens.

2. Accounts Section

Financial administration and its maintenance is the exclusive responsibility of the Accounts Section. This section deals with the preparation of annual budget, finalisation of annual accounts, audit, accounting for receipts and expenditure pertaining to the entire Urban Local Government. Prioritising items of expenditure and careful financial management in times of crisis is the sole responsibility of the Accounts Officer or Accountant, as he is called differently in different states. The Accounts section in a ULG should prepare a realistic annual budget clearly specifying the items of expenditure, both obligatory and discretionary, to which the municipal fund may be applied. Adequate provision will have to be made for everything necessary for or conducive to the safety, health, convenience, education of the inhabitants or to the amenities of the ULG and everything incidental to the administration. The Accounts Section should be capable of distinguishing the important item of expenditure from the unimportant and the more important from the less important item of expenditure.

The financial bankruptcy of most of the ULGs in the country and their inability to rise to the occasion in times of financial crisis is attributable to the inefficiency of the Accounts Section in prioritising the items of expenditure. There is a dire need for the Urban Local Governments to switch over to "Modern and transparent budgeting, accounting, financial management systems, designed and adopted for all urban services and governance functions" as envisaged under the JNNURM reforms. Accrual based double entry accounting system goes a long way in fulfilling this task.

3. Revenue Section

The entire activity of the ULG revolves round the Revenue section's capacity and efficiency. The revenues of the ULGs can be categorised into five heads: Taxes, Non-Taxes, Assigned Revenues, Non-Plan Grants and Plan Grants. While the latter three are devolved from the state government, the taxes and non-taxes are directly collected by the ULGs. The more the efficiency of the ULG the greater be the levy and collection of revenues from the two major heads. But there are several loopholes in the assessment, levy and collection of taxes and non-taxes by the ULGs which result in poor financial position that disable them to perform many of their important tasks properly.

4. Engineering Section

The most important section that holds the attention of the citizens captive is the Engineering Section. All developmental activities like the provision of urban infrastructure and its maintenance, preparation of projects for the development of the town/city come under the purview of this section. The main reason for the squalid look of most of the urban areas in the country is the incompetent and inefficient engineering staff who have no vision, commitment, dedication and expertise coupled with inadequate budget provision for maintenance of essential services.

5. Town Planning Section

This section is responsible for the regulated development of urban areas, prevention of reckless growth, removal of encroachments, widening of roads to enable the safety of vehicular traffic, preparation of master plan for the entire urban area as well as general town planning schemes, layouts, designs for housing, preparation of industrial, commercial, residential and agricultural zoning regulations and all matters related to the proper development of the town/city. This section, while preparing plans for urban development, has to follow the urban planning systems comprising long-term perspective plan, mid-term development plan and annual plan synchronising with the economic planning system of five year plans and annual plans. Planning is essential for effective urban development and urban development management.

6. Health Section

All health-related matters come under the purview of this section. Street sweeping, solid waste management, preventive medicine, control and prevention of seasonal diseases, epidemics and endemics, family planning, maintenance of medical institutions, pulse polio immunisation, health awareness programmes through information, education and communication activities etc. are the essential functions performed by the health section of Urban Local Government. The fast growth of urban areas, urban population and urban slums bring with them more and more health-related problems which the Urban Local Governments have to address properly.

Devolution of Powers and Finances to Urban Local Government

The Constitution (74th Amendment) Act, 1992 envisages the Urban Local Bodies to function as full-fledged local self government units and directs the States to take up confirmative legislation. Keeping in view the CAA on the devolution of powers and functions to Urban Bodies, most of the states in India have adopted conformity legislation by transferring some out of 18 functions enlisted in XII Schedule of the Constitution to the Urban Local Governments. These functions are detailed below:[9]

- Urban planning including town planning
- Regulation of land use and construction of buildings
- Planning for economic and social development
- Roads and bridges
- Water Supply for domestic, industrial and commercial purposes
- Public Health, Sanitation, conservancy and solid waste management
- Fire Services
- Urban Forestry, protection of environment and promotion of ecological aspects
- Safeguarding the interests of weaker sections of society, including the handicapped and the mentally retarded
- Slum improvement and up gradation
- Urban poverty alleviation
- Provision of urban amenities and facilities such as parks, gardens and playgrounds

- Promotion of cultural, educational and aesthetic aspects
- Burials and burial grounds, cremations, cremation ghats/ grounds and electric crematoria
- Cattle pounds, prevention of cruelty to animals
- Vital statistics including registration of births and deaths
- Public amenities including street lighting, parking lots, bus stops and public conveniences
- Regulation of slaughterhouses and tanneries

The Government of Andhra Pradesh has transferred the following subjects to the control of the ULBs[10]

- Urban Planning including Town Planning;
- Regulation of land use and construction of buildings;
- Roads and bridges;
- Water supply for domestic, industrial and commercial purposes;
- Public health, sanitation, conservancy and solid waste management;
- Fire Services;
- Slum improvement and upgradation;
- Provision of urban amenities and facilities such as parks, gardens, playgrounds;
- Burials and burial grounds: cremations, cremation grounds and electric crematoriums;
- Cattle pounds, prevention of cruelty to animals;
- Vital statistics including registration of births and deaths;
- Public amenities including street lighting, parking lots, bus stops and public conveniences;
- Regulation of slaughterhouses and tanneries;
- Urban Poverty Alleviation;

In addition to the above the following financial powers are also devolved on the Urban Local Bodies[11]

- Planning for economic and social development
- Urban forestry, protection of environment and promotion of ecological aspects

- Safeguarding the interests of the weaker sections of society, including the handicapped and mentally retarded
- Promotion of cultural, educational and aesthetic aspects

The Urban Local Bodies are authorised to outsource civic services wherever necessary.

Great hopes were raised about municipal bodies with the enactment of the Constitution (74th Amendment) Act, 1992. The Amendment empowers a State Legislature to endow the municipalities with such powers and authority as may be necessary to enable them to function as institutions of self-government and such law may contain provisions of the devolution of powers and responsibilities upon municipalities with respect to the preparation of plans for economic development, social justice etc. The sonorous terminology is pleasant to hear but the State Legislatures have not taken any action so far in pursuance of this Constitutional provision, except constituting a new elected body before the expiry of the term of the previous body and transferring responsibilities without devolution of adequate finances. It is impossible for an empty pocket to prepare plans and projects for economic development and social justice. Article 24-X provides that the Legislature of a State may assign a municipality such taxes, tolls and fees levied and collected by the State Government and provide for making such grant-in-aid to the municipalities from the consolidated funds of the State. Besides most of the states have not sanctioned any new taxes and new grants-in-aid to the urban local governments, even the profession tax collections are not adjusted to them. The State Finance Commission (S.F.C.) was constituted under Article 243-I to review the financial position of the municipalities and make recommendations for the distribution between the State and the municipalities of the taxes, duties, fees etc. collected by the State. While the subjects are transferred from the state domain to the local domain, adequate funds for development are not devolved.

Decentralisation of Powers

Decentralisation of administrative decision is not a new idea. Lord Mayo in his resolution of 1870 stressed the need to introduce certain changes in the administration of Municipalities. This resolution advocated that services like roads, education and medical relief should be treated as local issues and the funds required for their administration should be raised through taxation. The resolution also emphasised the need to raise local recourses for the management of local bodies.

Lord Ripon, a liberal minded Viceroy, known as the father of Local Self Government in India recognised the need to organise Local Self-government on sound lines. The resolution aimed at the devolution of Functions and finances according to local needs.[12] "By this system", Lord Ripon said "the tax payers have a satisfaction that they get a direct and immediate return for the services of sanitation, water, lighting, roads and education. To encourage public participation, men of respectable standing in native society may be induced to be elected as Chairman and conferred the title of *Rao Bahadur* or *Khan Bahadur*"[13]

The idea of decentralisation was to relieve the central government and state governments a large part of their excessive powers and responsibilities. Decentralisation means the transfer of certain powers and responsibilities from a higher authority to a lower or local authority. It connotes the establishment of a local representative government endowed with adequate administrative and financial powers to discharge the constitutional obligations and deliver their mandated services to their citizens. The Constitution (74th Amendment) Act, 1992 is the foundation for India's decentralisation efforts. The Amendment enables the participation of women and marginalised groups in government, ensures the existence of local political bodies and sets up a State Finance Commission to recommend guidelines for improving the financial position of the urban local governments. Decentralisation enables the ULGs to take decisions close to the scene of action. It allows active participation of citizens in the development process through identification of felt-needs, prioritisation of basic needs which leads to a sense of true ownership of the citizens (beneficiaries of urban development) and their commitment to the civic cause. Decentralisation efforts in the government should be complemented with necessary legal changes in the consumer laws so that they ensure better services to the people.[14]

Decentralisation has to take place at three stages: the functional and financial decentralisation from the State to the ULGs; decentralisation within the city from the city administrative units to the divisional levels; decentralisation from the divisional level to the community groups and civil society stakeholders, women and the marginalised to share in decision-making and implementation. The appropriate idea of decentralisation in the context of the Constitution (74th Amendment) Act, 1992 connotes citizen participation in urban local administration in its fullness.

References

1. Clark, J.J., *Local Government of United Kingdom*, London, 1948, p.1.
2. K.P. Jayaswal, *Hindu Polity,* Bangalore, 1955, p.12.
3. Sharda Chopra, *Dynamics of Municipal Administration,* Abhijeet Publications, Delhi, 2005, p.12.
4. Sriram Maheshwari, *Local Government in India,* New Delhi, 1966, p. 6.
5. Report of the Rural-Urban Relationship Committee, Vol. II, New Delhi, 1966, p. 6.
6. District Office Manual, Government of Andhra Pradesh, Hyderabad, p. 4.
7. Bata K. Dey, *Work Culture in India-Achievements and Failure*, Indian Journal of Public Administration, April-June 1989, Vol. XXXV, No.2, p.165.
8. Bata K. Dey, op. cited, p.165.
9. Toolkit on Comprehensive Capacity Building Programme for Improved Urban governance & Poverty Reduction, Ministry of Housing & Urban Poverty Alleviation, JNNURM Mission Directorate, New Delhi, 2009, p. 3.
10. G.O.Ms. No. 217, M.A., dated May 15, 2002
11. G.O.Ms. No.12, M.A., dated January 20, 2004.
13. Pillay, K.K., *History of Local Self-government in the Madras Presidency, 1850-1919*, All India Institute of Local Self-government, Bombay, 1953, p. 58.
13. Argal R., *Municipal Government in India*, Allahabad, Agarwal Press, 1950, p. 18.
14. Venkata Rangaiah, M., *The Development of Local Boards in the Madras Presidency,* Madras, 1938, p. 3.

5

Deliberative Wing vs. the Executive Wing of the Urban Local Governments

"The institutional characteristics of urban government play a part in determining its effectiveness, along with the people who run it and the environment within which it operates," (Davey, 1993)

The urban governance system has, *inter alia*, two important stakeholders—the political wing, also known as the deliberative wing, and the executive wing also known as the performance wing. The structural framework of the ULGs in the country is by and large the same. Every ULG consists of two wings-an official wing headed by an Executive Authority called the Commissioner or Secretary or Chief Officer, and a deliberative wing or political wing called the municipal council (in case of towns) or the municipal corporation (in case of cities) headed by a presiding authority called the Chairperson or President or the Mayor who is called the civic chief or city father. While the policy-making or decision-making power is mainly vested with the elected body, the implementation part vests with the official machinery. The strength of the elected body is fixed by the state governments as per the norms prescribed in the municipal acts of the respective states.

In every Urban Local Government the political wing is elected by the voters of the urban area and the executive wing consists of the official machinery appointed by the government. The two wings have a distinct role to play in the governance of the urban area, performing functions and discharging duties as specified in the laws of the respective states.

"A single wheel cannot run", says *Arthasastra*, "and so government is only possible with assistance." Likewise the political wing cannot run the administration of the Urban Local Government unassisted by the executive wing, nor can the latter take up appropriate decisions on its own in respect of public issues without the political wing. The advice tendered by the political wing is binding on the executive wing for implementation unless it is inconsistent with provisions of the law governing the urban local government. That is the relationship between the two wings of the urban local government and which speaks of the need for coordination between the two wings for efficient urban governance. The issues that are to be addressed by the ULGs require a partnership between the political wing and the executive wing for effective action. Both the wings of the ULG should function towards the broader goal of the welfare of the citizens.

An enlightened political wing and a dynamic, well-informed executive put together will provide the most accountable and citizen-friendly administration and deliver goods to the public. But this ideal is seldom realised in practice. Though the principal business of the political wing is only policy-making, it unduly interferes in the administration while the executive wing influences the political wing in the formulation of policy and even in decision-making in routine administration which completely disturbs the healthy functioning of the two wings of the ULG. Each wing in its efforts to dominate and control the other wing creates problems that ultimately reflect on the administration. Added to this, the terminology that defines the functions of the political wing varies considerably from the Act of one state to the Act of another state with the result that the political wing very often acts *ultra vires,* which disturbs the harmonious relationship between the two wings of the ULG. The infringement of the powers of one wing by the other wing leads to malfeasance like transgression of law in the discharge of duties, illegal activities, delay in service delivery, discourtesy towards the public and irresponsibility to public call, incompetence, suppression of facts etc. which cannot be easily checked and corrected and it ultimately leads to ineffective service delivery and improper accountability. Hence, there is necessity to clearly separate the policy-making function from the implementation function and to dissociate the political wing from the executive wing.

Deliberative or Elected Wing: The deliberative or elected wing of the ULG consists of the members elected by the electorate of the city or town with a presiding authority either directly elected by the voters or one of the members elected among themselves. The important functions of the political wing, as contained in many of the local governments' acts in general are:

- Making of bye-laws and taking policy decisions for regulation of business;
- Approval of annual budget;
- Sanction of civil works as per the budget provision;
- Ensuring the implementation of various developmental activities and all government sponsored schemes within the stipulated time;
- Ensuring financial discipline of the urban local body.

Executive or Performance Wing: The executive or performance wing of the ULG is headed by Chief Executive Authority and consists of staff partly appointed by Government and partly by the Urban Local Government. The CEA is appointed by the State Government and functions as per the legal provisions enacted by the State legislature. The important functions of the executive wing are to:

- Perform administrative and regulatory functions and implement all Government sponsored development schemes;
- Be in charge of the urban local government and implement all the resolutions of the political wing and be responsible for the due fulfilment of the objectives of the urban local government's act;
- Maintain financial accountability and ensure efficient service delivery;
- Prompt redressal of public grievances;
- Furnish to the political wing all the information received from the State and Central Governments;
- Assist the political wing with all relevant information for taking decisions.

Though the Chief Executive Authority is appointed by the Government and his functions and powers are clearly spelt out in the law, the political wing exercises tremendous influence on his functioning with the result that the executive wing has to succumb to the stress of the political wing. The CEA coordinates the work of all sections of the ULG, each section headed by a section head.

The two wings of the ULG have the common responsibility of fulfilling the constitutional obligations to the urbanites. But the problem with the present set up of the urban local governance is the total immunity of the political wing from accountability and punishment for any act or crime it commits. Absence of punishment for public representatives for any offence they commit and their total immunity from accountability are the root causes of inefficient and irresponsible administration in most of the ULGs. While the political wing takes credit for the good achievements of the executive wing, the executive wing is held responsible for the failures and offences of the political wing. The malfeasance of the political wing is never checked while the executive wing is held responsible even for the lapses and irresponsible deeds of the political wing, on the presumption of not guiding the political wing properly. In a position of such absolute irresponsibility the misdeeds and illegal activities of the political wing go unchecked and uncontrolled. The undue influence of one wing over the other creates problems that damage public interest. Good urban governance thus remains an utopia, unless the powers of the political wing are accompanied by responsibilities. Mere decentralisation of functions and devolution of powers from the Central and State Governments to the ULGs will not achieve the efficacy unless the powers, functions and responsibilities of each wing are clearly spelt out in the law governing the ULGs with penal provisions for their violation.

In order to promote greater accountability and a sensitive urban governance, the two wings of the ULG should function independent of each other, with interdependence only to the extent of the executive wing assisting the political wing with necessary information and legal guidance for policy formulation or decision-making, and the political wing supervising the functioning of the executive wing and ensuring the implementation of its decisions. Democracy at the town or city level becomes more meaningful and successful if, and only if, each of the two wings plays its roles within the framework of the established law and without encroaching into the functional domain of the other wing.

The ULGs in no state are empowered to legislate. They function as per the laws passed by the respective state legislatures. The ULGs can only frame byelaws to implement the provisions of the Urban Local Government's Act. The municipal laws suffer from certain lacunae since common legal provisions do not suit the local conditions of all ULGs in the state.

Majority of the elected local leaders have long since ceased to function as responsible public representatives, keenly interested in the welfare of their electors or development of their administrative jurisdiction. Local politics has long since ceased to be the pastime of the elite and the civilised people and has become one of the business activities of the majority of the elected ward members and local self-appointed leaders. The incapacity of the ULGs for delivering services efficiently and effectively is due to the reluctance of the elected ward members to enforce efficient governance for the benefit of the citizens. That is why they organise the governance structure in such a way that the official machinery functions as the henchmen of the elected wing so that the people's dependence on elected members maximises that ultimately increases their importance and promotes their election prospects.

It is observed in recent times that there is an abnormal increase of self-seeking cantankerous members in the political wing in most of the ULGs who treat the elective office as an opportunity to purchase a higher political office and very often abuse their powers to promote their personal or vested interests rather than fulfilling their constitutional obligations to the people even at the cost of development of the urban area with the result that the ULGs fail to function as efficient service providers. For example, in the execution of civil works, the members of the political body execute the works, as they themselves are the contractors, usually by proxy. This domination of self-interest over public interest among the members of the political wing coupled with their inadequate comprehension of the local issues and lack of capacity to address them has totally vitiated the very objective and purpose of urban local self-governance with independent decision-making powers. This attitude of the political wing and the total absence of harmonious relations between the two wings of the ULG, stunt the pace of urban development commensurate with the quick pace of urbanisation.

Another important matter of serious concern is that a considerable number of members of the political wing are practically without experience in dealing with public affairs and are quite unaware of the requirements of citizens and the nuances of urban local governance. They are quite unaware of the Government sponsored welfare schemes. Thus, the political wing fails to supervise and cheek the proper and effective implementation of these welfare schemes by the executive wing and rather pressurises the executive wing to cooperate with them in promoting their vested interests. The non-cooperation of the executive wing with the political wing in promoting their vested interests leads to conflicts between the two important stakeholders of urban governance, ultimately leading to administrative impasse in the ULGs. Thus, the bureaucratic work with democratic check, which is the underlying principle of democracy, fails to achieve the object set for. Adding insult to injury the legal framework that governs the relations between the two wings is not clear and effective in certain states. While the executive wing is entrusted with responsibilities and without powers, the political wing is entrusted with powers without responsibilities. While the executive wing has to perform its function and discharges its duties strictly according to the established law it faces tremendous influence of the political wing to violate law to promote their vested interest. Though the principles governing the roles and responsibilities of the two wings of the ULGs are well-defined and clear in the laws of certain states, in the actual working of the ULGs the clear division of responsibilities become blurred with the political wing encroaching upon the sphere of activities of the executive wing.

Meetings of the Council: The law has not properly streamlined the working of the political wing in certain states. While it is mandatory for political wing to regularly meet for discussion of the agenda at the appointed date and time, the presiding authority calls for meetings of the council at his will and pleasure. Furthermore, there is no meaningful discussion of any subject by the members of the political wing. What one observes from the deliberations of the meetings of the councils is only utter chaos, making charges and counter charges against one another and finally throwing the odium on the executive wing for their lapses or failures. This would naturally strain the relations between the two wings and the citizens become victims of the internal and internecine conflicts between the political wing and the executive wing of the ULG. In most of the ULGs the statutory meetings of the elected councils are held not with the objective of taking decisions but the meetings serve as a forum for settlement of personal scores between conflicting groups in the council. In view of the miserable failure of democracy at grassroots (town or city) level, and the conflicting interests between the members of the state legislature and the members of the local government, certain states do not go for periodical elections to the ULGs for several years in blatant violation of the law. It is only after the enactment of the Constitution (74th Amendment) Act, which has made it mandatory to hold elections to the ULGs well before the expiry of the term of the existing body that elections are held to the local bodies regularly and within the statutory period.

Election of the Civic Chief: The Civic Chief (Mayor, Chairperson or President) of an Urban Local Government is directly elected by the voters of the urban area in certain states while he is elected from among the elected ward members in other states. The direct election of the Civic Chief was introduced in Andhra Pradesh in 1987 and in certain other states in order to give him a status of irremovability from the elective office for the full term and to enable him to act independently in decision-making in certain matters. Experience gained over the last three elections shows that the direct election of the Civic Chief has certain inherent disadvantages also. It very often happens that the directly elected Civic Chief belongs to one political party while the Deputy or Vice Civic Chief, who is the leader of the single largest political party in the council, belongs to another political party with the result that the official machinery has to swing between two political authorities ultimately resulting in bad administration.

The Civic Chief: An independent empowered Civic Chief (Mayor or Chairperson) with independent decision-making power is no doubt necessary for efficient organisation of the urban local self-government but such a political entity is not always accountable to the council or the governing body of the ULG since he is not easily removable, and the cumbersome procedure prescribed for his removal from office, even for grave charges or his persistent failure to perform his functions according to the provisions of law, gradually makes him tyrant, irresponsible to public call and unaccountable to the council, while the Civic Chief, elected from among the elected ward members, functions in close harmony with the elected council and the scope for unilateral decisions or lopsided administration is minimised, since he is always in the hands of the ward members who elected him, as he owes his office to the ward members. Thus, both directly elected and indirectly elected civic chief offices have their own advantages and disadvantages.

The third and more important political authority under the Local Government Acts is the Chairman of the Standing Committee (in respect of Municipal Corporations) who exercises more powers than even the Civic Chief or the Deputy Civic Chief. In certain states there are very few matters that go up to the Council or Corporation presided by the Civic Chief, the rest being settled either by the Commissioner or the Chairperson of the Standing Committee. Thus, due to the concentration of political and administrative powers in two or three authorities the efficiency of administration of the Urban Local Government suffers. Realising this serious lacuna in the law certain states have restored indirect election of the chairperson or mayor so that the civic chief always belongs to the party to which majority of the elected members belong and the civic chief is also the ex officio chairperson of the standing committee so that the decision making lies with the city father while he remained a titular head of the ULG under the previous administrative set up.

Public employment is public wealth and public service is an opportunity for anyone to feel a part of something bigger than oneself. It is an elevation of one's personality and improvement of one's image in the public. Working for a town's or city's development is a highly rewarding career since it gives the utmost satisfaction of developing the town or city. The role of political wing is to encourage officials to give the benefit of their talent and expertise for the development of the urban area. But unfortunately the ULG service has become lacklustre for talented individuals, and the young career-minded individuals do not desire to seek a position in local government. The ULGs are losing their ability to attract and pluck out the smartest, most talented young professionals into their service. It is not only due to stagnant wages or frequent backlashes against officials but also because of lack of independence and security for the officials and lack of job satisfaction as well as the prevailing service conditions. The officials with innovative ideas and service motto are not able to give the best out of their ideas and talent, like working on plans to build new housing colonies, construct new parks and thereby create value for the surrounding lands or take up a major economic development project and the like. The highly gifted officials are unable to render service as they have to work with recalcitrant members of the political wing whose only motto is "get-rich-quick."

The executive wing very often finds itself in a fix, unable to comply with the demands of the self-seeking members of the political wing and on the other hand, unable to perform their functions in accordance with the established law. While refusing compliance with the demands of the political wing results in conflicts with it, violation of law results in punishment to the executive wing. In such a precarious situation, administration of the ULG very often comes to stand still, necessitating the interference of a higher authority of the State Government or the district administration to solve the deadlock. But the absence of such an appropriate constitutional authority to solve differences is another lacuna in the law.

The roles of the two wings can be better understood in the words of a great philosopher and that of an eminent jurist. Will Durant, the famous American philosopher, after a life-long study of various civilisations of the world has summed the lesson of history which has great significance for democracy in India: "Democracy is the most difficult of all forms of government since it requires the widest spread of intelligence. We forgot to make ourselves intelligent when we made ourselves the sovereign." These words clearly bring out the deficiencies in a local democratic set up that failed the ULGs to achieve the success that is expected of it. It shall be our endeavour to train the members of the political wing in appreciation of their role in a democracy so that they play their role effectively and constructively.

N.A. Palkhiwala, the eminent jurist and Constitutional expert rightly observes that "I have no doubt that the Government has at its disposal highly equipped man power-a large pool of talent, expertise and dedication more than the private sector or any other segment of society. But unfortunately there is something in the structure or system of a bureaucratic set up which prevents the highly gifted members of the civil service from giving their best to the country." This '*something*' is what needs a detailed examination by all administrators, legal luminaries and academicians so that its removal will pave the way for enabling the executive wing perform its tasks better and provide efficient governance through detached pursuit of action strictly in accordance with the established law.

Larry Diamond, a reputed authority in the world on democracy rightly observes that "if India wants to improve its democracy, it must create stronger institutions that allow for horizontal accountability" and that "India needs a counter corruption commission, which should be fully autonomous in its authority to check efficiency and punish corruption."

The growing inefficiency and ineffectivity of ULGs is mainly due to the official machinery acting on the basis of oral instructions of superiors and people in power which do not have legal sanction and which are not recorded. As a result, serious predicaments arise like deterioration of the standards of probity and accountability in the ULGs. The arbitrary and illegal decisions and acts of civil servants are the inevitable consequence of the evil influence of politicians who do not hesitate to force public servants of ULGs even to ruin their career for promotion of their vested interests.

It is impossible for the Chief Executive Authority of the ULG to maintain fearlessness, integrity and independence in the prevailing circumstances unless he is provided with certain special protection measures against undue interference of politicians *et al.* Special protection to the executive wing is necessitated by the greater role they have been entrusted with by the inclusion of several new subjects like urban poverty alleviation, weaker section housing etc. within the purview of the functions of the ULGs. There should be an independent statutory board or commission to effect promotions, transfers and postings of the Chief Executive Authorities of the ULGs in order to keep the important office, dealing with public affairs, away from political bickering. There should be a fixed tenure for all the important top brass officers of the ULGs to ensure stability and promote development and to implement various social welfare programmes. This would enable the officers to achieve their professional targets and help them to function as effective instruments of public policy. Minimum assured service is essential for effective service delivery and increased efficiency.

The official machinery of the ULGs should be responsive and citizen friendly, transparent, accountable and ethical in its actions and interface with the people. The Government should promote intellectual growth of municipal functionaries and upgrade their domain knowledge. The official machinery should be protected against pressure exerted by administrative superiors, politicians, business interests and other vested interests. There should be a healthy working atmosphere for the official machinery of the ULGs to perform functions, discharge duties and exercise powers entrusted to the officials in strict accordance with the established law. This will be possible only when there is a healthy working relationship between the two wings of the ULG which is critical for good urban governance.

In the due discharge of duties the officials of the ULGs have to take decisions from time to time in the interest of public welfare and safety which will have far reaching consequences on service delivery. Their decisions must be transparent and in public interest. But in the present scenario the role of officials of the ULGs has become very complex and onerous due to the dominance of the vested interest of politicising over public interests. While the executive wing is accountable to the urbanites for all their decisions and actions, they are forced to be answerable only to the politicians, totally ignoring public welfare. This situation calls for serious attention of law makers to ensure the prefect functioning of the official machinery of the ULGs in order to enable it to fulfil its legal obligations and to work out the objectives of the local governing laws. This is possible only when the official machinery is completely insulated against political interference.

There should be a high level supervisory committee at the state as well as regional level consisting of eminent men from all walks of life and urban governance experts to guide and advise the two wings who would bring in more professionalism, expertise and efficiency in the functioning of the urban local governments. Simultaneously a separate municipal cadre must be established in each state the members of which must be transferable periodically so that they function independently as per the established law uninfluenced by the local political bickering.

Conclusion

In order to improve the functioning of the ULGs the two wings should strictly adhere to their respective spheres of activity. The law governing the functioning of the ULGs has to clearly specify the functional domain and responsibilities of each wing in their respective acts to avoid infringement of the powers of one wing by the other. There must be a clear demarcation of functions for the two wings of the urban local governments in their respective acts. There must be a legal authority in every state to solve the conflicts that arise between the two wings of the ULG whose decision should be final in case of conflict of interest between the two wings.

The locals depend on the ULG for their local needs from cradle to grave. The successful functioning of the ULG lies in the development of a citizen friendly democratic government in which the deliberative wing and the executive wing function in close cooperation and with mutual respect and understanding, fulfilling the legal obligations to the citizens. The ULG commands respect and support of all sections of the people by virtue of its effective discharge of duties and prompt disposal of their grievances. There are no substitutes for honesty, integrity, equity and probity. No law or statute gives any positive results to ULGs unless both wings perform their functions with honesty and integrity with public welfare as the ultimate goal of both wings.

The political wing should take all steps for capacity building of the official machinery, planning for development of infrastructure commensurate with the quick pace of urbanisation, simplification of procedures, sensitising the public in respect of public delivery system etc. The political wing should inspire and serve as a catalyst to influence the best and brightest individuals to join the local self government service. Prioritisation of the felt-needs of the public and their welfare should be the guiding principle of decision-making by the political wing.

The executive wing should strictly confine its activities to implementation of the decisions of the political wing, perform its functions as ordained by law and desist from influencing the political wing in decision-making. Accountability to both the public and the political wing should be the guiding principle of official conduct of the executive wing.

The traditional administrative structure can no longer function efficiently in the fast changing urban scenario. Efficient urban local governance in the modern sense is one that has functional autonomy, financial self-sufficiency for due discharge of their constitutional obligations, empowerment of local functionaries to perform their functions efficiently and effectively and both the wings ensuring social accountability and transparency and allowing community participation in decision-making to achieve the desired objectives of urban local governance. It is the responsibility of the deliberative wing to ensure economy in expenditure, efficiency and effectiveness in service delivery while it is the bounden duty of the executive wing to possess loyalty, diligence, dedication, commitment, perseverance and integrity in the performance of their functions, discharge of their duties and exercise of their powers.

Both wings of the ULG should strive to fulfil the aspirations of the citizens as per the constitutional obligations envisaged in the Constitution (74th Amendment) Act, 1992 to the best satisfaction of citizens, which is the ultimate object of local self-governance.

The Constitutional (74th Amendment) Act, 1992 no doubt infused new blood in city governance in the country but the required and expected efficacy has not been achieved owing to various factors like inadequacy of urban administrative machinery and lack of a state wide broad based urban cadre, both administrative and technical. In order to improve the functioning of the ULGs the Chief Executive Authority of the town or city (Municipal Commissioner) is to be strengthened to function not only as a vital channel of communication but also as a staff agency to provide managerial and technical service. Besides, ULGs need for efficient functioning:

- A chief executive with demonstrable diplomatic skills;
- A management organisation with prestige, links with major sectoral public agencies and private enterprises, and ready-access to decision makers;
- Trained staff of multi-professional backgrounds working together towards common solutions;
- The involvement of client communities as an essential component of all urban projects.

6

Urban Finance and Resource Mobilisation

Urban Finance

'How to make cities better governed?' is the question before municipal functionaries. This question immediately raises the next question as to 'what resources are required to achieve it?' All ULGs in the country, irrespective of other aspects, face two serious problems-massive urban growth and concentration, and increasing cost of services. But the increase of revenues of ULGs has not kept pace with the increase in expenditure. About 60 per cent of the total revenue generated goes towards staff salaries and O&M charges. (This percentage differs from ULG to ULG). Most of the ULGs do not have revenue surplus to transfer to capital account. This situation reveals the need of the ULGs in the country to augment their local financial resources. There is the urgent need for cites to mobilise adequate resources to effectively address the issues arising from changing urban needs and demands since revenue generation must keep pace with the increasing expenditure on urban infrastructure and maintenance cost of essential services. Hence, augmentation of revenue sources at local (ULG) level is a must.

The problem of urban finance is that the fiscal role of the ULGs in India's economic framework has never been systematically assessed with the result that the finances of the ULGs have always been in doldrums.[1] The Constitution (74th Amendment) Act, 1992 points towards a larger role for the ULGs in the country's development affairs and suggests a larger fiscal space for them. The amendment provides for a review of the financial position of the ULGs once every five years, recognises the need and provides for a revenue-sharing arrangement between the ULGs and state governments, and encourages the ULGs to explore and experiment with revenue-enhancement measures. The assignment of functions to the ULGs should be matched by adequate finances. Unless finances are improved through local revenue generation as well as devolution of funds from state and central governments, decentralisation of functions serves no useful purpose. The Act has not improved the financial position of the ULGs but exacerbated the problem by the addition of new functions. There is a need to mobilise additional resources to cover the increasing financial requirements of service provision and fulfil the constitutional obligations ordained on the ULGs by the Act.

Sound financial management based on vigorous exploitation of local resources is essentially required for urban development and efficient urban management. Besides generation of internal resources, devolution of funds from Central and State Governments, the ULGs have to plug loopholes in levy, assessment and collection of local taxes and non-taxes etc. The ULGs have to improve their financial base to improve their revenue and expenditure performance, since provision of better infrastructure and service delivery efficiency depend on the availability of financial resources. In most of the ULGs there is a wide gap between the requirement of revenue and actual receipt which will hamper the growth potential of the urban areas. The growing demand for increased as well as improved urban services is pressing hard against the limited resources and poor administrative capacity of the Urban Local Bodies to cope with the problems of inadequate distribution and inequitable access to urban basic services. The ULGs have, therefore, to exploit the full potential of revenue under each source, since the standard of civic amenities provided is directly influenced by the availability of finances from all sources.

Municipal Own Revenues: The problems of finances for ULGs in India are due to scant attention urban managers have paid to critical issues of municipal finance management, imperfectly developed institutional mechanism for revenue generation and collection etc. Revenues locally generated by municipalities fall short of revenue expenditure in all states of India, except Maharashtra and Punjab.

According to P.K. Mohanty, "The share of own revenue sources in most ULBs was only about 1 per cent of city income," and hence he suggests that "equipping them with suitable revenue instruments could raise their own sources in the range of 6-7 per cent of city income."[2] Report of the Thirteenth Finance Commission (2010) reveals the per capita municipal expenditures and revenues in India in 2007 as follows:

Table 6.1 Grades of Municipalities

Year	*2002-03*	*2007-08*
Total revenue from all sources	Rs.734	Rs.1,430
Total expenditure	Rs.758	Rs.1,513

The above figures indicate the sorry state of finances of the ULGs. Despite genuine efforts to improve finance during the last decade or so, the efficacy is not achieved by the ULGs in India. The proportion of "own" revenues to total revenues of ULGs in most of the states of India is estimated to be less than 20 per cent, which clearly indicates that ULGs are desperately depending on devolution of funds from state and central governments. In order to minimise this dependence on governmental assistance ULGs have to generate their own local resources through updating accounts, revising taxes and non-taxes from time to time.

According to P.K. Mohanty, "Octroi has been the only tax within the jurisdiction of city government having capacity to keep pace with the growth of economic activities."[3] The abolition of Octroi had hard hit the finances of all ULGs in the country. The above situation calls for an adequate compensation to ULGs which should be equal to the realisation of income had Octroi been continued.

Basic civic services available in cities at present are unsatisfactory, and are far short of what is required to sustain faster and more inclusive growth of the economy. Cities cannot play their role as engines of economic growth if they are not financially sound to develop and maintain the infrastructure and services needed for fast expanding urban areas and burgeoning urban population.

Despite the growing vexed and vexing problems in urban areas due to various reasons, urbanisation is a positive, historical force and hence Urban Local Governments should make every effort to cope with quick pace of urbanisation and ensure that urban areas deliver a quality life that would enable them to become national assets and continue to be engines of economic growth. ULGs should develop a political and administrative system that responds to the ever-increasing needs of its people swiftly, flexibly and efficiently. Since the quick pace of urbanisation poses several new challenges relating to both governance and financing of urban services, ULGs have to take up two important issues-reforms in governance and augmenting their finances through exploiting local revenue generation to the fullest extent.

Cities are generators of revenue. Urban India is expected to contribute 75 per cent to the country's GDP by 2031. But as on date "cities are rich" but "city local governments are poor." This is due to the gross mismatch between the incomes to ULGs and the expenditure requirements. How to bridge the gap is the question before the ULGs. Each assigned function of ULG is not adequately funded. There is no broad clarity regarding how each and every particular service is to be adequately and predictably financed. For example, a flat rate is collected for protected water supplied for domestic use. The income realised from sale of protected water is not even 50 per cent of the expenditure incurred with the result that the balance of maintenance cost is met from other sources. This will result in recurring loss every year. It is, therefore, necessary to identify the revenue sources appropriate to finance particular type of services.

It is expedient for the ULGs to make genuine efforts to fill the gap between the expenditure required and income from all available sources of revenue to the ULG. In order to bridge the urban fiscal gap ULGs have to generate a current surplus so that they can take up development required for growing urban areas.

The need for development of infrastructure and its effective and efficient management commensurate with the rising levels of urbanisation and growth of urban population need no elaboration. The Indian cities are no exception to it. The development of infrastructure in cities is essential to sustain the quality of urban life and to enable the urban areas to continue their positive contribution to the national economy. The creation of urban development infrastructure, both physical and socio-economic, requires the ULGs to allocate a major part of their resources. The need for additional resources is further compounded by other functions like poverty alleviation, transport, medical and health, recreation facilities and so on. The ULGs have, therefore, to gear up themselves for exploiting the potential under the conventional resources to the fullest extent besides mobilising resources under non-conventional means for meeting the pressures of urbanisation.

Urban Finance and Infrastructure Needs

Governments have given lesser importance to urban areas and urban development than to rural development for several decades. It has resulted in low level of spending on urban development infrastructure that has adversely affected their fiscal sources to a great extent. Though the Constitution (74th Amendment) Act, 1992 gives importance to urban sector, it specified only functional base by expanding the list of subjects to be dealt with by ULGs but remained silent on the fiscal resources to meet the increasing expenditure on urban development infrastructure needed for fast expanding urban areas. In the era of globalisation, urban infrastructure development assumes greater importance to enable cities to play their positive role in making increasing contribution to country's GDP. The investment requirements for urban infrastructure development are estimated at Rs 79,300 to Rs 94,000 crores as per Rakesh Mohan Committee Report (1996) for 1996–2001 while the Central Public Health Engineering Organisation (CPHEO) has estimated the cost at Rs 1,72,905 crores by 2021 to cover 100 per cent urban population and Rail India Technical and Economic Services (RITES) indicates the cost at Rs 2,07,000 crores to cover cities with a population of 1,00,000 or more in the next 20 years. The Government of India constituted a High Powered Expert Committee (HPEC) to deal with the new challenges that urban India faces. According to the Committee's report the investment for urban infrastructure for over a period of two decades (2011–31) for covering eight specified areas like water supply, sewerage, solid waste management, storm water drains, urban roads, urban transport, traffic support infrastructure and street lighting is estimated at Rs 39.2 lakh crores at 2009-10 prices. The committee in its "Report on Indian Urban Infrastructure and Services, March 2011" opined that the urban areas in the country are visibly deficient in the quality of services provided by the ULGs even to the existing population. The Indian economy is one of the fastest growing economies in the world, but the current service levels are very low relative to the needs of the urbanites while the requirements are very high to sustain the economic productivity of the urban areas. In the prevailing economic situation of ULGs, they are unable to assimilate and fulfil the aspirations of rate-payers with a positive outlook, foresighted planning and prudent fiscal management. It is, therefore, important to study the origin of the problem of inefficiency and incapacity of Urban Local Governments, and work out suitable solutions to overcome these deficiencies in order to achieve the objectives set for in the CAA, and to improve the functioning of the ULGs to the best satisfaction of urban dwellers.

Meagre finances and limited financial capacity of ULGs to plan and manage cities to meet the challenges of increasing urbanisation in the country are due to a host of factors both financial and non-financial in nature. They include: (1) inadequate resource mobilisation from local principal sources of income, viz., property tax etc; (2) high proportion of expenditure on establishment; (3) a very high expenditure commitment in urban slums and outskirts of the urban areas; (4) politicisation of expenditure; (5) unrealistic budgeting; (6) lack of realistic fiscal planning; (7) Low levels of assessment; and (8) Inefficiency in tax collection and rampant corruption. Unusual pressure for services by citizens demanding more services with improved quality coupled with restricting revenue availability, require unusual counter measures. Such a situation is, at best, administratively and politically naïve and, at worst, potentially devastating to an ULG's financial health. ULGs have, therefore, to augment their finances through property tax reforms, including the introduction of the scheme of self-assessment of property tax, revamping of advertisement tax, trade licence fee system, and use of land as a resource, increasing and improving remunerative enterprises. The search for additional sources of revenue to meet the ever-increasing urban challenges is, therefore, of paramount importance.

A critical analysis of the sources of income and collection efficiency of several ULGs reveals that the income is not really as poor as it seems to be but for the poor performance of ULGs in exploiting the potential under each source to the fullest extent. For example, the potential under property tax is not exploited fully due to non-revision of taxes for several years, sometimes even decades. The same is the case with the levy, assessment and collection of trade licence fees. It is imperative for the ULGs to take up a comprehensive evaluation of their sources of revenues, levy methods and collection efficiency and fully exploit the potential from each source in order to protect the financial health of ULGs to minimise the ULGs' dependence on Government grants or external support and to increase their credit-worthiness.

Financial Resources of Urban Local Governments

Cities are reservoirs of major financial resources such as income tax, corporation tax, service tax, customs duty, excise duty, value added tax, stamp duty on registration, entertainment tax, profession tax, motor vehicle tax etc. But the ULGs are not given their due share of all these taxes except a few. There is a close relationship between urbanisation and economic growth, and hence it must be ensured that the positive effects of urbanisation are not affected by neglect of urban life. The ULGs cannot function effectively without a sound financial administration.[4] Government at all levels-central, state and local-must take up all measures to make urban life more meaningful and purposeful through sound financial management of cities so that they continue to their positive role in country's economy is not adversely effected.

Empowerment of the ULGs through functional devolution is an important objective of the CAA. Certain states have transferred some of the eighteen functions listed in the Twelfth Schedule to the ULGs but have not, at the same time, contemplated measures for strengthening them financially. Despite incorporation of these provisions in the local municipal acts in certain states like West Bengal, Madhya Pradesh, Andhra Pradesh etc. the over-all progress of decentralisation of powers and devolution of funds by state governments to the ULGs has been very slow and there is a lot to be done in this regard.[5] Constitutional Amendment for decentralisation of financial powers is not sufficient for augmenting resources of the urban local governments.[6] The central government must provide special capital support to the ULGs in the states which are not in a position to allocate requisite funds to their urban centres for development commensurate with requirement. The small and medium towns need financial support from the centre for their infrastructural projects as their economic bases are not strong enough to generate adequate revenues locally for the purpose. At the same time the ULGs should contemplate measures to increase the inflow of capital from institutional sources and the private sector. It is the primary responsibility of the ULGs to ensure access to infrastructure to all sections of their population, irrespective of their income and affordability.[7] The government can fulfil this responsibility through sub-contracting arrangements with the private sector or by strengthening the ULGs financially, administratively and technically. Such strengthening of the ULGs helps to generate non-agricultural employment and diversify their economic base, since there is a correlation between the availability of urban infrastructure and amenities, and manufacturing activities. In view of the increased responsibilities of the ULGs coupled with their poor financial base and lack of local financial sources like cash flow from local tax resources or other charges, the governments have to make available to them additional financial resources to enable them to meet urban development expenditure and financing shortfalls in towns and cities. Since direct user charges are not affordable by a majority of the urban dwellers, the government should be the legitimate financier of these services.

State of Local Finance: The principal criterion for assessing the performance of the ULGs is the mobilisation of their internal resources. Urban Local Governments in India are always starved of the required finance to discharge their statutory responsibilities and they depend on the benevolence of the Central or State Governments for grants since most of the major sources of finances are with the State or Central Government. As the State Governments have gradually usurped the financial resources of the ULGs, their financial position has been going from bad to worse with the result that they are unable to generate their local sources of revenues to fulfil their constitutional obligations.

State Governments under the guise of some policy reform, without a corresponding compensation, have usurped taxes, which, previously the ULBs were empowered to collect. In certain states: (a) animal and vehicle tax; (b) octroi; (c) commodity market cess and (d) profession tax are some of the taxes which were listed among the Municipal Laws which the Urban Local Governments were formerly empowered to levy, asses and collect and utilise for development. But some of these taxes were abolished and the others were taken over by the State Government. While the upper ceiling fixed on the Local Bodies' share of these taxes has further deteriorated their financial position, the statutory responsibilities of Urban Local Governments have further increased over the years without a corresponding increase in the devolution of finances. And there are no efforts to build up the financial capacity of Urban Local Governments at the municipal level. As a result the ULGs face severe financial crunch. What is worse, the ULGs have not been prudent in their expenditure and in minimising wasteful expenditure and financial irregularities. The elected bodies generally oppose enhancement of the tax base since the electorate has voted them to power on a promise of service without any financial burden to them. When certain municipal taxes gained good potential they were taken over by the State. The State exercises abnormal control over local governments without giving them a free hand to raise their resources from various sources. Besides, the services provided by the ULGs are charged at the rates fixed by the State Government which do not even cover the cost of services. In such cases, there is no budgetary support from the State to compensate for the deficit. Thus, the ULGs have to fend for themselves. This very often results in poor quality of service.[8] Thus, the capacity of the Urban Local Governments will automatically continue to suffer as long as they do not set themselves right through prudent financial practices and innovative measures for generating financial resources.

The Government of India has introduced certain measures to help urban infrastructure such as tax exemption for municipal bonds, fiscal incentives for private sector participation in urban infrastructure etc. Though these measures indicate the possibilities of change, mark the beginning of change, and also indicate further possibilities of change, the change is yet to make an impact. Certain states and cities in the country have introduced taxation and accounting reforms, set up State Finance Commissions to suggest measures for devolution of funds to the ULGs for urban infrastructure development and encourage private sector participation in civic services. Even these steps have not given the efficacy to the required level.

Resource Sharing: This situation could be remedied by a resource sharing mechanism, which lays emphasis on the urban government's maintaining better financial discipline and ensuring better realisation of its revenues. Some of these measures are:

- The ULGs should be empowered to make all municipal services cost-effective.
- Where the income from the services rendered is less than the cost of the services, the deficit should be filled by grants from the State.
- Resources raised by the ULGs should be utilised exclusively for maintenance of services.
- All capital works, developmental works, recreation facilities should be financed by the Central and State governments in the form of grants.
- The ULGs should have an effective machinery to realise their revenues and should be empowered by law to disconnect essential services like electricity, water supply, drainage etc for tax defaulters or tax evaders in order to ensure cent per cent realisation of all locally generated revenues.

The Urban Local Governments in certain states have been demanding the State Governments to apportion a share of all State revenues to them including a share of sales tax proceeds, a share of motor vehicle tax and a reasonable amount of annual road grant for the upkeep and maintenance of thoroughfares in municipal areas.

The transfer of 18 functions in the Twelfth Schedule to the exclusive domain of the ULGs, necessitates them to identify the service beneficiaries and measure the service benefits in respect of these functions, so as to make them user charge financing.

Tax collection efficiency: In order to make certain services cost-effective, certain reforms have to be initiated in the property tax levy and collection.

- Collection of water charges on metered system which substantially improves the revenue from sale of water supply;

- Levy of drainage and sewerage charges at such rate as would meet the cost of operation and maintenance of the services;
- Levy and assessment of house tax at such rates that major services like roads, conservancy, street lighting etc. become cost-effective;
- In respect of other services cross-subsidisation needs for the urban poor should be provided;
- The funds required for projects/services of town-wide or city-wide importance to be linked to the general component of the property tax; and
- Transport development levy to be levied as a component of property tax in order to improve transport projects in urban areas.

The financial resources of the ULGs have to keep pace with the budgetary requirement for essential services. The Budget requirement for providing essential services should be assessed by a valuation committee consisting of experts in the area of service in the department concerned and municipal officials. The cost of providing water supply, sewerage and drainage services shall be linked to water, sewerage and drainage charges. In respect of other services the estimated cost of services shall be calculated and should be apportioned into components of property tax.

"Infrastructure projects are generally capital intensive and have long gestation period. The financial structure should, therefore, provide a proper framework for resource mobilisation, phasing of project expenditure in relation to resource raising ability, servicing and maintenance requirements, cash flow and risk management. In this regard a commercialisation approach needs to be followed which should attract finance from non-traditional sources including debit/equity from multilateral funding agencies. A schedule for recovering user charges is an important determinant for a feasible cash flow profile of the project and for making it a commercially viable project. Commercialisation of projects would necessarily require government support and it should be perceived as complementary and not supplementary to the development efforts by the private sector."[9]

Internal Sources of Revenue to Urban Local Governments

(1) Taxes : (a) Property Tax; (b) Vacant Land Tax; (c) Advertisement Tax.

(2) Non-Taxes: (a) Water Charges; (b) Water supply donations; (c) Drainage Cess; (d) Market fees; (e) Slaughter Housefees; (f) Shop Room Rents; (g) Encroachment fees; (h) Building Licence fees; (i) Layout fees; (j) Betterment fees; and other town planning receipts (k) Trade License fees; (l) Birth & Death certificate fees and (m) Miscellaneous Receipts.

(3) Assigned Revenues: (a) Entertainment Tax; (b) Profession Tax; (c) Surcharge on Stamp duty

(4) Non-Plan Grants: (a) Per Capita Grant; (b) Profession Tax Compensation; (c) Offset Loss Compensation; (d) Motor Vehicle Tax

(5) Plan Grants: (a) Environmental Improvement of Urban Slums; (b) Assembly Constituency Development Programme Grant; (c) Member of Parliament Local Area Development Grant;(d) Swarna Jayanti Shahari Rojgar Yojana Grant ; (e) Flood Relief Grant; (f) Road Widening Grant; (g) Urban Infrastructure Development Scheme for Small and Medium Towns Grant; (h) Integrated Low Cost Sanitation Scheme Grant; (i) Clean and Green; (k) Building Regulation Fees; (k) Drought Relief Grant; (l) Rain Water Harvesting Grant; (m) School Building Grant.

Despite tremendous potential of income assured from property tax, it is not fully exploited by the ULGs. Since direct taxes are considered by the tax payers as a burden to them, urban local governments have to look into indirect taxes, assigned revenues and government grants.

Resources Mobilisation

Mobilisation of resources for providing the needed infrastructure is a Herculean task for most of the cities and towns in India. Search for resources consists of three categories: mobilisation of domestic investment resources; devolution of funds from provincial (state) and national (central) government; and foreign investment. (The Andhra Pradesh government could successfully get foreign investment of Rs 745 crores from the Department for International Development, Government of United Kingdom for providing infrastructure; improve service delivery through better performance of urban local governments and for strengthening civil societies in 42 Class-I towns in the State during 2000-2007.

Resources have to be mobilised not only for enabling urban local governments to function effectively but also to tide over the inadequacy of governmental (both national and state) assistance. There are possibilities for mobilisation of additional financial resources at the local level both through taxation and through charging for services. ULGs should have built-in efficient mechanism for promoting local resource mobilisation and better financial performance. In most of the ULGs in India real property is the main local tax base; but in certain Urban Local Governments its tremendous potential is not fully exploited. That is why property tax revenues decline in real terms in many states particularly because of improper valuation. The fiscal powers of Urban Local Governments and their ability to generate resources should be strengthened.

As regards charging for services, emphasis has been laid in recent years on the need for cost recovery and appropriate charging policies for urban projects and urban services. "There are strong reasons from both the points of view of economic efficiency and equity for charging at least marginal costs, if not full cost recovery, for such urban services as water, sewerage, land development and urban transport"[10] Urban Local Governments should adopt a methodology for appropriate pricing policies of urban services. Once these are reasonably well-developed, they can easily be implemented e.g. certain Municipal Corporations had resolved to collect user charges for collection of garbage from bulk garbage generating units in order to meet the cost of providing additional vehicles and men for clearing the bulk garbage generated, which was cost-effective and had given good results). Cost recovery has certain risks like excluding the poor etc. but it is inevitable and unavoidable for Urban Local Governments to adopt it in respect of certain essential services which cannot be satisfactorily maintained unless the methodology for cost recovery is adopted. There are several problems in local revenue administration in regard to levy and collection of taxes and non-taxes. Despite a fine array of local revenue sources

ULGs are unable to exploit their potential fully due to ineffective systems of valuation, assessment, collection and enforcement.

Most of the urban development programmes and service delivery measures "face severe constraints in mobilisation of local resources, mainly because the local tax base is usually very narrowly prescribed... some increase in revenue yields can generally be achieved through increasing the effectiveness of existing systems and procedures. However, it will ultimately be necessary to broaden the local government tax base by enhancing local government taxation powers."[11]

The reforms in property tax have not been effective. Dissatisfied with the ambiguity in the rules relating to levy and assessment of property tax, certain states including Andhra Pradesh, Tamil Nadu, Gujarat, Karnataka and Bihar undertook property tax reforms in order to fully exploit the property tax potential and to remove subjectivity in the determination of the hypothetical annual rental value.

Suggested Reforms in Levy and Assessment of Property Tax

1. Tax Base

The significant problem of Municipal property taxation pertains to the basis of taxation. The fixation of tax base is the first question to be tackled in property tax reforms. There are two alternatives suggested: one is Annual Rental Value and the other is Capital Value. The shift from rental-value based taxation to capital-value based taxation is expected to improve the yield of tax since the capital value of buildings increases faster than their rental value. Another advantage of it is that it will obviate the necessity of arriving at a hypothetical rental value. But this system would abnormally increase the tax with the result that protest from cash-poor and property-rich rate payers is unavoidable, while the capital value system is inevitable and is the only adoptable system for assessing vacant land tax.

2. Vacant Land Tax

Vacant Land Tax is levied to discourage owners of lands to keep them vacant to avoid their misuse, and to encourage housing. There has been an unearned increase in land values. But Urban Local Governments are unable to tap even a fraction of it. Further vacant land is taxed at a rate much higher than land with built-up property with the result that evasion of tax by vacant landowners has become the routine rather than the exception. Besides, such owners often do not reside within municipal limits and thus collection of vacant land tax from them poses another serious problem. A huge demand from Vacant Land Tax remains accumulated in the Assessment registers since Vacant Land Tax is assessed @ 1.00 per cent of the capital value of the land per annum and with poor collection. In view of this inherent problem certain Urban Local Governments have decided to collect Vacant Land Tax at the time of granting permission for construction of building in the vacant land in question by adopting the following criteria:

- In respect of vacant lands in approved layouts, from the date of approval of the layout;
- In respect of vacant lands in built-up area, for the last five years;
- In respect of vacant lands on which assessment has already been made, from the year of such assessment.

3. Advertisement tax: The increasing commercial activity in urban areas should quite naturally lead to increasing advertising of their products. The increasing publicity and advertising has become another major source of income to ULGs if all advertisements are correctly assessed and tax fixed as per the rates notified. But most of the advertisements in cities are not assessed to tax and the large scale of evasion of advertisement tax results in loss of revenue to the ULGs. When advertisement tax collection is privatised in certain ULGs there is a tremendous increase in income from this source since the private entrepreneur leaves no single advertisement without collection of tax. Privatisation of advertisement tax is, therefore, seems quite beneficial to the ULGs instead of their own collection. But there are legal constraints to privatise collection of advertisement tax. The ULGs should, therefore, make genuine efforts in the assessment and collection of advertisement tax to the fullest extent since it is a major source of revenue to the local bodies.

Property Tax Administration in Various Stated

Property Tax is a major source of income to Urban Local Governments and in most of the ULGs it amounts to 20 per cent of the total revenue to the urban local government. Several experiments were made during the last more than two decades to rationalise the administration of property tax in order to maximise the yield from this source and minimise dissatisfaction to the genuine tax payer. Urban Local Governments have the responsibility to ensure that while a genuine taxpayer is not overburdened with arbitrary taxation, the potential of this major source of income to them is fully exploited.

The method of assessment of property tax has undergone several reforms. It is of interest to study as to how to levy, assess, collect property tax, and account for the property tax levied and collected. This tax is assessed and levied on immovable or tangible property. Property tax consists of four components: tax for general purpose, for water, for lighting and for sanitation. Different methods are in vogue to fix the tax base in different states of India. Certain State Governments have prescribed the maximum and minimum rates between which a Municipality or a Municipal Corporation can levy and assess property tax.

The power of Urban Local Governments to levy property tax is circumscribed by a number of limitations-either by State legislation or Central Act. For instance, Central government properties are exempt from payment of property tax except for actual services provided. This results in considerable loss to the ULBs. However, Government of India permitted ULBs to levy service charges on central government properties. The central government undertakings are liable for property tax like any other person/institution. Hence, all public utility undertakings of the Central Government and Port Trust properties have to be taxed while central government properties are to be levied tax at least for the services provided.

Property Tax System in Andhra Pradesh

The Method of Property Tax administration in Andhra Pradesh has passed through many phases during the last three decades. After the Andhra Pradesh Municipalities Act came into force in 1965, the first quinquennial revision of property taxes was conducted in all the Municipalities in the state in 1970. Under the system the annual rental value of the buildings or portion of the buildings occupied by the owners was arrived at 9 per cent of the capital value of the buildings or portion of the buildings while the rental values of the rented portion were calculated on the basis of the hypothetical rent for which it was reasonably expected to be let from month to month or from year to year. This rental value is not the actual rent paid by the tenant to the landlord, but a reasonable rent arrived at based on the rental values prevailing in the locality for similar buildings.

The capital value system of Property Tax Administration had resulted in abnormal increase of tax on every holding necessitating the inevitable withdrawal of the system. After its withdrawal, the state Government ordered a quinquennial revision of Property Tax in one fifth of the Municipalities in the state every year on a staggering basis in a phased manner. Under this system every building was assessed together with its site and other adjacent premises occupied as an appurtenance thereto and the annual rental value of lands and buildings was deemed to be the gross annual rent at which they were reasonably expected to be let from month to month or from year to year with reference to its location.

This system of Property Tax Administration worked well. But it involved the discretion of the assessing authority in arriving at a reasonable or hypothetical rental value of the property and as such the assessment of hypothetical rent differed from one assessing authority to another. The discretionary power of the assessing authority led to corruption, miscalculation of rental value and such other irregularities. Besides, the provisions of Rent Control Act were to be applied to building constructed prior to 1957 under which the enhancement of fair rent was limited, despite exorbitant increase in rental values. After several years of intellectual exercise, the Government has amended the provisions relating to the calculation of rental values based on the plinth area of the property in order to:

- Remove the discretion on the part of assessing authorities in the levy of tax thereby avoiding arbitrary taxation,
- Delink property tax from Rent Control Act provisions,
- Simplify the procedures relating to assessment and levy of tax, and
- Facilitate self-assessment of property tax by owners themselves.

In this system the entire Municipal area is divided into convenient territorial zones based on the availability of civic amenities like water supply, street lighting, roads and drains, markets and shopping centres, educational institutions, banks, postal services, public offices, medical institutions, factories and industries and such other relevant facts. After dividing the Municipality into territorial zones, the buildings situated in each zone are classified into six categories viz., 1. RCC posh buildings 2. RCC ordinary buildings 3. Madras Terraced or Jack Arch roofed or Stone slab roofed buildings 4. Mangalore tile roofed or asbestos roofed or G.I. roofed buildings 5. Country tiled buildings, and 6. Huts or thatched roof accommodation. After classifying the buildings based on their type of construction, they are further classified into six categories taking into consideration the nature of use of the buildings, viz., (a) Residential (b) Shops (c) Public Use like office complexes, Educational Institutions, Hospitals, Nursing Homes and Banks (d) Commercial purposes like Hotels, Lodges, Restaurant etc., (e) Industrial purpose like Factories, Mills, Workshops and other industries and (f) Cinema Theatres and places of entertainment.[12] Based on the above criteria of type of construction and nature of use of buildings there are 36 categories of rental values arrived at for each zone. For the purpose of arriving at rental values a survey is conducted taking into consideration the actually let out buildings and the actual rents paid by the tenants. The assessing authority then arrives at the monthly rent of each category in a zone per square metre plinth area and notifies the rates for fixation of monthly rental value of buildings in a zone for information of the public. The rates so notified shall be in force for the purpose of levy and assessment of property tax on buildings in the municipal area until they are revised after next revision.

A comparative study of the old and new systems of assessment of buildings to property tax will enable us to reach a proper conclusion. In the old system (which withstood the test of time and which was the result of several experiments and which remarkably improved the financial position of Municipalities and Municipal Corporations from 1978 to 1984) the assessing authority would make a personal inspection of each and every property, determine the reasonable rental value of the building taking into consideration the nature of construction, use to which it was put, the location of the building, the rental values prevailing for similar buildings in the locality. The rental value of exactly similar buildings also differed from one another, since the location of the building, length of time occupied by tenants, proximity to highways would determine the rent apart from the amenities and accommodation in the buildings. Hence, the rental value of each building had to be determined separately by considering various factors. Contrary to this well-established system of fixing the rental values of buildings, the new system introduced in 1993 provided for a uniform rental value for all similar buildings in a particular zone, which extends to several kilometres, without considering the various aspects described above. This results in abnormal under assessment of certain buildings which are fetching exorbitant rents, and arbitrary increase in respect of buildings the rental values of which are comparatively low due to distance from developed areas and lack of facilities. The new system resulted in reduction of the existing tax on commercial buildings and industrial houses, while the already existing high tax has further increased on old residential buildings. The net result for the whole municipal area due to the revision of taxes on the new system was a slight increase over the existing tax demand benefiting many rate payers and hard hitting a few others. Contrary to this new system, the old system enabled the increase of property tax demand by more than 100 per cent without causing the slightest burden to any taxpayer. The new system has not given the expected potential.

When the new system was proposed without any concessions, it led to a multi-fold increase of the existing tax rousing cries of anguish of the rate-payers all over the state. Then the government came forward with a concession to limit the increase of tax to 75 per cent over post 1983 assessments and 100 per cent over pre–1983 assessments. This again resulted in continuing the existing discrepancies since a grossly under-assessed building would continue to enjoy grossly low increase while arbitrarily assessed buildings would suffer arbitrary increase. Furthermore, a building constructed just before the commencement of the new system would enjoy the limitation of increase of tax to 75 per cent over the existing tax, while a building constructed just after 1993 juxtaposed to it would be heavily taxed since it would not have limitation in the levy and assessment of tax. Another important reason for low income from property taxes is due non-revision of property taxes for several years although the Municipal Acts provide for quinquennial revision of property taxes. The ULGs should revise property taxes once every five years to update taxation and realise adequate revenue for the satisfactory maintenance of municipal services.

It is necessary to take up property tax reforms from time to time so as to ensure reasonable assessment of property tax to fully exploit its potential and to avoid arbitrariness in its assessment, minimise discrimination and maximise efficiency in the levy, assessment and collection of taxes.

Patna Experiment

Patna Municipal Corporation has revised rates of property tax in order to prevent its tax assessing authorities from constantly harassing property owners and to avoid threats of arbitrary taxation. The Annual Rental Value (ARV) according to the Patna Municipal Corporation Act, 1951 is "the gross annual rent at which the holding may reasonably be expected to be let". Since no Rules were framed till 1993, properties (holdings) were assessed to property tax inconsistently and irrationally by the tax inspectors. The rates of taxation were as follows:

Holding Tax (Tax for General purpose)	: 12.50 Per cent of the ARV
Scavenging Tax	: 10.00 Per cent of the ARV
Water Tax	: 10.00 Per cent of the ARV
Education Cess	: 6.25 Per cent of the ARV
Health Cess	: 5.00 Per cent of the ARV
Total	: 43.75 Per cent of the ARV

The exorbitant rate of taxation led to arbitrary and unreasonable assessment of properties by the tax officials leading to corruption besides heavily taxing a genuine taxpayer. A simple tax structure with lower rates of taxation acceptable to the tax payers was keenly felt. The Rules relating to taxation were amended in 1993 and the rate of tax was reduced from 43.75 per cent to a mere 9.00 per cent of the Annual Rental Value. As per the amended Rule, the Annual Rental Value is defined as the rent that a holding is capable of fetching over a period of one year, and the rates of taxation are as follows:

Holding Tax	: 2.50 Per cent of the ARV.
Scavenging Tax	: 2.00 Per cent of the ARV.

Water Tax	:	2.00 Per cent of the ARV.
Education Cess	:	1.25 Per cent of the ARV.
Health Cess	:	1.25 Per cent of the ARV.
Total	:	9.00 Per cent of the ARV.

In order to assess the annual rental value of a building under the new system, an area based assessment method was introduced totally eliminating the powers of discretion of tax officials. The definite criteria for assessment included: (i) Location of the holding (property); (ii) Use of the holding; (iii) Type of construction and (iv) Carpet area of the holding. The new Rules eliminated any scope for arbitrary, erroneous, subjective and monocratic assessment of property tax. The locality was defined as: (1) Principal Main Roads, (2) Main Roads and (3) Other Roads; for ascertaining the use of buildings, they were categorised as: (i) Commercial or Industrial holdings; (ii) Residential holdings and (iii) All other holdings not falling in the first two categories. In respect of the type of construction the buildings were classified into three categories, viz., (i) Pucca Buildings with R.C.C. Roof; (ii) Pucca Building with Asbestos or Corrugated Sheet roof, and (iii) Other Buildings which did not fall in the above two categories.

Thus, it became a matrix of three multiplied by three multiplied by three. The Corporation would notify the rate per square foot for each type of construction, type of use and each location. This method of taxation had a number of practical disadvantages over the previous method of determining the Annual Rental Value. In brief: (1) the new system divided the buildings (holdings) into only three categories while there are several categories in respect of the nature of construction; (2) the uses of buildings are divided into only three categories while the holdings are used for different purposes all of which do not have the same rental values; and (3) dividing the city into locations based on the type of roads would not do justice in the determination of rental value.

The classification of buildings based on the nature of construction and use is no doubt an endless quest. But the Patna example of classification into three rigid categories is an over-simplification of a complex issue. The classification need not be too elaborate and at the same time should not be over-simplified either.

The Patna experiment, however, achieved the object of eliminating the discretionary powers of the assessing authority in the calculation of Annual Rental Value of holdings. The new system of property taxation has become acceptable to the rate-payers because of its corruption-free nature, its simplicity and the lower rate of taxation, besides transparency.

The reduction of tax from 43.75 per cent to 9.0 per cent of the Annual Rental Value remarkably increased the demand to Rs 17.00 crores from the earlier Rs 4.00 crores. This is, however, not universally acceptable or achievable since the increase in demand due to reduction of tax rate was only due to large scale evasion of tax by tax payers when the tax rate was high. In respect of Urban Local Governments where the collection of property tax demand is as high as 90 to 98 per cent, reduction of tax rate would lead to decrease of demand (tax yield) considerably leading Urban Local Governments to financial bankruptcy.

Kolkata System

The method of assessment of property tax in Kolkata was based on the annual rental value of a building. The assessment was based on the discretionary powers of the assessing authority giving scope for subjectivity. The system suffered from inherent legal lacuna, inviting excessive litigation, thus resulting in loss of revenue to the Municipal Corporation. There was no transparency in the system and left no scope for self-assessment. It suppressed the actual rent and property value due to the absence of a well-regulated real estate market. The low rent paid by the long-standing tenants, irrespective of other considerations like the nature of construction, location of the building, rents paid for similar buildings in the vicinity etc. led to low taxation, thus disabling the Municipal Corporation from fully exploiting the potential under property tax. There was no well-established procedure for the determination of annual rental value and assessment of property tax. Thus, a genuine tax payer was likely to be burdened while a tax evader enjoyed low tax benefit. This system was almost similar to the system that prevailed in Andhra Pradesh before the introduction of the Restructuring of Property tax in 1993. Kolkata Municipal Corporation, after an in-depth study and discussion of various successful practices, decided to adopt the Unit Area System, which is a simple method of arithmetical calculation of property tax based on the area of the building, adopting the unit area value or unit area tax for the building. The system makes it possible for the rate payers to assess their properties to tax by themselves and file self-assessment forms.

The unique advantage of the Unit Area System is that it simplifies the concept of assessment, removes subjectivity, is transparent and easily understood, raises sustainable revenue demand and enables efficient tax administration and monitoring.

In this system of assessment, the entire urban area is divided into specific areas and each area is categorised into five classes based on scientifically verifiable nine mandatory factors and four optional factors with points on gradation scales. Each ward is divided into sub-wards on the basis of perceivable parameters and along some principal roads of the ward. The factors taken into consideration for categorisation of wards into sub-wards are: Average Rental Value; Market Value of Land; Water Supply Position; Drainage System,; Conservancy Services; Availability of Medical and Educational facilities and Entertainment Centres; Availability of Transport Facilities; Average Width of Street; Daily Market Facilities; Locality of the Building and the Type of Locality like Posh Area, City Central Area or Commercial Area etc.; Economic status of the Residents; Availability of Park, Playground, Greenery etc.

There are five multiplicative factors considered for calculation of tax according to their distinctive features:

- Means of access to the building/property
- Occupancy
- Structure or nature of construction
- Age of the Property
- Nature of usage.

Ahmadabad System

Ahmadabad Municipal Corporation, which had a financial deficit of Rs 35 crores and a bank overdraft of Rs 22 crores, could tide over its financial difficulties and generate considerable surplus within a limited time period through intensification of tax collection. This could be possible through updating of tax records, plugging of leakages and evasion of tax payments, efficient disposal of property tax disputes and realisation of 100 per cent collection through strengthening the enforcement mechanism.

Non-taxes: Non-taxes are directly collected by the ULGs. The section-wise sources of non-tax revenue can be categorised as follows:

1. Revenue Section: (i) Market Fee; (ii) Slaughter Fee; (iii) Rent from Shopping Complexes; (iv) Rent from Municipal Quarters; (v) Parking Fee; (vi) Mutation Fee; (vii) Sale of Forms etc.

2. Health Section: (i) Trade License Fee: (ii) Fee on Birth and Death Certificates; (iii) Sale Proceeds of Swept Material and Compost: (iv) Burial Ground Charges; (v) Fee for Issue of No Objection Certificates etc.

3. Engineering Section: (i) Contribution to Water Supply Connections; (ii) Water Charges for non-Residential/Commercial/ Industrial purposes; (iii) Contribution to Sewerage Connections (iv) Sewerage Connection Charges; (v) Road Cutting Charges etc.

4. Town Planning Section: (i) Building License Fee; (ii) Layout Fee; (iii) Development Charges; (iv) Betterment Charges; (v) Compounding Fee (on unauthorised constructions); (vi) Encroachment Fee; (vii) Building Penalisation Scheme (BPS) / Layout Regularisation Scheme (LRS) etc.

We shall discuss here only the important sources of non-tax revenues and measures for realising their full potential.

Measures for Improvement of Finances under Non-Taxes

The expenditure on provision of essential services like piped water, sewers, drains, roads, electricity, garbage collection, transport, health care and education has gone high up. The cost-effectiveness of infrastructure is significantly reduced due to the widening gulf between the expenditure incurred on provision of these services and income derived from the recipients.

Inadequate finances or bankruptcy of ULGs disable them to effectively address issues relating to slums., poverty, pollution, congestion, environmental degradation, crime, social unrest and the like. Hence, additional sources of revenue are to be searched to meet the ever-increasing expenditure on infrastructure and maintenance of essential services. Efficient collection of non-tax revenue will solve the problem to some extent.

Every ULG collects various fees and charges under different non-tax sources. The most important of them are Excess Water Charges, Drainage Cess, Market Fees, Shop Room Rents, Encroachment Fees and Trade License Fees. These are important sources of income directly collected by the ULGs, after property tax. Most of the ULGs do not properly watch the income from these sources.

1. Water Charges

In almost all the ULGs in India including the Metropolitan Cities, water charges are collected on flat rate basis irrespective of the quantity of water consumed by consumers. As a result there is a heavy loss of revenue in respect of charges collected for the supply of protected water. In no single ULG, the income from water charges is equal to the expenditure incurred for supplying protected water. In certain lower grade ULGs there has always been wide protest against collecting water charges on metered system with the result that the gap between expenditure on and income from water supply widens from year to year. The deficit is met from other sources. Besides the loss of revenue there is a heavy loss of safe drinking water due to unauthorized water tap connections given to the public by the field level staff who are interested in illegal earnings. The mismanagement of water supply system by the field level staff is largely responsible for heavy financial deficit in the ULGs. Efforts to arrest this trend have not been sincere and honest since local politicians are deliberately involved in all the irregularities.

When a survey of civic amenities available and required to residents was conducted in certain cities, about one-third of the total water tap connections in the city were found to be unauthorised ones. Regularisation of these connections duly collecting the water supply tap connection charges together with penalty brought adequate revenue to the Municipal Corporations and could be utilised for development. In order to prevent the loss of revenue from this source, the ULGs introduced an integrated demand notice for all taxes and fees that each tax payer had to pay to the ULGs. This has enabled the ULGs improve their revenue as well as timely collection of taxes.

Use of excess water or bulk usage of water is quite common in major industries, well-established business houses, firms etc., but the municipal authorities collect water charges from them on a flat rate system without providing metres to measure the quantity of water used. Consumers of bulk quantity of water bribe the field level functionaries who manage to collect water charges at the flat rate with the result that the ULGs incur heavy loss of revenue. This loss can be avoided by introducing metered water tap connections to all consumers including domestic consumers so that water charges can be collected for the actual quantity of water consumed.

2. Drainage Cess

Drainage cess is levied from building owners for each drainage connection provided to the building. This cess is levied if, and only if, there is an underground drainage system with sewerage treatment plant. Towns/cities which have this system must concentrate on providing drainage connections and by assessing drainage cess separately and not as a component of property tax as this source will fetch considerable income.

3. Market Fees and Shop Room Rents

This is another important source of income to the ULGs. Though the revenue from the market fee is considerably large, inadequate and inefficient officials are passive in realising the full amount from it. Every year the ULGs conduct auction of lease hold rights for collection of fees in the municipal markets. The bidders offer huge amounts at the time of bid but, by taking advantage of the lacunae in the law or by conniving with the municipal officials, evade payment of a part of the lease amount, thus causing considerable financial loss to the ULGs. Income from shop room rents is an equally important source of income. Though there would no loss of income from this source if properly collected, the revenue collection staff with an ulterior motive delay timely collection of shop room rents and it results sometimes in inordinate delay in the realisation of revenue from this important source.

Another way of loss of revenue is delay in renewing the lease of shop rooms at an enhanced rent or in reauctioning the shop rooms which would fetch a higher rent on par with the prevailing rental values for similar shop rooms in the vicinity.

In certain towns and cities of India it is very often observed that the rents fetched for municipal shop rooms is comparatively much less than the rents fetched for similar private shop rooms in the vicinity. Whenever the municipal authorities try to rectify the anomaly the local politicians deter the officials either though political power or muscle power from enhancing the shop room rents, despite steep rise in the rents of private shop rooms. If this obstacle can be successfully overcome by the official exercise of legitimate authority, this would be a reliable and recurring source of income to the ULGs.

Certain state governments ordered the municipal authorities to put municipal shop rooms to auction for goodwill and the goodwill so realised should be kept in a separate account in the bank to be utilised exclusively for the construction of remunerative enterprises as per the existing demand. This had resulted in realising adequate income for developmental activities. The shop rooms in certain ULGs were thus leased out through auction against goodwill and fixing the monthly rent similar to the rents for similar private shop rooms in the vicinity. The income it fetched through this method was double the cost of the construction of shop rooms.

4. Encroachment Fees

Encroachment fees fetch considerable income to the ULGs if properly assessed. Most of the municipal sites and road margins are encroached upon by business establishments, and they are classified as unobjectionable encroachments. Since there would be no immediate necessity to remove these encroachments, encroachment fees can be levied and collected from encroachers of municipal lands to realise adequate revenue.

5. Building Licence Fees

Another important source of income is Building License fees. Building licence fee is collected as per the notification of rates issued by the ULG and within the limits prescribed by the Government. The calculation and collection of building licence fee as per the rates notified will fetch huge revenue. But municipal authorities generally mismanage Building Licence fees by miscalculation of the fees that has to be levied, misinterpreting the rates prescribed for different types of constructions in different localities and such other means. In fast growing urban areas building activity is very high where a huge income can be expected from building licence fees.

It has been observed that there is a large scale misappropriation of building licence fees in certain ULGs by appending duplicate or fake bank receipts in support of the building licence fees. The field level staff collect the building licence fee but do not remit the fees collected from the applicants in the municipal treasury and manage to mislead the licensing authority by producing fake receipts that results in loss of revenue to the municipal treasury. Such cases are detected only long after the misappropriation took place. The municipal authorities at the higher level should, therefore, evolve an effective method of ensuring correct calculation of the building licence fee payable with each building application and remittance of the fees so collected to the respective head of account to avoid possible loss of revenue from this important source of income to the ULGs.

6. Trade Licence Fee

Licence fees for running shops and business establishments are another important source of non-tax income to ULGs. If all trades are listed and licences are granted duly collecting trade licence fee, it will fetch considerable income to the ULGs. But "the present system of issuing licences and the common flouting of regulations by shops and establishments provide erroneous and highly undesirable rent-seeking opportunities for local officials."[13] Most of the trades in urban areas are generally not assessed and licence fee collected by the field level health staff. It was observed in certain cities that the number of trades levied and assessed to licence fees was not even five per cent of the actual number of trades functioning. Thus, there is heavy loss of revenue from this source due to non-booking of trades for granting licence. The number of trades in the city can be nearly identified by the number of non-residential property tax assessment so that the evasion of trade licence fee can be minimised. If income from this source is not adequate, it is due to the non-listing of trades for collection of licence fees from the traders by the licensing authorities and awful corruption among the field level staff of the ULGs.

Preparation of an inventory of the existing trades in every urban area by a private agency will considerably improve income to the ULG from this source. Trade licence must be collected from all trades without leaving a single trade unassessed to avoid loss of revenue from this important source of revenue.

7. Building Regularisation/Penalisation Scheme: Several unauthorised constructions have come up in all cities of India for various reasons. Certain state governments have issued orders for regularisation of the unauthorised constructions by collecting regularisation or penalisation charges at fixed rates. The amount thus collected was kept in a separate account which was utilised exclusively for infrastructure development or other developmental activities. The municipalities and municipal corporations in Andhra Pradesh have realised huge revenues under this scheme during 1996-2000 and again during 2007–2010.

8. Parking Fees: Parking fee collected in most of the cities including metropolitan cities is very low. This is an important source of revenue, particularly in big cities but the potential is not fully exploited with the result that development and maintenance of parking spaces is stunted. Improper maintenance of parking spaces results in traffic congestion on roads. Reasonable enhancement of parking fee from time to time is not treated as a burden by the users of parking space since it is essential for them. Fast growing towns and cities can generate substantial revenue if parking places are privatised, particularly in congested and busy commercial localities of towns and cities.

Tax vs. Service Charges

Urban Local Governments in India have been faced with endemic problems of poor cost recovery and low quality of services. Certain essential services are not cost-effective, for example, in most of the municipalities and corporations, the expenditure incurred on protected water supply is double the income derived from it, with the result that the Urban Local Governments have to divert other funds to water supply maintenance to meet the cost of supply to the entire population in the town/city.

Where the services can be measured and beneficiaries can be identified (like water supply, garbage collection etc.) user charges are the best financing instrument, since user charges promote efficiency in respect of general services where services cannot be measured and beneficiaries cannot be identified (street lighting, traffic control, security etc.) the best way of financing them is through taxation on local residents; in respect of infrastructure services like roads, public utilities etc., the appropriate source is borrowing.

In most of the ULGs of India, less than 10 per cent of the cost of services was recovered through user charges, and in a few others cost recovery was between 10 to 20 per cent. There are hardly three or four ULGs in India in which cost recovery ranges from 50 to 75 per cent. User charges are grossly underexploited while property tax, which constitutes the primary source of local tax revenue to ULGs in India, is regarded as an unbearable burden by the tax payers. "The share of tax revenues in total municipal revenues has dwindled, eroding local fiscal autonomy. User charges are yet to dominate the municipal scene. Borrowing constitutes a far less important source in India compared to many countries."[14] Hence, certain Urban Local Governments have attempted to link certain service costs to municipal user charges and benefit taxes. ULGs have to focus their attention on user charges and cost recovery to meet the O&M charges of water supply. This needs to establish a link between the costs of services and charges imposed or taxes levied. There are certain services like protected water supply, excess water usage, clearance of bulk garbage from bulk garbage generating units, sewerage etc, which can be measured and for which the beneficiaries can be identified and can be financed through direct user charges so that the services would be cost-effective and the quality of services can be maintained at a high level and to finance public services. Cost recovery of certain important services is an important measure of the municipal finances, for retaining the self-sustainability of the service. Low cost recovery results in poor service quality. Levy of user charges enables the consumers understand the scarcity value of the services and enables the service providers the quantum of demand that needs to be met. User charges must be revised from time to time regularly in order to keep pace with the increasing cost of services and to generate a minimum surplus.

Even after all taxes and charges are collected efficiently duly exploiting the potential to the fullest extent, there remains a wide gap between the cost of the services provided by the municipal government and the income generated through levy of local taxes and non-taxes. This fiscal gap is to be filled only through plan grants, that is, grants for specific purpose. In order to assess and fill the gap there should be a good inter-governmental transfer of revenues which should be at a predetermined percentage of sales tax, other shared taxes or general state revenues. The formula for the distribution of funds out of the general revenues of the state should be the gap between total revenue generated locally by the ULG and the total annual expenditure incurred by the ULG from all sources. Each plan grant should be released for a specific purpose and it should be mandatory for the ULGs not to divert the said specific plan grant for other purpose, as a measure of maintaining financial discipline.

Market Borrowing: Since smaller town governments will not have access to market funds, there should be an intermediary institution at the state level which can pool risks and borrow with ease and at a lower cost that can approach the capital market, national level financial intermediaries and bilateral and multilateral lending institutions on behalf of these smaller entities. They can also assist municipalities in project formulation, preparation of capital development plans and projects and designing of suitable cost recovery instruments.

Economic self-sufficiency of ULGs: The ULGs have to financially strengthen themselves with their own sources of revenue at least to meet the maintenance cost of essential services. Economic self-sufficiency of ULGs in India has been an impossible task since neither the ULGs have made genuine efforts to improve their financial base nor did the State nor Central Governments give adequate thought about making ULGs economically sound by proper allocation out of revenues generated from urban areas. Though most of the cities in India have become regions of relative industrial growth during the last four decades and increase in GDP, the financial position of the ULGs has not recorded similar increase owing to various reasons. Besides, the powers of ULGs to raise taxes and levy user charges are limited by statutes. Unless Governments-State and Central give serious thought of this issue, the ULGs cannot discharge the larger responsibilities assigned to them by the Constitution.

In order to raise revenues, Government should enhance the taxation and revenue raising powers of the ULGs; create of special funds for infrastructure development; make provision of statutory payment to local governments at fixed percentage of recurrent revenues of central and state government departments' budget as grants, thus giving urban local governments more flexibility to meet local needs and demands. The Government of Tamil Nadu has created such a fund which could be utilised exclusively for creating infrastructure facilities in urban areas. All other states will do better in this aspect by creating such a fund by pooling up sufficient funds from various sources-central government grants, state government grants and mobilisation of local resources. The central and state governments must also provide technical assistance and training to officials of the ULGs in improving tax administration and collection procedure and improving revenues from the existing resources; empower the ULGs to draw from nationalised banks or credit authorities to provide services and facilities for which users can be changed so that the services become cost-effective and the loan can be repaid with the revenue generated from user charges.

Additional resource mobilisation for infrastructure development is not only inevitable in the present situation for meeting the challenges of fast urban growth but also due to the fact that in the absence of such development infrastructure, the quality of urban life deteriorates; and it ultimately hampers the economic and human development. If ULGs are to respond to the needs of the urbanites and to contribute to the growth momentum, they must be administratively empowered, financially strengthened and efficiently governed. Since the local tax base of all ULGs is very low and generation of revenues beyond a certain limit is not possible for the ULGs, there must be constituted an infrastructure development grant or capital works grant to be released to all ULGs as per a specific or needbased formula.

Measures for Improvement of Local Revenue Generation

ULGs have to take certain immediate measures to improve municipal revenues which include:

- Updating of tax records and computerisation of all tax records such as property tax records, trade licence fee records, town planning records etc;
- Focusing on all major tax payers and benchmarking;
- Bring all tax payers into the tax network and revise tax periodically;
- Eliminating ineligible and unnecessary exemptions;
- Assessing all unauthorised constructions to tax and impose penalty;
- Plugging of leakages and evasion of tax payments through enhancing collection efficiency;
- Efficient disposal of property tax disputes; and
- Realisation of 100 per cent collection through strengthening of enforcement mechanisms; and
- Instituting rewards for good performance and punishments for non-performance.

Devolution of Funds

In regard to the devolution of funds from the government to the ULGs there should be a systematic method of transfer of state resources to support the developmental activities of the ULGs. At present the new urban infrastructure projects are funded through budgetary support from the central and state governments laid down in the five-year plans and annual plans, but it is inadequate. In order to fill the gap between supply and demand of urban infrastructure services the government has no alternative but to increase the allocation of resources for the most required basic services. The devolution of additional finances to the ULGs is further necessitated by the dissatisfaction with the quality of urban infrastructure services which is constantly pushing investment out of the fringes of prominent urban agglomerations. The State Finance Commissions constituted under Article 243Y of the Constitution must review the financial position of the ULGs and make recommendations to the government as to the measures needed to improve their financial position in such a way that the fiscal gap is filled.

The devolution of funds from central to local administration is another area of consideration. The release of funds project-wise to local administration has not been effective. Most of the local projects have not been fully financed by the centre with the result that the projects either remain incomplete or take an inordinately long time for completion. The pattern of central-local financial relations should be such as to ensure that grant distribution systems are not only equitable between the regions, but they should be so designed as to provide correct incentives to local governments to mobilise local revenues and to pursue appropriate policies.

Even in advanced countries like the USA and the UK, ULGs depend on the devolution of funds from the governments when they cannot generate revenues locally. In U.K. central grants constitute more than 50 per cent of the local body expenditure, while in USA, sales tax will meet most of the expenditure on maintenance of essential services besides federal assistance. In India, contrary to developed countries, ULGs have to generate their own local sources or have to suffer financial stringency that ultimately results in poor quality of services.

ULGs have to improve their financial position through all possible means to make India's burgeoning urban areas better places to live. But the ULGs with their limited powers to raise taxes and limited capacities to generate local resources, predictable and guaranteed transfer of funds from higher tiers of government is inevitable and unavoidable for ULGs to fulfil their constitutional obligations since the resources available to ULGs are not adequate to serve even the present population and even to maintain basic services, leave aside development of new infrastructure to keep pace with the fast urbanisation.

The main reason for the sorry state of finance of ULGs is that broad based taxes are with the higher levels of government while the brunt of expenditure functions is with the ULGs. This situation necessitates transfer of funds from higher levels of government to ULGs to offset the fiscal disabilities of ULGs. For such devolution of funds from states to the ULGs the best criteria for adoption is the per capita own revenue as the most feasible summary indicator of a city's vulnerability to volatility. There is the need for a formula-based regular devolution of funds to ULGs from state and national governments to provide better infrastructure, improve governance and to build a modern urban India that is economically productive, socially just and environmentally sustainable, since the future of Indian economy wholly depends on urban India. The formula for such devolution of funds from the government to the ULGs should be the difference between the total income of the ULG and the expenditure both capital and maintenance.

Huge amount of finances are required to invest in planned infrastructure and services in urban areas so that it enhances their working efficiency and productivity and contributes to increased GDP. The fiscal gap in ULGs can be redressed by strict economy measures that include:

- rationalising local responsibilities and service norms;
- reducing service costs and avoiding avoidable and extraordinary expenditure;
- enhancing municipal revenue base and the powers to raise local revenues;
- considerable increase in the devolution of funds from higher authorities to ULGs; and
- stepping up measures to mobilise local resources etc.

The own sources of revenues of ULGs should ideally be sufficient to enable them to finance the maintenance of essential services that primarily benefit their residents and at the same time they should not be a burden to the local residents but should be in relation to the benefits they receive from the services provided by ULGs. This means that tax payers pay tax as per the services they use. Funds devolved from higher levels of government must be specific plan grants which should be utilised for development or capital works. Plan grants should not be considered in isolation without augmentation of the local tax base of the ULG since that would take away the initiative and autonomy of ULGs to levy, assess and collect the local taxes and local revenue generation. In the levy, assessment and collection of local taxes efficiency, equity, transparency, economy, local autonomy, adequacy, revenue stability and immobile tax base are required.

The establishment of a Municipal Development Fund is very essential to finance local development projects. The Urban Local Governments till now have relied on *ad hoc* capital flows from the central government for their development projects. The establishment of the Municipal Development Fund enables Urban Local Governments take out loans to finance development projects as required. Such funds can provide a mechanism for recycling investment resources and for mobilising additional resources from the public.

Borrowing: Most of the laws relating to collection of local revenues are not perfect and the mechanisms have not been entrusted with powers to initiate penal action against tax defaulters. Borrowing from agencies like LIC, HUDCO for development of infrastructure have become a routine affair for ULGs and certain ULGs could not utilise the loan properly but only repaid the loan with interest. Thus, borrowing by ULGs resulted in financial bankruptcy and indiscipline. There shall only be market-based approach to financing urban infrastructure, so that investment through borrowing sets in economic regeneration. Private sector or commercial debt finance will be available only for those ULGs whose local finances are sound enough and have the ability to repay the debt over a reasonable period. Thus, efficient and adequate internal revenue generation is a necessary condition for attracting private financing into public infrastructure. Property tax and user charges are the most prominent internal funding mechanisms for ULGs in India.

Current Efforts and Reforms

The ULGs are required to evolve an effective system of financial management since paucity of funds impedes development of towns and cities. All the committees constituted by the Government of India starting from Local Finance Enquiry Committee in 1951 till the Rural-Urban Relations Committee 1966 concluded that the finances of the ULGs was in a pitiful condition and that measures were required to augment their finances.

The CAA gives urban local governments a constitutional status as opposed to their being mere creatures of a state enactment. However, other than placing them in the constitution and ordaining regular elections, the impact of the amendment has been minimal. Mere handing down of responsibility by itself is not likely to yield the desired results. The state governments still have overriding powers over the ULGs. Their finances are tied up in a similar manner. Hence, reforms in revenue generation are required to enable cities to access private commercial finance at reasonable cost to fund public infrastructure. The High Powered Expert Committee in its India Infrastructure Report 2011 suggests a municipal finance list for incorporation into the Constitution of India as follows:

- Exclusive Taxes: Property tax, including vacant land tax, profession tax, entertainment tax, and advertisement tax.
- Revenue-shared Taxes: All taxes on goods and services levied by the state government.
- Non-tax Revenues: User charges, trade licensing fee, floor space index (FSI) charge/betterment tax/ impact fee/development charge.

Unless urban local governments achieve the required financial viability they cannot meet the demand for core urban services required for expanding urban areas. Furthermore, the services must be provided as economic goods rather than as welfare measures so that the services would be cost-effective and infrastructure development and maintenance would be sustainable. This necessitates the modification of the existing tax structure and introducing or bringing in innovative financial measures to keep urban finances on a recurring base as urban India has to address the huge challenges of development in the presence of serious resource constraint.

Owing to their limited sources of raising revenue the ULGs are perennially searching for funds to provide basic services. The prevailing financial situation warrants greater financial autonomy to the local governments duly enhancing their power to levy taxes as well as set the rates of taxation and user charges to ensure sustainability of the project under the strict oversight of local representatives and civil society. The increasing cost of urban services necessitates the need for strengthening the financial viability of municipalities and reducing their dependence on central/state government funds. The important considerations in this regard are:

(1) to enhance local government's revenue generation capability and its borrowing capacity: and

(2) to increase the cost effectiveness of local government expenditure, both of investment and maintenance.

Although very considerable income is derived from urban areas, the national and provincial governments are consistently reluctant to empower Urban Local Governments to raise their resources to maintain urban areas as efficient producers of goods and services. It is necessary to lay emphasis on increasing the efficiency of urban infrastructure investment, with measures relating to increasing revenue generation capacity as necessary complements to secure the financing of investment programme. All revenue enhancement measures have to be directed at improving existing systems and procedures of valuation, assessment and collection systems of revenue accounting. Besides, the Government has to evolve new fiscal instruments which envisage reduction in subsidies, improved pricing and cost recovery mechanism.

References

1. Om Prakash Mathur, *Urban Finance,* India Infrastructure Report 2006, Oxford University Press, New Delhi, 2006, p. 85.
2. *Cities and Public Policy*, p. 152.
3. *Cities and Public Policy*, p. 167.
4. Amareswar Mishra, *Urban Government and Administration in India,* Anu Books, Meerut, India, 1986, p. 66.
5. David Savage and Shubhagato Dasgupta, *Governance Framework for Delivery of Urban Services*, India Infrastructure Report 2006 Oxford University Press, New Delhi, 2006, p. 44.
6. Amitabh Kundu, *Trends and Patterns of Urbanisation and Their Economic Implications,* India Infrastructure Report 2006, Oxford University Press, New Delhi, 2006, p. 38.
7. Amitabh Kundu, *op. cited*, p. 38.
8. G. Sai Prasad, *Accountability of Urban Local Governments in India*, Atlantic Publishers, New Delhi, 2007, p. 72
9. D.S. Meshram & M.L. Chotani in *Theme of Urban Infrastructure Development,* Urban Infrastructure Development: Issues and options. The

47th National Town and Country planners Congress, December 1998, Bhuvaneswar p. 8.

10. Richard Batley and Nick Devas in *The Management of Urban Development,* p.182.
11. Emiel A. Wagelin in *New Approaches in Urban Services Delivery*, p. 255.
12. Rule 6 of A.P. Municipalities (Assessment of taxes) Rules, 1990. A.P.M. Act, 1965, A.L.T. Publications, Hyderabad, 2001, p. 577.
13. Govinda Rao and Richard Bird, *Urbanisation in India*, New Delhi, 2014, p. 214.
14. P.K. Mohanty, *Cities and Public Policy*, p. 149.

7

Urban Infrastructure

It is an established fact that the urban sector has increasingly become an important drive of economic growth. Cities are recognised as engines of growth both at the regional and nation levels. As a result of the rapid urbanisation most urban settlements are characterised by short falls of infrastructure, inadequate housing and water supply, inadequate sewerage, insurmountable traffic congestion, air and water pollution, abject poverty and social unrest making urban governance a difficult and challenging task. ULGs in the modern context are not merely service providers but facilitators. Besides civic service delivery, they have to address all urban issues including spatial planning, infrastructure development, social inclusion, and resource mobilisation. Cities are to function as engines of economic growth while being liveable.

Urban India has tremendous potential to harness the power of urban agglomeration externalities and planned infrastructure development in towns and cities to achieve the desired goals of economic development and poverty reduction. But inadequate infrastructure investment is largely responsible for the failure of ULGs to keep pace with the requirements of fast urbanisation and exploit these goals.

The contribution of urban areas to GDP is as follows: 1950-51: 29 per cent; 1980-81: 47 per cent; 2007: 63 per cent. This figure is likely to rise to 75 per cent by 2031. If the positive aspect of urbanisation is carefully exploited it enables urban areas enhance economic growth and improves the lives of millions of poor people.

Planned urbanisation is, therefore, the immediate task for ULGs. Urban Managers have to convert urban challenges into opportunities. In view of the positive role the rapid pace or urbanisation plays in the country's economy the positive side of urbanisation should be ensured to continue by bringing about the needed urban infrastructure development.

While urbanisation contributes to increased GDP, urbanisation in India, like in most of the developing countries, is more a severe handicap than an asset for the economic development. It is because of inadequate infrastructure made available in fast expanding urban areas. Urbanisation in India is mainly due to rural-urban migration since diminishing returns in agriculture push rural labourers to urban areas in search of livelihood opportunities. Though urbanisation and development are correlated, urbanisation does not inevitably increase development but necessitates development to cope with urbanisation, while development inevitably triggers urbanisation. A quarter of urban population in India lives in slums, which are in degraded, hazardous and unhygienic conditions. India has been urbanising fast but with low levels of per capita income. In the prevailing urban scenario, slums and urban poverty are two important issues that need immediate serious attention.

The development of key infrastructure and efficient delivery of essential services play a decisive role in augmenting agglomeration, minimise congestion and finance planned urbanisation. India has made genuine efforts to prevent rural-urban migration by concentrating mostly on rural development since Indian economy, until recently, was more agricultural than industrial. The efforts of urban planners to impose restrictions on immigration have proved futile in view of the increasing demand for unskilled labourers in urban areas.

In view of the futility of the efforts of urban planners to prevent or restrict immigration from rural areas, adequate investment in urban infrastructure assumes greater significance in order to make cities vibrant, generating employment particularly in the unorganised sector. Despite the potential of the informal sector to attract into its expanding fold migrants from rural areas, master plans in India did not include the informal sector. But of late, some master plans have allocated land for activities of the informal sector, realising its role in urban economy.

It includes rehabilitation of slum clusters, night shelter for the shelter-less, housing for the urban poor and work places for workers in the informal sector and street vendors.

ULGs have to respond to large scale migration by increasing level of local services to augment agglomeration and reduce congestion. The best way to cope with quick pace of urbanisation is through the provision of public goods. As observed by P.K. Mohanty, "Cities improve and innovate. It is principally cities that create the wealth of nations."[1] But the prevailing state of affairs of urban areas is far from satisfactory. The provision of infrastructure facilities and services required to support the increasing urban population is lagging far behind the pace of urbanisation. As a result, urban environment is deteriorating rapidly due to serious shortages of water supply, power, sewerage, developed land, housing, transportation and other civic facilities. Considerable urban population is below the poverty line. This has led to proliferation of slums, growth of the informal sector, inadequate educational facilities and deteriorating health facilities to the urban inhabitants. In most of the urban areas in the country, only 60 to 85 percentage of the population is served by safe drinking water and 50 per cent have no sanitary facilities. The following tables exemplify this fact:

Treatment of waste water and solid waste in the mega cities of India is as follows:

Table 7.1: Waste Water and Solid Waste Treatment

Serial Number	*Name of the City*	*Percentage of Solid Waste Disposed*	*Percentage of Waste Water Disposal*
1.	Mumbai	97	Less than 50
2.	Delhi	90	78
3.	Chennai	90	63
4.	Kolkata	75	50
5.	Hyderabad	75	Less than 50
6.	Bangalore	70	75

Source: Central Pollution Control Board Survey, 1996.

The above table shows the inadequacy of solid waste disposal and waste water disposal in the mega cities of India. The infrastructure deficiency in urban India can be known from the following table:

Table 7.2: Infrastructure Deficiency in urban India

Basic Amenity	*Deficit Percentage*
Without water source within the premises	34.6
Without taps	31.3
Without electricity for lighting	12.4
Without bathroom within the house	29.6
Without latrine within the premises	26.3
Without kitchen within the house	24.0

Source: India Infrastructure Report, 2006

Besides the above service shortage, the following is the housing shortage in the country:

Table 7.3: Housing Shortage in urban India

Type of Housing	*Shortage in Millions*
Economically Weaker Sections	21.78
Low Income Groups	2.89
Middle Income/Higher Income Groups	0.04
Total	24-71

Source: India Infrastructure Report, 2006

Weaker Section housing: The housing shortage in India is 26.53 million units while unofficial estimates put the figure around 40 million units. Most of the weaker section housing programmes had seen a failure as beneficiaries are not willing to pay their share even over a long period of a decade and an half even at the smallest possible EMI. Most of the weaker section houses taken up in urban areas have stopped at different stages.

Basic Infrastructure: Urban India as on date is in awfully bad shape as indicated by the availability of minimum basic services.

Table 7.4: Basic Infrastructure in Urban India

Serial Number	*Type of Revenue*	*Percentage of population covered*
1	Individual Taps	70.6
2	Toilets	81.0
3	Drinking Water	71.0
4	Treatment of Waste Disposal	62.0

Still worse are urban transportation problems, public transportation, housing and slums.

The above infrastructure deficiency shows the need to take up measures for providing the needed infrastructure as well as services in order to facilitate and sustain urban growth and to provide a high quality of life to urban dwellers. Urban Local Governments have, therefore, to organise, manage and finance the infrastructure needed for the increasing urban population. If the above situation in urban areas is not mitigated through appropriate measures, it leads to serious repercussions on the vital economic base itself. It is in this context that governments at all levels-central, state and local-should address serious urban issues like huge unmet demands for basic services like water supply, housing, drainage, solid waste management, slum clearance, traffic needs etc. in order to make urban life qualitative one. Investment in infrastructure in cities leads to greater efficiency in resource allocation and efficient urban development. "A strategy of planned urban development can generate a win-win situation for both urban and rural areas. This can also contribute to the broader social objective of accommodating rural migrants trying to escape poverty."[2]

In order to mitigate the infrastructure deficiency in urban areas Urban Local Governments have to improve water resource management duly diverting water from other uses to meet the requirements of urban, particularly larger urban, areas; introduce institutional reforms for efficient delivery of services to urban dwellers in most effective and efficient manner; design effective urban planning and management strategies; expedite housing programme through creating suitable delivery mechanism in the housing implementing agencies; improve resource mobilisation and cost recovery; encourage the beneficiaries of urban development to actively participate in decision-making and so on.

The ULGs have to meet the infrastructure needs from time to time since urban infrastructure development plays a crucial role in supporting faster and more inclusive growth of the country's economy. Besides implementing the Government sponsored schemes for infrastructure development, the ULGs should design schemes at local level in such a way as to leverage their own sources for urban infrastructure development with an identifiable link to improve service delivery. Furthermore, master plans for Indian cities should be inclusive in accommodating the needs of the low income group and the poor people since they provide the much needed semi-skilled and unskilled labour who are essentially required to sustain urban life.

The increasing demand for urban services is proportional to the rapid increase in urbanisation. Demographic projections indicate a dramatic shift in the incidence of poverty from rural to urban areas in the coming decades. World Bank studies indicate that more than half of the absolute poor will be concentrated in urban areas. Most of the urban areas in the country experience continued high rates of migration from rural areas to urban slums and squatter settlements during the recent years, making the extension of basic services and facilities to these migrants a complex and difficult task. Increasing the access of urban dwellers, particularly the poor, to urban basic services is not only likely to become a crucial problem in the near future, but the solution for the problem requires a combination of innovative approaches. The significant migration of rural poor to select urban locations in search of livelihood increased both the urban population below poverty line and urban slum population significantly during the last three decades. (BPL population increased from 60 million in 1973-74 to 80.7 million in 2004-05, while the slum population increased from 26.0 million in 1981 to 61.8 million in 2001). The already existing severe strains on urban services are further exacerbated by the constantly increasing concentration of the poor in cities. These migrants, however, have become vital contributors to the city's economy without whom many of the support systems for city life would collapse. But their influx has led to the growth of slums in cities which are the centres of problems. The non-recognition of this fact has resulted in the improper planning of the cities that has led to enormous strains on urban infrastructure.

It is, therefore, imperative to find innovative and effective solutions to meet the growing demand for urban basic services. Besides the efforts at the local level, the central and state governments must explore alternative policies and organisational arrangements for meeting the basic needs of the urban population.

The principal objective of all urban planning is to create planned, well managed and responsive cities with effective delivery of services to all residents, cultured and caring societies with concern for equity. ULGs can achieve this objective, through an integrated approach that blends urban development and infrastructure planning with sound fiscal policy and system to manage and deliver urban services effectively. "Infrastructural development is considered to be the key to improving the urban environment. For example, the construction of flyovers and the widening of roads are expected to ease congestion and reduce air pollution. Water supply and sanitation infrastructure are designed to reduce water pollution. These projects are usually funded by international loans; however, only large cities are able to prove that they are credit-worthy and they have, therefore, been the main recipients of these loans."[3]

The ULGs have to find alternative sources for bringing about the necessary development. The potential alternatives are: improving service delivery through using market surrogates; reducing cost and improving the quality of service through privatisation of the management of urban basic services; actively supporting self-help and service upgrading schemes by the poor; encouraging private sector participation in urban development and service delivery; and the adoption of policies that attempt to redistribute migration to small and medium towns. The alternatives suggested will have both advantages and limitations that planners and policy makers should take into consideration in forging sustainable urban development strategies. "Sustainable human development emphasises that development should be broad-based and bottom-up, redistributive and just, empowering and environmentally sustainable; seeking to meet the needs of the present generation without compromising the ability of future generations to meet their own needs."[4]

All the expanding urban areas in the country need improved urban basic services on par with the existing or developed areas. It is clear that the strain on basic urban services arises not only from broader problems of rural-to-urban migration, inadequate employment opportunities both in rural and urban areas, and the continued concentration of the poor in larger urban areas but also from the limited financial resources and administrative incapacity of central, state and municipal governments to provide greater coverage.

Maintenance of Urban Infrastructure

Cities are engines of growth and they need huge investment for development of infrastructure in order to enable cities to be the catalysts of economic dynamism. Good quality infrastructure is essential for fast growing urban areas if the cities are to function efficiently and quality of urban life is to be maintained. In view of the growing importance of Indian cities and the role they play in the country's economy, cities are to be provided with well-developed infrastructure and efficient systems of public service delivery to fully respond to the increasing infrastructure needs of growing urban areas, so as to create conditions that attract investments in industry that contributes to rapid economic growth. The institutions of service delivery built in through traditional designs are not efficient enough to satisfy the citizens as they are created on political and bureaucratic forces. This can be addressed through institutional innovations under partnership mode to operate them in the right direction.

Investment in infrastructure enables a self-financed process of urban development. As long as cities languish in squalor and poverty due to inadequate investment in infrastructure development, the economic growth and development of India stagnates. Adequate infrastructure investments would generate adequate employment opportunities in non-agricultural sector and sustains urban life. The ULGs have to address the serious infrastructure bottlenecks in cities in such a way that they attract labour into their expanding fold unabated. The main objective of infrastructure development policy should be the exploitation and augmentation of agglomeration economies, and management of the problems of urban growth, environment and poverty which accompany urbanisation. Provision of infrastructure base for the economic growth of urban areas and effective civic services for urban dwellers are critically important to exploit agglomeration economies and to minimise the negative impacts of population growth in urban areas. The development infrastructure and rejuvenation of cities accelerate economic growth by contributing to the productivity of firms and households. The prevailing situation in urban areas of the country calls for an urban agenda that revitalises urban management structures, systems, procedures, legal framework, financial management, urban reform etc.

The maintenance of infrastructure needed for rapidly increasing urban population is always a serious problem and a top priority item for all urban mangers within the urban management cycle since the failure or inability to maintain urban infrastructure not only leads to wastage of resources but results in the breakdown of services which will seriously impair the efficient functioning of the city or town. The reasons for failure to maintain urban infrastructure are unclear responsibilities, lack of resources, obsessions with new investment etc.

The aid donors are generally willing to finance new infrastructure, leaving the task of maintenance to the host countries, despite their obvious lack of resources to meet the maintenance costs and lack of the needed administrative and technical skill for maintenance. While creation of new infrastructure is a difficult task, maintenance of the existing as well as the newly developed infrastructure is an equally presumptuous task. In order to improve maintenance, responsibilities have to be clearly assigned and resources identified.

Financing of Urban Infrastructure

Experience gained over the past decades in the financing of urban projects and their state of affairs indicate the need to probe into the methods/ strategies of urban financing in the present times in order to make investment in urban projects more meaningful and purposeful. Investment made in urban projects should be such that it is imaginatively planned so that it can contribute to the vitality and progress of the urban area chosen for financing, keep the project in the mainstream of self-generating growth of finance for its maintenance, raise the standard of urban services, bring forth maximum benefit for the full development of the urban area. The translation of such an idea into action necessitates constructive thinking, meticulous planning, imaginatively planned investment, and frugality in expenditure. It is not possible to estimate the financial requirements of urban infrastructure since it involves the setting of standards which is a judgemental exercise. The estimates prepared by various organisations like Expert Group on Commercialisation of Infrastructure Projects (EGCIP, 1996), the IIR 1996, the Central Public Health Engineering Organisation (CPHEO) and others indicate the urgent need to upscale investment into urban infrastructure to meet the large unmet demand of services.[5]

Weaker Section Housing: The ULGs have to take up bankable urban housing projects that promote affordable housing for low-income households, the upgrading of slums, and the provision of infrastructure in settlements in towns and cities of the country. The Government of Andhra Pradesh has taken up the weaker section housing programme for the below poverty line population by linking the loan component to Banks. The infrastructure required for these housing colonies is provided under Integrated Housing and Slum Development Programme (IHSDP), which is sponsored by the Government of India. The key clients of slum upgrading and weaker section housing are municipal authorities, community based organisations, non-governmental organisations and the departments concerned in the Central and State governments.

The activities involved in urban housing and infrastructure programme are: to mobilise domestic capital for upgrading activities by facilitating links among the local stakeholders by packaging the financial, technical and political elements of development projects and to prepare local projects for potential investment by international financial institutions and investors in the global capital markets. The ULGs will have to consult a team of specialists on international and domestic financial institutions and financing models. ULGs must develop mechanisms to mobilise domestic saving and capital for affordable housing and liaise between financing institutions and the beneficiaries of housing schemes. Improving the living conditions in urban slums is a serious issue the ULGs all over the country are facing. In order to improve the urban situation in the country Urban Local Governments have to develop commercially viable infrastructure projects, adopt credit rating of urban infrastructure entities and encourage private sector participation in urban infrastructure provision etc.

Improved infrastructure has become the crying need of cities since economic growth and poverty reduction are linked to infrastructure development. Progress in creating the infrastructure needed for the constant influx of urban population is very slow while the demand for it is burgeoning.[6] Besides inadequate infrastructure for the increasing urban population, the neglect of urban sprawls by civic authorities has made urban areas vulnerable to natural disasters and disease. While urban polity so far focussed on metropolitan cities, even Tier-II cities, which are growing fast, need policy attention. Pursuant to the enactment of the Constitution (74th Amendment) Act, 1992 and the Twelfth Finance Commission award to Urban Local Governments, the Government of India has decided to merge all its urban improvement programmes into three schemes viz., (i) Jawaharlal Nehru National Urban Renewal Mission (JNNURM); (ii) Urban Infrastructure Development Scheme for Small and Medium Towns (UIDSSMT); and (iii) Integrated Housing and Slum Development Programme (IHSDP). The JNNURM is a reform-driven, fast-track and planned development programme to address the issues of infrastructure and basic services to each urban poor in all cities and towns. This is a path-breaking step of the central government in formulating a reform-oriented urban infrastructure programme which aims at developing urban infrastructure at an accelerated pace.[7] The infrastructure projects admissible under the JNNURM cover *inter alia* water supply and sanitation including desalination plants, where necessary; sewerage and solid waste management; widening of roads and bridges to remove transport bottlenecks and truck terminals; environmental improvement and city beautification schemes; construction of working women's hostels, homes for destitute children, night shelters, community toilets, street lighting; slaughter houses; and civic amenities like playgrounds/ stadiums, community halls etc.

The JNNURM envisages the achievement of the following outcomes at the end of the Mission period by the Urban Local Governments:

- Modern and transparent budgeting, accounting, financial management systems must be designed and adopted for all urban services and governance functions;
- City-wide frame work for planning and governance will be established and become operational;
- All urban poor will have access to a basic level of urban services; financially self-sustaining agencies for urban governance and service delivery will be established through reforms to major revenue instruments;
- Local services and governance will be conducted in a manner that is transparent and accountable to citizens;
- E-governance applications will be introduced in core functions of Urban Local Governments resulting in reduced cost and time of service delivery.[8]

In order to become eligible for assistance under the scheme the assistance-seeking Urban Local Governments have to undertake a series of reforms at the state level and the local level to address the issues of urban governance and poverty alleviation, including the provision of basic amenities to the poor in a sustainable manner. The governments of certain states have proposed the following Mandatory Reforms which are at various stages of implementation:

- Implementation of decentralisation measures as envisaged in the Constitution (74th Amendment) Act, 1992;
- Repealing of Land (Ceiling and regulation) Act, 1976;
- Reformation of Rent Control Laws;
- Rationalisation of Stamp Duty;
- Enactment of Public Disclosure Law;
- Enactment of Community Participation Laws; and
- Associating elected municipalities with city Planning functions.

The ULGs are also required to prepare a City Development Plan (CDP) based on a Rapid City Assessment (RCA) in order to help the Urban Local Governments to: (a) develop a vision for the city; (b) ascertain the gap between infrastructure and investments; and (c) set out priorities for undertaking reforms and investments.[9]

Policy Alternatives and Organisational Choices

The increasing demand for urban services cannot be met entirely through rapid and substantial increases in central, state or municipal government expenditure. Many services such as urban housing, transportation networks, citywide sanitation systems, public safety, education and health care can best be provided only by central and state governments because they require large-scale capital financing and a political base of protection.

According to Emiel A. Wagelin, "Cities are engines of economic growth and sources of employment particularly in the service sector. Cities are also major sources of national, provincial and local tax revenue, in many cases outstripping rural areas not only on a per capita basis but often in absolute terms as well."[10] The positive economic functions which cities fulfil can be made more effective through appropriate investments in infrastructure, urban services and shelter improvements. These investments can be financed out of the revenues generated locally if the capabilities of urban local governments are quickly and substantially improved. It means the reduction of dependency of the ULGs on national fiscal resources through increased generation of local revenues to finance more cost-effective urban infrastructure/services development. This does not, however, mean the enhancement of taxes or tax rates but rather improved assessment and collection practices, improved local administration techniques, more effective budgeting systems as well as more efficient infrastructure investment planning and programming and operation and maintenance improvements. The crucial prerequisites for the development of an effective service delivery system are increased attention to urban services delivery, strengthening of municipal management and finance practices.

The Central Government has initiated certain measures in this regard with considerable success during the last three decades. During the year 1974–79, the Government implemented the Integrated Urban

Development Programme (I.U.D.P.) for towns in all states with a population of 3.00 lakhs and above and areas of national importance as a central government support scheme through the provision of conditional soft loans to state governments. The project cost was to be shared by the central, state and local governments. Though there were major deficiencies in the scheme, it led to the pooling of investment resources from various layers of the government and generated additional attention to urban development in the state governments and the local agencies. The nature of the scheme was such that it made its operation more flexible than the schemes funded through annual budget allocations. Both the achievements and deficiencies of the scheme provided interesting lessons for a similar support mechanism established in 1979 and directed at small and medium towns. A similar programme called the Integrated Development of Small and Medium Towns (IDSMT) was introduced in 1979 on a financial pattern similar to that of the IUDP. The scheme enabled the ULGs provide sites and services, remunerative enterprises (shopping complexes), development of parks and play-grounds, tourist spots etc. The objectives of all these urban development programmes were the strengthening of municipal management and improved infrastructure. The results of the programmes depend on the increasing effectiveness of planning and programming of urban services investment in which more emphasis was to be laid on improving managerial structures and procedures, and ways and means of increasing local government revenues.

Innovative combinations of policy alternatives and organisational arrangements are required to reduce urban services deficiencies in the face of rapidly growing urban population and the increasing concentration of the poor in cities, as a result of large scale rural-urban migration which could not be discouraged by attempts to restrict urban services to the existing or long-term residents of urban areas. The major policy alternatives suggested in this direction are:

- Considerable enhancement of the governmental provision for improved urban service by building up the capacity of the ULGs;
- Improving the organisational efficiency and responsiveness of service providing public agencies;

- Reduction in the cost of services through necessary changes in regulations and methods of delivery;
- Encouraging self-help and service upgrading by the beneficiaries;
- Encouraging private sector participation in urban development and service delivery;
- Generating employment and higher income to the poor by increasing effective demand among the poor for urban services; and
- Effecting the distribution of urban population and channel migration of urban population to smaller urban and rural areas where per capita cost of providing services is comparatively lower than in larger urban areas.

The policy and organisational alternatives have advantages as well as limitations. The policy analysts should weigh the appropriateness of each policy alternative for deficiency of service as per the results they are expected to produce in regard to the access of the poor to urban services in future. During the recent past the magnitude of the problem of urban basic services has grown well beyond the financial and administrative capacity of the ULGs. There is no accurate data on the cost of meeting the public service needs of urban residents. It is estimated that even if the total savings of the country are mobilised to provide housing and infrastructure for the additional migrants expected to come and settle in urban areas in the next two decades, they would fall short of the amount needed. Hence, the first and foremost solution to the growing deficiencies in urban services is to expand central, state and municipal government expenditure for service provision. The government should play the lead role in the provision of basic services and facilities in urban areas.

Weak administrative and financial capacities of urban local governments are the most critical institutional issues which have hampered effective formulation and implementation of urban development policies and programmes. Since local governments are short of financial resources, they fail to attract qualified administrative and professional staff who prefer to work for government ministries/ departments, semi-autonomous organisations or the private sector.[11]

Therefore, if the capacity of ULGs to improve service delivery is to be expanded, there are two options to be seriously considered: (1) Empowering the ULGs to raise the required revenues to meet the increasing cost of urban services and (2) Capacity enhancement of the ULGs through strengthening their technical, administrative and organisational capacity to deliver urban services.

In the prevailing financial circumstances of most ULGs in the country, it is imperative that they adopt policies and innovative ways that lower the cost of providing services through changes in regulation and methods of service delivery, duly ensuring that there would be considerable reduction in the cost of services, without reducing their access to the poor. The ULGs should adopt urban development and service delivery regulations that are tailored to local conditions and which are appropriate to the needs of the poor and which will substantially increase the access of the poor to urban services. The rapidly rising land prices and land speculation practices in all urban areas have a tremendous impact on driving up the cost of urban services, on service delivery costs and on the access of the poor to urban services.

Dennis A. Rondinelli outlines a number of actions that national and municipal governments can take to control land costs and guide land uses in ways that will lower the costs of extending services. They are:

- Location of public facilities in such a way as to encourage or discourage private activities dependent on them in various parts of the city;
- Purchase of land by government in advance of need to guarantee its availability for the construction of public facilities, parks, offices, or recreational areas;
- Acquisition and reservation of property through 'land banking' for later use or to control the density of development in various parts of the city and to reduce the costs of public services and facilities in areas where congestion might occur;
- Adoption and enforcement of appropriate zoning, sub-division, and building ordinances that guide or restrict the use of private land;

- Control or regulation of building types and locations, land coverage and structural standards through appropriate building permission requirements;
- 'Value freezing' of land designated for future construction of public facilities, utilities or infrastructure to discourage speculation; and
- Adoption of special levies on land held out of development for speculative purposes, and on 'wind-fall profits' from increases in land values due to the installation of public services and facilities on nearby tracts.

"Some combination of appropriate controls, together with land-use planning, can assist municipal governments to reduce the cost of providing services and increase the access of poor to them".[12]

The cost of extending urban services can be reduced and a large number of people can have access to them if they are designed for multiple purposes and tailored specifically to suit local needs. For example, opportunities do exist for providing basic housing and shelter and related services in less costly and more effective ways. Housing shortages are very acute in the urban slums and squatter settlements that abound in almost all urban, particularly the larger urban, areas. It is established by experience that the housing programme taken up by governments have not satisfactorily met the housing needs of the houseless slum dwellers. Besides, financial institutions do not come forward to provide the poor with the capital needed to buy or build their houses. The urban slums are overcrowded, squatting has proliferated and thus the conditions in urban slums have only gone from bad to worse. Appropriate financial and administrative arrangements for dealing with the housing problem do not exist in most of the states. Therefore, alternative policies have to be adopted if the housing problem of the weaker sections of society has to be tackled effectively.

Suggested Policies for Consideration

- Support to programmes that assist the urban poor to improve their own housing conditions through sites and services, core housing and shelter upgradation. The sites and services projects allow poor families to improve their houses and to add and build upon basic dwelling units and expand their structures slowly as their income increases. This programme can help low income groups, through community action, extension of water and sewerage facilities, street lighting, preventive health services and construction training programmes. Low cost loans should be provided to poor families to upgrade their basic dwellings. Governments should go in for simple core dwellings so that the beneficiaries of the programme can improve them incrementally. This would be more beneficial to the low income groups since low income households are allowed to repay in monthly instalments of loans at affordable level, besides using locally available building material.

- Provision of minimum basic services to allow self-help programmes to operate effectively. The self-help projects require for their operation provision of essential pre-conditions from central and local governments. They cannot be successful as isolated or unsupported activities undertaken only by neighbourhood groups. Some of the important conditions are basic infrastructure and utilities that must be extended from an existing net work, land tenure and low-cost credit. Greater financial and legal security is essential to making self-help group programmes work more effectively.
- Promotion of public-private cooperation and private sector participation in infrastructure development and service delivery. The access of the poor to urban basic services can be extended most effectively by promoting cooperation through voluntary and private organisations. Community groups and voluntary organisations can play a major role in organising the poor to obtain certain essential services by establishing proper conditions to work with government agencies in finding appropriate solutions to their service needs. In certain situations services can be extended to newly developing areas or extension areas through joint efforts of the ULGs and the

private sector. In order to fulfil this objective satisfactorily, the ULGs as well as national government should—

(a) Adopt administrative practices and make organisational arrangements to allow voluntary organisations to actively participate in providing as well improving services in poor settlements. This includes the active community participation in improving service delivery, the use of well-trained personnel chosen by the community; the application of technology appropriate to local social, cultural and economic conditions; and contributions from the community in the form of cash, kind, labour and other services to help finance basic services.

(b) The service needed for particular localities of urban areas should be privatised and adequate finance should be mobilised so that with the active role of the community the projects can be successfully implemented. Community participation in providing and improving urban services inculcates a sense of responsibility in the community in the efficient management of services.

(c) Service extension programmes create opportunities for private sector participation and market mechanism can be used for providing services and facilities where appropriate. The cost of extending urban basic services can considerably be reduced if service delivery programmes are designed to create opportunities for participation by the private sector. Public-private partnership provides best solution in respect of land readjustment. This enables the extension of services to new areas at no cost to ULGs and allows private owners to profit from the provision of services required for development.

It is primarily the poor and vulnerable sections that are excluded from basic services in all urban areas in the country and they are often the last groups to receive services and facilities when the ULGs extend them. The high levels of unemployment and under-employment coupled with low levels of income among large sections of urban dwellers are the reasons for their inability to pay for the services, either directly through user charges or indirectly through taxes. The urban basic services problem in most of the towns and cities of India cannot be really solved until their high levels of poverty are substantially reduced. The best approach to alleviate poverty and ameliorate the living conditions of the urban dwellers is to provide services in such ways that promote employment among the beneficiaries and take up employment generation in the areas where the poor live so that they can obtain services more effectively on their own. Certain programmes should be taken up to increase the capacity of the informal sector to provide appropriate services which, if strengthened, will serve as a source of employment. These programmes include:

- Generation of employment for the beneficiaries of those services by designing service improvement programmes.
- To strengthen the informal sector as a source of employment. A number of public services could be provided through informal sector activities at comparatively lower cost since regulations and restrictions are eliminated in the informal sector.
- Providing services and assisting small-scale enterprises in slum localities and squatter communities as a source of employment and income. Employment can be generated for the poor through encouraging the participation of local small-scale industries in service extension projects. For example, low cost weaker section housing can be taken up by using indigenous materials that can be easily produced by local small scale industries in the areas where the housing project is taken up which uses local contractors and labour.

The problem of providing services in fast growing urban areas and to a burgeoning urban population is likely to become more critical over the next two decades. Urban population will continue to grow and the shifting incidence of poverty will increase the needs of poor households concentrated in towns and cities at a rate that outpace the capacity of government to extend the coverage of basic services.

The administrative capacity of ULGs remains low and their revenue raising authority is constrained. Their ability to formulate and enforce appropriate land use and urban development regulations is usually weak. Where the infrastructure needs of urban areas are to be met through services from multiple government agencies, problems of conditions and cooperative action often undermine effective delivery. The hierarchical structure and control oriented approach to administration used by government agencies reduces their flexibility and responsiveness to the needs of the urban population, especially the urban poor.

In view of the above situation it is inevitable for the union and urban local governments to make adequate investment in infrastructure, utilities and services to support small and medium scale enterprises in urban areas to cope with the demand for urban services. The appropriate market surrogates that increase the effectiveness of the ULGs to provide better urban service are: encouraging direct competition among public service institutions; encouraging the active marketing of local government services and using performance agreements for urban service delivery.

Outsourcing of services: Experience of certain ULGs has conclusively proved that outsourcing of certain services like sanitation, maintenance of street lighting, collection of advertisement tax etc. is highly economical and at the same time very efficient. When inadequate financial sources are a major impediment for providing and extending urban services, outsourcing is the best way to improve the ULGs' service delivery capacity.

Urban Innovation

Urban areas, with increased industrialisation and growing commerce have become a focal point of attraction to the villagers in search, primarily, of livelihood. This has led to massive urbanisation which has, in turn, led to the explosive growth of large urban centres, which is an inventible and an unprecedented world phenomenon. "In effect, the static city of colonial days has become the dynamic city of today. Yet many of the most productive large urban centres are in a critical condition as successive ways of population growth and economic changes have increased the gap between the demand for satisfactory living and working environments and the capacity of the public sector to deliver the required services."[13] Urban Local

Governments in India, responsible for urban affairs, encounter serious difficulties in responding to the mounting pressures of rapid urbanisation, economic and technological changes and cultural transformation. Since the Dynamic city has become a Problem City, it is the burden of urban managers to find out solutions to the growing urban problems. Most of the critical problems common to almost all urban areas in the country as in the world are:

- Unbalanced population, spatial and economic growth;
- Large-scale deprivation and unmet provision of land, housing, employment and transportation needs;
- Deteriorating environments, and inadequate basic services;
- Shortage of public fiscal resources and qualified manpower for effective plan implementation and management;
- Uncoordinated national and municipal urban policies and inadequate organisational structures;
- Costly imported finance and inappropriate planning ideas and technology; and
- Absence of meaningful public participation in the planning and development process.[14]

It is clear from the above that urban managers have to think of the measures to fill the yawning gap which remains between the reality of urban development and the goal of balanced social, economic and physical development. Urban manages have, therefore, to answer two questions:

(1) To what extent urban policymakers, planners, government, the private sector and international aid agencies have dealt with these problems?

(2) What are the prospects for the future?

The urban managers in India should take a close look at the experience of urban local governments in addressing the ever changing urban areas, contrasting situations, formulating, implementing and evaluating policies for improving urban settlements, especially low-income communities. The issues for consideration before the urban managers and Governments are:

- Urban policies and settlement planning;
- Urban Management and Finance;
- Urban Plan Implementation and Public participation;
- Education and Training; and
- National and International action for settlement development.

Case studies of the needs and demands of various cities and towns in India point out that it is not possible to identify successful examples of public policies, strategies and guidelines for meeting urban settlement needs, particularly in regard to housing, employment, urban basic services and resource generating activities. In regard to urban finance and urban management also, there are no conventional financial practices which are capable of wider application to all cities and towns of India. The same is the case with urban planning and management.

An integrated approach to urban plan implementation involves community participation, local resource mobilisation and appropriate technology. Certain appropriate changes should be brought about in public policy and international action, aid and investment activities which are required to implement development programmes and the effective improvement of settlements, especially low-income groups. Planned management of urban growth is an essential pre-requisite in national and metropolitan policies in order to counter the adverse effect of rapid urbanisation in India. These include measures to improve living conditions and working environments in urban areas, create new centres of economic growth and employment supportive of national development requirements.

Provision of shelter and services for the large mass of slum dwellers living in sub-standard housing areas and squatter settlements in all urban areas in the country, is a key issue for immediate action. Provision of low-cost housing to slum dwellers needs a range of new approaches. These include:

- Government provision of land for sale as serviced plots to encourage self-help building;
- Granting security of tenure to tenants and squatters to stimulate their improvement effects;

- Encouraging trading, commercial and industrial development in designated residential areas to broaden the local tax, employment and resource generating base;
- Introducing a "betterment' taxation system so that government can recapture costs of land use for development and redistribution in poor areas; and
- Rationalising public service networks and provision of utilities in areas of greatest social need.[15]

The state governments should direct the Urban Local Governments to allocate all plan grants to prospects benefiting low-income communities and the unemployed. The Urban Local Governments should be enabled to play a more strategic role in urban development, guiding the growth of urban investment productivity and incomes, training of qualified personnel in urban management, development operations and policy implementation. A development agency must be created within the urban local government which is action-oriented, flexible in outlook, sensitive to human and material resources issues, and based on realistic assessments of achievable objectives.

Urban Development Authorities

Urban planners have to show a concern for planning and management at the town or city level. They have to: (a) deal with urban problems which extend beyond an individual local governmental jurisdiction; (b) improve urban infrastructure and (c) increase the efficiency of certain services through economies of scale. It is presumed that urban local level planning is conducive to providing a minimum level of services to disadvantaged groups which ensure coordinating planning and management activities in the area.

Coordinated efforts of various agencies involved in urban development are required:

- to make the most efficient use of limited resources and to avoid wastage;
- to eliminate conflicts among the goals of rapidly proliferating urban-oriented government agencies;

- to attain uniformity in government policies at the operational level;
- to establish effective linkage among public agencies so that these may assist each other.

"There are several methods, techniques and mechanisms which have been utilised to ensure coordination. These include: (a) exchange of information; (b) negotiation to resolve differences; (c) specification of each agency's functional areas; (d) institutionalisation of procedures to ensure that views of relevant agencies are incorporated in decision-making; and (e) delineation of guidelines by the supreme coordinating body."[16] There are no universally applicable institutional arrangements or structures for coordinating urban development activities. They depend upon the scope and size of urban development efforts. Since it is difficult to achieve project-based coordination every time among various agencies, there must be an agency to bring about the required urban development duly achieving this coordination. Hence, Urban Development Authorities are constituted to achieve this objective. The UDAs in Andhra Pradesh are developed and organised in such a way that all agencies, performing different tasks right from policy formulation and decision-making till the implementation of the project, are created within the administrative system of each and every Urban Development Authority. This kind of system is conducive to increasing the capacity of the agency to negotiate and informally influence organisational decision, besides making available the necessary technical and professional competence within the organisation and improve the quality of task performance.

The Urban Development Authorities in A.P., endowed with special powers and finances, are playing the above role to some extent in bringing about sustainable urban development. The Urban Development Authorities work totally independent of the elected municipal councils/ corporations to bring about sustained urban development since local politicians with vested interests generally impede the progress of urban planning and management in all urban areas. The UDAs have been established to undertake wider planning, coordinate activities of local governments and provide selected services requiring higher levels of technological and managerial skills, keeping in view the future needs of urban areas. Though the government in consultation with Urban

Local Governments designs a plan to guide urban growth and urban planning, the role played by the local politicians often not only stunts the development process but even ruins the life of city dwellers. Unless these recalcitrant elements are replaced by an educated, qualified, broad-minded patriotic body, urban development would be an impossible task in the country despite its well-defined policies, keen focus of officials on all development issues, meticulous planning, good governance and effective institution building. Owing to the existence of elected bodies in all urban areas, urban governance has completely failed to respond adequately to the towns' or cities' explosive population growth, urban sprawl, slum and squatter settlements and the resulting pressures on housing and public services. Urban Local Governments cannot take up planning and implementation of development programmes outside their jurisdiction since their administrative jurisdiction is limited. The Urban Development Authorities can bring about effective development both on-site and off-site since their jurisdiction extends beyond the municipal limits covering several municipalities and municipal corporations. The activities of the UDAs have rapidly increased from time to time.

The UDAs have developed in themselves a planning wing, an engineering wing and an administrative wing. Thus, the UDAs need not coordinate the services of other agencies for implementation of their plans or programmes. They are now able to mobilise and sustain large scale infrastructure investment and lay emphasis on the provision of primary facilities, leaving the maintenance part to the ULGs concerned, with the result that the improvement in service delivery has been effective and purposeful. The UDAs are able to implement and manage several sectoral projects such as water supply, sanitation and road projects.

The inability of the Urban Local Governments to provide the minimum basic services to urban dwellers and to bring about sustainable urban development is due to the involvement of multiplicity of agencies in providing public service among which there is no coordination. Under these circumstances the needs of the urban poor cannot be met and the achievement of overall urban improvement and development will naturally be stunted. In order to avoid this undesirable effect, Urban Local Governments must be encouraged to reform their administrative, fiscal and management structure for the coordinated implementation of urban development policies. One important step in this direction is to constitute more and more Urban Development Authorities, without the involvement of politicians, to take up urban infrastructure projects, leaving only the maintenance aspect to Urban Local Governments. It is high time Governments realised the urgent need for a reappraisal of the issue with a view to making the needed changes in the national policy on urbanisation and in the programmes for urban development.[17]

The Management of Urban Development

Urban management should above all be concerned with economic development. Management is organisation of policy-making and implementation rather than dealing with policy issues. The role of urban managers in the management of urban development is to support and influence policy-making rather than direct it. In the changed urban scenario the role of government institutions is not to monopolise decisions and impose undesired solutions on the poor and undesirable regulations on entrepreneurs. The tendency, expected in the present situation, is to move away from the idea of developing institutions and professional managerial capacity as ends in themselves. Instead, the present attempt should be to create a more responsive, public service oriented administration which involves beneficiaries more directly in organisational control. Managers of public affairs are expected to adopt a more restrained, selective and supportive role; action should be arrived at by negotiation with the stakeholders of urban development as well as beneficiaries, rather than merely direct. This means a drastic change in the management practices and training of officials who should act as regulators, providers and bearers of solutions to urban problems and problems of management of urban development. Regulatory bureaucracy, professional arrogance, elitism and inappropriate standards are not valid. As the monopolistic, unresponsive and centralised administration could not bring about the expected efficacy, it should be replaced by institution building.

In the management of urban development there can be no generalisations and pre-packaged solutions. What was successful or appropriate earlier may no longer be so and prove inappropriate later.

The managers of urban development should, therefore, develop ideas and techniques which are relevant to the present situation or local circumstances and needs.

Important Issues in Urban Development

1. The Intrinsically Inefficient Public Sector

The public sector is now realised as being monopolistic, lacking in competition. It has an unresponsive bureaucratic nature leading to professional and bureaucratic interests and become an agent of underdevelopment. The solutions are, therefore, regarded as outside public administration-either in popular mobilisation or in non-state action i.e., in self-help and the freeing of private enterprises.

2. External Obstacles

The failure of policy implementation is due to a lack of commitment and support from others: lack of finance, lack of political will, the deadweight of established and outmoded practices, the unwillingness of different stakeholders of urban management to collaborate, and the apathy and irresponsibility of the clientele.

"In India, for example, the public service is typically composed of elite and transitory administrators, professional staff and clerks. Administrators are drawn into general policy issues and crisis management, rather than the systematic and long-term management of implementation. The professionals see problems narrowly and expect their plans and designs to be implemented without there being effective structure for implementation."[18] The solution for these obstacles is "to overcome political obstacles and managerial deficiencies by imposing programme by-passing the normal processes so as to get things done quickly and to strengthen the local political role in policy determination and to increase the local managerial presence, capacity and discretion. This would indicate that the aid programmes should work through regular agencies, make a long-term commitment, build local powers of fund-raising, coordination and problem-solving, encourage local political influence and raise the expectations and demands of excluded sectors. (Model: Hyderabad UCD project). This builds political will by mobilising the constituency of the poor; promoting decision-making and responsibility of local politicians; increasing local managerial capacity to recognise and resolve managerial problems"[19]

3. Organisational Competence and Effectiveness

The promotion of institution-building, that is, the development of organisations with clear structures, leadership and trained staff is of paramount importance. "The very virtues of democracy-impersonality, standardised rules and procedures, fairness-may break down in situations of dire scarcity, acute need, incomprehension of the rules of the game, and extreme local diversity. The rules cannot cope with the diversity and volume of demands, and situation becomes a crisis demanding reference to the top-or else there is breakdown and free-for all."[20] What is needed is the ability to respond to local demands, requirements and opportunities. The principles to be followed for increasing organisational competence are: decentralisation; local political control as the means of prioritisation and coordination; more discretion at local and technical level etc., "The big question for development administration is whether it is possible to combine the virtues of impersonality and fairness with those of responsiveness and discretion."[21]

4. Growth with Redistribution

In respect of provision of urban services like roads, water supply, sewerage, garbage collection, housing and transport services, the middle classes and the upper classes are the beneficiaries. Hence, redistribution with growth could be achieved through targeting on the people i.e., aiming the benefits at identified target groups and tailoring public provision to their basic needs. In order to fulfil this objective, adequate support should be given for the informal sector, access to safe drinking water from public taps and security of land occupancy. Urban Local Governments must be able to identify the requirements of the poor and then put in their efforts to provide them.

5. Access to Service

The question to be considered for providing access to basic services to the urban dwellers, particularly to the poor, is how to make the distribution of basic goods and services systematic and "as of right" without making special arrangement for the poor who effectively trap them.

Different problems have different kinds of solutions. The problems, opportunities and management approaches are to be considered as they occur in particular towns and cities, rather than trying to identify standard solutions. The major issues of concern for urban management are identified here and briefly described one after another.

Major Issues of Concern for Urban Management

1. Keeping pace with Urbanisation

While the process of urbanisation cannot be stopped paradoxically it plays a positive role in economic development. This is particularly true in case of towns and cities where urban employment is the only option for many for eking out livelihood. Urban development polices should be so designed as to accommodate population growth and also aim at harnessing the economic growth potential of urban development. Certain national economic policies have unduly stimulated urbanisation. For example, *Swarna Jayanti Shahari Rojgar Yojana* (SJSRY), National Slum Development Plan (NSDP) etc. Hence, there has to be a proper distribution of scarce resources between the rural and urban areas in proportion to their needs.

2. Project Formulation

The Government has to carefully study the processes within which particular interventions, programmes and projects fit in. This includes a thorough analysis of: (a) Economic development patterns and opportunities; (b) Urban Markets in land, housing and services; (c) The existing institutional system and (d) Existing local and national policy framework.

Planning for urban development and to ensure regulated growth of urban areas is an important function of ULGs. This planning includes provision of basic infrastructure services. In order to perform this important task ULGs need strategic vision, technical skill and adequate finances.

Greater Bangalore City Corporation has undertaken certain initiatives as part of its infrastructure development, which made visible improvements in the city. They include:

- Road infrastructure like flyovers and underpasses at critical junctions to regulate traffic, improved bus stands, introduction of low floor disabled friendly buses;
- Better social waste management through door-to-door garbage collection and provision of modern type toilets for public convenience; and
- Improvement of urban environment through renovation of parks, improvement of pavements and pedestrian ways and upgradation of slums.

Each ULG has to prepare a comprehensive development plan in consultation with well-established and experienced international consultants incorporating all the requirements for two decades ahead and implement the plan as per the priorities fixed.

3. State Intervention

The provision of urban infrastructure and facilities, including housing, is primarily the responsibility of the government. But its role alone is not enough, since it has excessive bureaucratic control of access to scare resources which very often results in corruption and manipulation by the powerful and discourages individual and community initiatives. Even then the Government has to play its role. In fact it has to concentrate on:

- Those services which the public sector or individuals cannot provide;
- Providing the environment and structures within which individuals and community groups can provide services for themselves rather than relying on public sector provision;
- Facilitating private sector provision through deregulation, appropriate pricing and fiscal policies; and
- Encouraging private sector or community provision of public services such as construction, waste collection, disposal etc.

4. Relaxation of Regulation

There is a dire need for deregulation since urban development is stunted by excessive regulations particularly relating to land issues like minimum plot size, regulations on the availability of affordable housing land for people etc. Excessive regulations have a negative impact on incentives and initiative.

5. Institutional Framework for Integrated Urban Development

The need for integration, particularly of infrastructure provision has been recognised. Special institutions have to be established for particular functions which are not related to the overall urban development context, for example, a housing corporation with special power for providing housing for the weaker sections etc. These special institutions/organisations would not have the traditional responsibilities for regular service provision and for operation and maintenance of the infrastructure provided by the development authorities. In recent times steps have been taken to strengthen the existing local institutions like local government, municipal corporations etc rather than creating new or special institutions.

6. Decentralisation

Local political institutions and political control must be encouraged through decentralisation to build up their sense of accountability by giving them a proper role and entrusting responsibilities. This process can mobilise local opinion in the formulation of policy and feedback for implementation. The decentralisation process provides the mechanism for accountability which may be absent where programmes are handled by other agencies/authorities. Decentralisation of decision-making to Urban Local Government level encourages effective participation of local beneficiaries of urban development in decisions affecting their interests.

The central and state governments exercise a very high degree of control over the ULGs in all matters including development planning and management in cities. A highly centralised system of planning and management is adopted in the country since the capital intensive industrialisation and urbanisation strategies adopted in the country required strong intervention by the central and state governments in investment and production process. But this over-centralisation often results in inordinate delay in plan formulation and implementation. For example, proposals under the Integrated Housing and Slum Development Programme (IHSDP) prepared by the ULGs are not accepted by the Government unless they are prepared and finalised by consultants appointed by the Government, which clearly shows that decentralised planning is absolutely necessary to expedite planning and implementation. Central planning was introduced in the country in order to promote rapid growth in industrial output, mobilise capital for further investment, generate employment and accelerate social and political change. Though planners and practitioners have firmly believed that central control and management would certainly lead to a more effective and expeditious programme for capital investment it has, in the long run, proved to be ineffective since central planning and management cannot take, or fail to take, into account local priorities and conditions. The trend towards central planning and control-oriented administration was strengthened since the administrative capacities at the local level were often inadequate and since the local units of government and administration were (and are) financially and technologically weak. But this should not be taken as grounds for central planning. Instead, the financial and technological capacities of the ULGs must be strengthened to enable them to plan and implement programmes at the local level so that the principal interests of the urban residents would be fulfilled. The disillusionment with the results of central planning has necessitated decentralised planning.

Development is a complex and uncertain process that cannot be easily planned and controlled from the centre. There are adequate reasons for decentralised planning duly transferring more responsibility for urban development planning and administration to the ULGs and regional authorities. Decentralisation can overcome the severe limitations of centrally controlled national planning by delegating greater authority to officials who are working in the field and thus closer to the problems. Decentralised planning cuts through the red-tapism and the highly structured procedures characteristic of central planning and management. "By decentralising functions and reassigning central government officials to local levels, these officials' knowledge and sensitivity to local problems and needs can be increased. It can allow greater representation for various political, religious, ethnic and tribal groups in development decision-making that could lead to greater equity in the allocation of government resources and investments, thus institutionalising participation of all citizens in urban development planning and management."[22] Greater centralisation in programme planning and implementation limits the role of urban local authorities. Another important ground for the statutory authorities at both national and state level playing the entire role in project formulation and implementation is that the ULGs lacked skilled man-power. This has several negative effects on the functioning of the ULGs. For example, over centralisation disables the ULGs to improve their resource base and formulate and implement plans at local level duly fixing priorities as per local needs. Thus, over-centralisation has led the ULGs to ineffective functioning as full-fledged local self-government units. On the other hand, decentralisation leads to the development of greater administrative capability among the ULGs and private institutions in urban areas, thus expanding their capacities to perform such functions as development and maintenance of infrastructure more efficiently and satisfactorily than the state or central government departments can do. When the development implementation part is left to the exclusive domain of the ULGs, the planning part is more carefully performed and supervised by the state or central governments by concentrating on formulation of development policies. Decentralisation provides a structure through which activities of various government departments and agencies involved in development could be coordinated more effectively with each other and with the ULGs and non-governmental organisations within various towns/cities. Thus, it leads to a more flexible, innovative and creative administration. According to G. Shabbir Cheema, the main advantages of municipal (local) level planning and management are: "regulation of local activities; mobilisation of community resources; provision of a framework for local participation; decentralised coordination of urban development activities; familiarity with local social, economic and political situations; and making locational decisions."[23]

7. Responsiveness to Citizen Satisfaction

Most of the urban development programmes at present appear to have little consideration of the real needs and preferences of the beneficiaries. Urban Local Governments, therefore, have to invent the ways in which programmes could be made more responsive to the needs and choices of the citizens. This is possible through introducing market mechanisms to provide greater choice to consumers; encouraging and enhancing the operations of those organisations which best serve beneficiaries' needs, and greater decentralisation of field management to the local level or through the local political process.

8. Management Discretion

The existing bureaucratic systems involve long bureaucratic chains which are unsuited to conditions of rapid change, acute need and local diversity. The hierarchies have to allow scope for more local discretion and responsiveness. Managements should avoid mere implementation of pre-conceived plans and policies and instead should become more capable of assessing the needs and analysing opportunities and negotiate towards objectives. A good and successful example of this method is the way the Department for International Development (DFID), Government of U.K. implemented the Andhra Pradesh Urban Services for the Poor (APUSP) project in 42 Class-I towns of Andhra Pradesh during 2000-07. The Municipal Action Plan for Poverty Reduction (MAPPR) was prepared by involving the beneficiaries in identifying the felt needs of the community in each slum. The team consisted of both officials and select beneficiaries (Community Volunteers) who prepared the plan duly considering and analysing the available strengths, weaknesses, opportunities and threats. This is simply a shift from planning as control to planning as development and a continuous interactive process. In order to achieve the object full well the management function should be strengthened at the local self-government level and professionals should be made more aware of their management role.

9. Asset Management and Service Delivery

This is essentially a question of internal management and the need to increase and improve the effectiveness and efficiency in service delivery and asset management. Besides the above, certain other approaches are to be considered in the aspect.

- There should be a corporate approach to management in which the objectives are clearly defined and plans, policies and strategies are well developed. The layout should clearly reflect the policies and plans in order that the plans are implemented through budgetary decision.

- The functions, duties, responsibilities and powers of urban managers should be clearly defined so that they can be held publicly accountable for the services they render and the functions they perform.
- Low staff productivity and poor motivation stunt public services in Urban Local Governments. Hence, it is necessary to adopt new approaches towards staff appraisal, supervision, career planning incentive schemes, training for skill upgradation etc.
- There should be a correlation between service outputs and input costs. In most of the Urban Local Governments in India, the services rendered are cost ineffective (for e.g. supply of protected water for human consumption). The gap between the cost of rendering service and income derived from it can be reduced by greater use of indirect provision, through contracting and private or community provision which facilitates the explicit examination of cost effectiveness.
- There needs to be implemented an improved system of financial management that provides appropriate control mechanisms and prevents fraud and corruption besides providing updated financial information from time to time which enables the urban managers to run their services effectively and efficiently.
- The magnitude of corruption has always been a critical issue in almost all the Urban Local Governments in India that prevents effective service delivery which often discriminates against the poor. "There is need for deeper analysis of systems prone to corruption and for personal and incentive system which discourage it and machinery to permit greater accountability and transparency."[24]

10. Public-Private Partnership in Urban Management

The maintenance of certain services is becoming a problem day by day both from financial and management points of view. Since the rate-payers feel all direct taxes like House tax, Vacant Land Tax, Agriculture land tax etc., as an unbearable burden on them, the ULBs have to find out alternative sources of revenue to meet the increasing expenditure on the development of infrastructure and maintenance.

'A weak cow has many bugs', so goes the proverb. Many of the problems the ULGs face are the result of poverty and the inability of national and local governments to create institutions and raise the required revenues to provide sustainable solutions to the urban problems. The only alternative left is to invite private sector participation in developmental works and maintenance of civic services. Public-Private Participation (PPP) in urban development is the best way of developing infrastructure which plays a decisive role in accessing private sector expertise and efficiencies in service delivery. Private sector comes forward to invest in projects that are technically simple, have small gestation period and allow easy estimation costs and that are profitable to the investors.

Privatisation of services: Almost all the Urban Local Governments in the country have been facing severe financial crunch. ULGs cannot march ahead with development without the active participation of the private enterprise. Privatisation of certain services is desirable to reduce the cost and improve the quality of services.

The private sector's role in urban infrastructure development is of vital importance. The 47th National Town and Country Planners Congress held in Bhubaneswar, India, during 1998 laid emphasis on "incremental approach for development of urban infrastructure services, tapping of non-traditional sources for funding of urban infrastructure, evolving of self-financing mechanism, rationalisation of norms and standards for provision of urban infrastructure, multiple use of facilities and services, sharing of operation and maintenance responsibilities by public, private and community organisation",[25] which would strengthen the efficacy of urban infrastructure development and management.

Substantial private sector involvement is essential to finance the quantum of investment required for urban infrastructure development and for executing the complex urban infrastructure projects since the public sector alone cannot finance, create, operate and maintain urban infrastructure with the same efficiency as when private sector is involved, particularly for large scale delivery of public services to the urbanites. Private sector participation in the development of urban infrastructure mobilises private finance and deploys private sector's technical and managerial expertise in the design and development of infrastructure projects. The inadequacy of local finance to develop the infrastructure required for expanding urban areas, financial incapacity of state government to subsidise a municipal debt, inadequate borrowing capacity of ULGs also necessitate private sector's active role in the development and maintenance of infrastructure in cities. Its unique advantage is that it creates value by channelising innovative and modern management practices from the private sector in project management, structuring, resource mobilisation, asset management and project implementation.

PPP provides benefit to both ULGs and the private sector participant. The ULGs continue to own the underlying assets, they can share in the project, leverage inadequate budgetary resources, and at the same time bring in innovative practices, expertise, and efficiency in the delivery of public services, while the private sector benefits because ULG's participation enhances lender confidence and resolves bottlenecks during the project period. It must, however, be noted that the ULGs can access private capital only for creation of infrastructure that is remunerative.

In India the public infrastructure projects were completely financed and implemented through government grants until 1990. But later the need for private sector participation in infrastructure including urban infrastructure development are felt to make them cost effective and improve efficiency and quality of the project and to enhance the accountability of ULGs in service delivery. PPP model in urban infrastructure like roads, sewerage, solid waste management, water supply etc. have given exceptionally good results besides benefiting both ULGs or Government and the private sector participant. The state government must establish a PPP cell to develop/formulate a PPP policy framework which gives private partner a clear sense of the risk-sharing arrangements for PPP, and they will have a greater clarity on how to design and implement projects under PPP mode. It is the responsibility of the state governments to create an enabling environment for PPPs to flourish, so that private partners are encouraged to come forward to develop and maintain urban infrastructure, since PPP is an essential pre-requisite in view of the magnitude of the challenges of infrastructure and service delivery confronting urban areas of India. Cities have realised that private sector can play a valuable role in public infrastructure creation and maintenance. The private expertise and private investment must be optimally utilised so that ULGs can get better infrastructure outcomes. Each ULG has to work out its own terms and conditions for private sector participation in infrastructure development and service delivery based on local conditions and needs.

The Government of Andhra Pradesh has initiated the PPP for specific schemes and projects like pay and use toilets, development or modernisation public parks, construction of foot-over bridges (with escalator) on state highways, street lighting, market complexes, bus shelters, advertisement on medians and electric poles, development of islands, improvement and beautification of traffic junctions etc.

The Grater Hyderabad Municipal Corporation has invited private sector participation for construction of city bus shelters all over the city. A large number modern bus shelters have been constructed in the city by private entrepreneurs where they advertised their products. Besides the Greater Hyderabad Municipal Corporation (GHMC) has incurred no expenditure in the project, the GHMC has collected advertisement tax from the private entrepreneurs. Thus, the private sector participation has brought considerable revenue to the GHMC besides providing an essential civic service.

Individuals, organisations and community groups with different resources and needs can play a role in the urban development process through public-private partnership. Under this innovative approach the public sector will ensure the functioning of the city as a whole and the community will ensure the provision of services at the household level. Public-Private partnership will develop a sense of responsibility in the community to own and operate the services and thus better efficiency is assured in the system. Furthermore, it emphasises the importance of decentralising and strengthening local administration.

The advantages of PPP is that it improves both efficiency and effectiveness in a service delivery, unlike the public sector in which the general distrust of bureaucracy and the oppressiveness of the state are clearly visible that hampers development and efficiency. Involvement of community leads to empowerment of citizens. PPP enables cost effectiveness, higher productivity, accelerated innovative delivery, enhanced customer satisfaction, dedicated social service, prompt recovery of user charges in harmony with local prevailing conditions. In the PPP model of service provision the government is: the funding agency that provides asset support to the private sector to provide public service; a buyer that buys the services on a long-term basis; and a coordinator that welcomes private sector participation. PPP involves a long-term relationship between the public sector and the private sector in the form of a contract binding on both the parties. Besides, it enables the provision of service or implementation of a project speedier and provides operation skills.

The success of PPP depends on improved ULG accountability and performance. The ULG must be able to understand costs and performance standards. In order to make the partnership effective, the ULGs must create incentives and simultaneously exercise control over the performance of the private partner.

In certain countries the private sector has demonstrated the capacity and willingness to tackle critical problems in the provision of certain services. Public-private partnership has already been tried in some parts of the country and has achieved great success. The best examples of this mode are Tirupur water supply project and Vizag Industrial water supply project. PPP augments the level of services, enhances the efficiency of service delivery systems and brings in new technology.[26] In order to improve the efficiency of the system, certain measures such as the following are to be taken.

- There should be clarity in regard to the scope and framework for private sector participation in the provision of urban infrastructure;
- Project and contract development should be specific and clear, duly including risk management and adequate concern for financial viability;

- The Government at the higher level should provide policy support and appropriate regulatory framework; and
- Active participation of stakeholders of urban infrastructure development must be encouraged.

There is a dire need to improve service quality rather than mere capacity augmentation. Focus should be laid on institutional restructuring to separate the role of policy, regulation and operation in order to bring in consumer and commercial orientation.[27]

Private sector participation is sought not only in physical development activities but also in the provision of basic services such as transport, communications, solid-waste collection and recycling and provision of various other utilities. This approach is advantageous as far as satisfactory quality levels are ensured, and provided services are made available at affordable prices. To get the best advantage of private sector participation in the provision of urban basic services the public sector must be able to maintain its role in establishing quality standards and enforcing them, detailed assessment should be made of the performance and capabilities of private sector in providing the same services at comparable quality and costs, and an assessment is also to be made of the competitiveness of the private sector. Another advantage of preferring private sector to public sector in service delivery is that the private sector can control illegal practices at the intermediate levels while prevalence of high level of corruption impedes efficiency in public sector.

In a period of severe economic constraints, the rational utilisation of what already exists in the built environment of human settlements needs more attention than it has received in the past. The development of approaches to the operation, maintenance and rehabilitation of infrastructure is a difficult task which requires political commitment on the part of national and local governments. Massive investment in infrastructure has been largely nullified by failure to operate it properly owing to various reasons. That is why public-private sector partnership in urban development and management is the best way out.

11. Community Participation

Another important aspect of urban infrastructure development and management is community participation. Urban infrastructure projects are planned and implemented by governments without keeping in view the local needs. Infrastructure investments were made without any clear understanding of local demand. The infrastructure built without involving its beneficiaries ended up by being inadequate, of poor quality and very often useless as it was unrelated to their needs. Hence, active community participation in infrastructure development is absolutely necessary. The community can participate in four stages.

- Participation in planning, which helps in defining the objectives, strategies and priorities;
- Participation in programming and budgeting, which guaranties the effective employment of resources to fulfil objectives;
- Participation in implementation, which creates responsibilities for maintenance and management; and
- Participation in operational activities, which ensures more cost-effectiveness and efficient maintenance and management.

Active community participation in planning and implementation of urban services and facilities is essential for the effectiveness of policies and programmes. In most of the ULGs the disadvantaged sections are usually unable to utilise these services due to poverty and lack of their own viable social and political organisation. Hence, it is necessary to create an institutional mechanism in every ULG for popular involvement in the provision of urban services. Innovative leadership, egalitarian power structure and effective community organisation should be encouraged in order to ensure that participatory urban development programmes are implemented more effectively and meaningfully reaching the genuine beneficiaries. The participatory method of planning and implementation of the urban development projects yields spectacular results since the community participation enables to identify the felt needs of the community and fix priorities, enables the right choice of locations, choice of genuine beneficiaries, choice of community leaders, control of allocation of project resources, mobilisation of community resources and choice of implementing agencies.

In order to encourage the community to participate in urban development projects policy framework must be made favourable to them particularly in view of the risks involved. Unless the governments assure the sanction of required funds at rates of return appropriated and adjusted for risks, the private sector cannot actively participate in infrastructure projects in a big way.[28] There must be a separate budget allocation for funding projects for infrastructure under public-private partnership. The government has proposed the establishment of Indian Infrastructure Finance Company (IIFC) and designed a scheme to support public-private partnerships in the provision and development of infrastructure like roads, power, railways, ports, airports and tourism. The establishment of IIFC is expected to accelerate the financial closure of many infrastructure projects and increase the size of infrastructure loan market to move forward. The government has also formulated a scheme to provide a viability gap fund to infrastructure projects in order to make infrastructure projects commercially viable by providing the money required to make the projects feasible. In this system the infrastructure will be built and maintained by a private sector entity and the asset is indirectly owned by the government and the government will provide the viability gap fund, which shall not exceed 20 per cent of the total project cost and predetermined user charges would be collected from the users of the project. The new institutional mechanisms are yet to bear fruit.

The diversification of responsibility for urban governance is an innovative concept in modern urban governance since it provides administrative decentralisation, besides improving urban services. The privatisation of civic services, active association of business organisations and non-governmental organisations in local urban improvement and management are a few steps in this direction. The possible areas of privatisation are: solid waste management, water supply, waste water treatment and street lighting. Privatisation of certain civic services like sanitation, street lighting etc. has given good results besides achieving economy. For example, privatisation of street light maintenance in Greater Visakhapatnam Municipal Corporation has given spectacular results whereby it could save about Rs 10 lakhs per year.

Public-private partnership, backed by the IIFC and the viability gap fund scheme, holds the promise of faster financial closure of infrastructure projects without over-burdening the country's public finances, and is also expected to reduce fiscal constraints on infrastructure investment and boost efficiency. The Urban Local Governments have to make an assessment of infrastructure needs of the towns and cities and find out the projects that could be taken on the PPP basis in order to enhance the quality and quantum of infrastructure services, to realise the full potential of public sector assets so that the stakeholders receive a fair share of benefits from public-private partnership.

References

1. P.K. Mohanty, *Cities and Public Policy*, An Urban Agenda for India; New Delhi, 2014, p. 67.
2. P.K. Mohanty, *Cities and Public Policy An Urban Agenda for India*, New Delhi, 2014, p. 60.
3. Darshini Mahadevia in "*Sustainable Urban Development in India: An Inclusive Perspective*", UNRISD Publication, Geneva, 2002, p. 6.
4. *Ibid.* p. 1.
5. David Savage and Shubhagato Dasgupta, *Governance Framework for Delivery of Urban Services,* India Infrastructure Report 2006 Oxford University Press, New Delhi, 2006, p. 48
6. Anupam Rastogi, *India Infrastructure Report 2006,* Oxford University Press, New Delhi, 2006, p. 1.
7. Rajiv B. Lal, Indian Infrastructure Report 2006, Oxford University Press, New Delhi, 2006, p.v.
8. Tool kit on *Comprehensive Capacity Building Programme for Improved Urban Governance & Poverty Alleviation,* Ministry of housing & Urban Poverty Alleviation, New Delhi, 2009, p. 2.
9. Anupam Rastogi, *The Infrastructure Sector in India,* India Infrastructure Report 2006, Oxford University Press, New Delhi, 2006, p. 21.
10. Emiel A. Wagelin, *New Approach to Urban Service Delivery*, pp. 244-45.
11. G. Shabbir Cheema, *Strengthening Urban Institutional Capabilities: Issues and Responses,* UNCRD, Nagoya, Japan, 1990, p.160.
12. Dennis A. Rondinelli, *Extending Urban Service in Developing Countries,* p. 9.
13. Thomas L. Blair, *Urban Innovation Abroad, Problem Cities in Search of Solutions,* ed. by Thomas L. Blair, p. 1.
14. *Ibid*, p.2
15. *Ibid*, p.4.
16. G. Shabbir Cheema, *Strengthening Urban Institutional Capabilities: Issues and Responses* UNCRD, Nagoya, Japan, 1990, p. 155.

17. Dr V. Nath, *Urbanisation, Urban Development and Metropolitan Cities in India,* Concept Publishing Company, New Delhi, 2007, p. 65.
18. Richard Batley and Nick Devas in *The Management of Urban Development,* Birmingham, U.K., 1980, p. 175.
19. *Ibid*, p.176.
20. *Ibid*, p.176.
21. *Ibid*, p.177.
22. G. Shabbir Cheema in *Strengthening Urban Institutional Capabilities: Issues and Responses,* UNCRD, Nagoya, Japan, 1990, p.155.
23. *Ibid*, p.164.
24. Richard Batley and Nick Devas in *The Management of Urban* Development, p.184.
25. D.S. Meshram and M.L.Chotani in *Urban Infrastructure Development: Issues and Options.*
26. Sujatha Srikumar in Urban Infrastructure Development in India, IL & PS Infrastructure Development Corporation Ltd., 2008, p.10.
27. *Ibid*, p.11.
28. Anupam Rastogi, *The Infrastructure Sector in India, 2005* in Urban Infrastructure Report 2006, Oxford University Press, New Delhi, 2006, p.1.

8

Accountability, Transparency, Grievance Redressal and Service Delivery

Accountability and transparency are the hallmarks of modern urban local self-governance and they expedite the process of enhancing actions that work and curtailing those that do not. The public are entitled to disclosure of full information on what is going in the ULGs. All decision-makers in the ULG are responsible for the consequences of their actions and all their actions are subject to review audit and the public can freely access to the outcomes of such reviews. Accountability is the obligation of the holders of public office to take responsibility for their actions. It is a democratic principle enshrined in the legal framework of the ULGs. Accountability in urban governance is an agreed relationship between the municipal functionaries and the citizens of the urban area. Accountability is a *sine qua non* of every public authority established under a statute since citizens demand increased accountability and their own active participation in the formulation of projects and their implementation for public welfare. As per the reform agenda of the JNNURM every state has to enact legislation of a public disclosure law for accessing central grants. It calls for a quarterly disclosure of audited financial statements to the public within two months of the end of each quarter. Recently there is considerable pressure from the public to make the Urban Local Governments and officials accountable for the use of public money. Transparency enables efficient functioning of democracy at grassroots level. The decision-making process should be transparent and open to scrutiny since public in a democratic set up governance have a right to know how public institutions are functioning and how the public fund is utilised.

Municipal accountability is two-way: they are responsible to the people for their decisions and they are equally responsible to the Government in regard to proper and timely utilisation of the grants released to ULGs.

Accountability is as essential pre-requisite or a key requirement for achieving the desired outcomes of urban governance processes and standards in public life to ensure the well being of urbanites. Accountability and transparency play a vital role in ensuring effective and efficient governance and well-being of citizens duly enforcing a corruption free and more equitable form of governance. The best way of avoiding corrupt practices among local government officials is to make managers accountable to the public in one form or other.

In the U.S.A. Government enacted Government Performance and Results Act, 1993 in order to create a frame work for more effective planning, budgeting, programme evaluation and fiscal accountability for public servants and to improve public confidence and performance of government agencies. The Act has created tools like strategic planning and performance measures to ensure accountability of governments and public servants to their citizens. A similar legislation is felt necessary in India also to improve governance and increase accountability of governments at all levels and to enhance overall effectiveness.

Urban Local Governments in India, as has been observed during the last three or four decades of their practical working, pay enormous attention to furnishing progress reports periodically but perform duties and render services perfunctorily. Seldom do ULGs focus on practical results and citizen satisfaction. At present the ULGs suffer from several inherent organisational defects which include:

- Governments at any level-central, state and local- have not specified the areas in which the ULGs have to excel, keeping in view the felt needs and demands of the citizens;
- There are no strategic organisational plans to achieve the specified goals or targets;

- There are no specific legal provisions defining its processes or steps to be taken for achieving the goals and add values; and
- The public are quite unaware of the programmes meant for their welfare, the objectives, activities and the targeted beneficiaries, nor is a system evolved to keep the public informed of these programmes and to invite their active participation in them to achieve better results.

In the above prevailing situation, ULGs have to evolve a system of performance accountability in all wings of the ULGs. The ULG and its officials must be accountable to citizens to whom they owe their existence. It must be two-fold: while the official machinery (performance wing) is accountable to the district and state administration, both wings (deliberative wing and performance wing) must be accountable to the citizens in regard to the goals established and achieved within the time frame prescribed by statute. In order to achieve this objective, these goals should be reflected in the Annual Performance Plan and Budget which should contain, *inter alia*, the established performance goals and the level of performance to be achieved under each programme or activity which should be specific, quantifiable and measurable, and should describe the human and material resources required and the operational procedures adopted to achieve these goals. These details enable the deliberative wing to assess the progress achieved *vis-à-vis* the targets fixed, deficiencies in the achievements and to find out reasons for the short-fall of progress and to workout solutions for better performance. This can be achieved through a performance management framework, Performance Management System (PMS) duly fixing the Performance Indicators. The PMS must assess the availability of resources, the circumstances and constraints in implementing various urban development schemes, and fix priorities, objectives, indicators and targets to be achieved during a specific period. The system should promote a culture of performance management and focus on results to be achieved. Although Governments have enacted laws and framed rules to insist the public servants to perform their duties faithfully and conscientiously with commitment and dedication to duty without fear or favour, affection or ill-will, these laws could not be implemented effectively as there is no official machinery above the ULGs to exercise strict vigilance in respect of funds received from the Government and taxes collected from the rate-payers and expenditure incurred by ULGs for the specific purpose and avoid wasteful expenditure.

Accountability in ULGs can be better ensured through civic engagement in local affairs. The citizens should participate directly or indirectly in exacting accountability. Good and efficient urban governance requires systematic measures such as greater transparency, increased accountability, reduced discretion and well-defined procedures for removal of corruption. In certain states accountability has been achieved through e-governance, use of information technology, citizen awareness brochures, decentralisation, simplification of procedures, monitoring and evaluation, time-bound service delivery, grievance redressal, periodical auditing and such key mechanisms. The Right to Information Act (RTI), Citizens Charter, incentives to honest and diligent officials, stakeholders' involvement in delivery of public services, public involvement in decision-making and social audit of local government expenditure are some of the instruments of accountability. Besides, reform in urban governance like public disclosure of information, e-governance, single window system for delivery of services, transparency, citizen participation in decision making, social audit of local government expenditure are some of the tools initiated to provide citizen-friendly, public accountable local governance. Accountability through performance evaluation will ensure that its activities meet the needs and expectations of the urbanites.

We have adopted democratic system of government at local level also in order to give a greater say to the local community in addressing their local needs. In such a system of democratic government all officials are answerable to the people as well as to the elected representatives for their decisions and actions. Such accountability, enforced through enacted laws, rules, regulations and byelaws, should focus attention both on compliance with law in force and on achievements of results. The Nolan Committee on Standards in Public Life in the United Kingdom enumerated seven principles for strict adherence in public life. They are: selflessness; integrity; objectivity; accountability; openness; honesty and leadership. Certain states in

India have prescribed efficient accountability mechanism through administrative procedures, annual audit, agency performance evaluation etc.

Accountability is the devising of concrete and effective steps that enable ULGs to fulfil their constitutional obligations, redress grievances and deliver services to the public promptly and efficiently with honesty and commitment. This can be achieved through drastic reforms in the law dealing with public utility service.

Good and efficient urban governance is possible through well developed institutional framework, well-structured organisation of the local government and human resource management. The Global Campaign on good urban governance suggests certain norms for good urban governance which include:

- Sustainability through the balancing of environmental, social, and economic needs of present and future generations;
- Subsidiarity of authority and resources to the closest appropriate level;
- Efficiency in delivery of civil services and in local economic development;
- Equity in access to basic civic necessities and decision-making processes;
- Transparency in local government operations with information disclosure on all aspects of local government functioning;
- Accountability for actions to the public at large;
- Civic engagement and citizenship development; and
- Security to individuals and their living environments.

The four key aspects of good urban governance, according to Constitution (74th Amendment) Act, 1992 are: democracy and representation; effective civic service delivery; transparency and accountability; and civic engagement and participation. The edifice of good urban governance rests on four pillars, namely, ethos, ethics, equity and efficiency. Ethics and social accountability are essential requirements of efficient urban governance. The widely prevalent awful corruption is the main problematic issue that stunts development and adversely affects the efficiency of governance. The primary concern of victims of corruption in public life is not just punishing the erring official on a complaint lodged by them but the prompt delivery of service. All the anti-corruption measures initiated by Government should reckon with this ground reality. Punishing the corrupt personnel is entirely different from ensuring accountability on the part of the officials entrusted with the responsibility of delivering service to the public. Corruption is an important manifestation of the failure of ethics. Ethics is grounded in the notion of responsibility and accountability. Management of ethics in public life is an essential aspect of ensuring accountability in urban governance and it is the responsibility of ULGs to enunciate those principles in their respective laws.

The primary concern of ULGs today is to take up measures to provide a better accountability frame work in order to focus on service delivery that is consistent with citizen preferences, and to minimise corruption, waste and inefficiencies which generally permeate public governance. The top-down hierarchical controls should be made more effective. Citizens should be empowered to hold governments accountable to them.

In order to remake urban governance more ethical and accountable there is the dire need to bring about reforms in urban governance and to bring in new perspectives. A policy options paper was prepared in 2004 with the following salient features:

Salient Features of Accountability

Constitution and Government

- Executive powers should vest with Empowered Standing Committee;
- Five-year term for Mayors/Chairpersons;
- Provision for wards and ward committees;
- Classification of functions into core functions, functions assigned by government and other functions;
- Supersession of elected bodies only after review by a committee;
- Re-election of dissolved council within six months.

Financial Management

- State governments to prepare municipal accounting manual;
- Municipalities to prepare annual balance sheets;
- Provision for appointment of a Municipal Accounts Committee;
- Provision for appointment of Chartered Accountants as auditors;
- Heads of accounts to be separated for capital, maintenance, water supply, roads etc;
- Preparation of annual inventory of municipal properties;
- Comprehensive debt limitation policy by state government; and
- Enabling access to capital markets and financial institutions for capital investments.

Municipal Revenue Generation

- Property tax assessment system on capital value or plinth area basis;
- Self-assessment of property tax by rate-payers; and
- Implementation of State Finance Commission's recommendations.

Urban Environmental Infrastructure and Services

- Participation of the private sector, the NGOs and CBOs in urban service delivery.
- Service charges to reflect Operation and Maintenance and capital costs.
- Implementation of Solid Waste Handling Rules and Hazardous and Bio-medical Waste Handling Rules of Government of India.
- State-level regulatory commission on municipal services.

Others

- Representation to municipalities on District/ Metropolitan Planning Committees.

- Implementation of development plans by Urban Local Governments.
- Regulatory powers to manage illegal construction activities.
- Easy access to information on various activities of municipalities.[1]

Accountability Mechanism

There must be an institutional framework in the ULGs for ensuring ethics and public accountability in urban local governance in order to foster responsive and responsible municipal governance. The performance of municipal functions by municipal functionaries must be made transparent, that is, open to law, regulation, prudent judgement and scrutiny; all participants in the governance from decision-making till implementation must be responsible to the citizens for the consequences of their actions; and all actions of municipal functionaries must be subject to candid review. This objective can be ensured through:

- Decentralisation of responsibilities among various functionaries in respect of day to day operations;
- Transparent, simple and easily understandable service delivery processes;
- Enforcement of accountability standards to functionaries of the Urban Local Government;
- Public hearing of complaints relating to long-pending issues;
- Dissemination of updated information relating to implementation of various schemes and utilisation of public fund; and
- Access to information so that accountability is clear, utilisation of public fund is transparent and public expenditure is people's welfare-oriented and is effectively controlled.

The Ministry of Urban Development has suggested certain steps to implement the recommendations of the Model Municipal Law. The Government of Andhra Pradesh has taken up the preparation of a Unified Municipal Law applicable to all Urban Local Governments in the state based on the Model Municipal Law, which is expected to replace the existing five different Acts, namely, The Andhra Pradesh Municipalities Act, 1965, Greater Hyderabad Municipal Corporation Act, 1955, A.P. Municipal Corporations Act, 1994, Greater Visakhapatnam Municipal Corporation Act and the Vijayawada Municipal Corporation Act. The Government of Andhra Pradesh started e-Seva Centres in all municipalities and municipal corporatism in 2003. They have been functioning effectively by rendering electronic service in respect of eight services pertaining to different governments. It is proposed to include a total number of 36 services under the e-Governance.

Citizen Charter

The Citizen Charter is a document which represents a systematic effort to focus on the commitment of the Urban Local Government to its citizens in respect of standard of services, information, choice, and consultation, non-discrimination and accountability, grievance redressal, courtesy and value for money. It is also a commitment of the Urban Local Government to improve service delivery, and guarantee citizen satisfaction. The system worked marvellously well since under the charter the official concerned was penalised @ Rs 50/- per day for delay in delivering the service beyond the time frame prescribed by the Government. In order to implement the Charter effectively, a service centre was opened in every Municipal Office in the entire state of Andhra Pradesh in May, 2001 and citizens were required to submit their applications for any of the above services only through the service centre and the service would be delivered through the same centre within the time-frame specified in the Government Order as well as in the acknowledgement of the application.

The Department of Municipal Administration, Government of Andhra Pradesh, prepared a Citizens' Charter which was approved by the Government of Andhra Pradesh in order to root out corruption in public service especially at the service delivery end of the system, by prescribing a timeframe in respect of four important services, namely, (1) Assessment of property tax and allocation of Door Number, (2) Disposal of Building Applications, (3) Sanction of water supply house service connections and (4) Issuance of birth and death certificates.[2]

Besides, the system was designed to ensure prompt delivery of services like adequate and effective sanitary arrangements, adequate safe drinking water, proper maintenance of roads, drains and street lighting, to provide for and maintain sufficient number of parks and ensure prompt registration of births and deaths. The above system could put a check on the field staff that would generally harass the public at the service delivery end and could at least minimise, if not totally eradicate corruption.

Besides corruption in Urban Local Bodies, the incapacitated, ill-informed and lethargic official machinery, and too many laws for too simple matters also contribute to ineffective service delivery and improper accountability. What is required in these circumstances is to train the service delivery officials in decentralised planning, simplification of procedures and sensitising the public in respect of the public service delivery system. Besides imparting expert training in service delivery methods, the Local Government employees are required to maintain the highest standards of character and integrity in the performance of their functions, the discharge of their duties and the exercise of their powers. The Local Government employees should ensure that, in the discharge of their duties, they are never influenced by personal gain or advantage, their conduct does not give rise to suspicion of any self-centred motives, and that they remain impartial in implementing the policies of the Local Government regardless of their personal or political opinions.

In Sweden there is an official called Ombudsman entrusted with the responsibility of receiving complaints from the public against officials and redressing public grievances. He is an autonomous inquisitorial authority into complaints. Official malfeasance like transgression of law in the discharge of duties, illegal activities, delay in service delivery, discourtesy or rudeness, incompetence, suppression of facts or furnishing false information etc. are covered under the powers of enquiry of the Ombudsman. A similar institution called Lok Pal at the centre, and Lok Ayukta at the states is established in India. Their role is, however, confined to the complaints referred to them, but the accountability of Urban Local Governments to public call and need is not ensured by them. A more acceptable alternative, therefore, would be to reorganise the Urban Local Governments in such a way that meritorious services are rewarded and corruption, inefficiency and delay are exemplarily punished promptly. The most practicable and effective arrangement to achieve this end is by introducing incentives for meritorious service and penalty for delay in service delivery. Though the Service Centres established in all Urban Local Governments under the Citizen Charter has ensured prompt delivery of service in respect of the four important services mentioned above the problem is not completely addressed, and much has yet to be done in regard to grievance redressal. The district level and regional level officials exercising vigilance and control over Urban Local Governments must be empowered to play a more effective role to set right wrongs resulting from corruption, inefficiency and official malfeasance. They should be free from undue and unwarranted interference in the discharge of their duties from people of influence and power. Besides Government, the private sector and the civil society organisations, which play an important role in decision-making, must be accountable to the public and to their institutional stakeholders.

It is not possible to ensure that the employees of Urban Local Governments strictly adhere to the above code for reasons quite obvious. The appointing authority in Urban Local Bodies is the Chairperson who is elected on political party lines. The Chairperson quite naturally expects the staff appointed by him to be loyal to him, totally disregarding other factors. It is pertinent to mention that the staffs of Local Governments are exempted from duty in the elections to Local Bodies since they are apt to involve themselves in active local politics and their involvement in the election process may vitiate the very purpose of free and fair election. In order to ensure that the conduct of officials, particularly those involved in the service delivery end, meets the above standards, drastic changes in the law relating to the appointment, service conditions and punishment of officers and servants of Urban Local Governments are needed. Certain state governments had amended the provisions dealing with appointment and punishment of municipal employees in order to ensure that they would not be influenced by local political considerations.[3] The pernicious evil, however, has remained unchanged in most of the states. The question before us, therefore, is how to ensure that the officers and employees strictly adhere to the code of conduct designed for them. This is possible through ensuring that the employees of the ULGs meet the minimum requirements of commitment to achieve the objectives set for, total dedication to the work allotted to him or her, reasonable knowledge of the rules, regulations, byelaws and other legal procedures governing the Urban Local Government and candid nature in the discharge of duties, performance of functions and exercise of powers. The fundamental principle that should govern the employees' conduct is efficient and prompt service delivery with impartiality and judging things in the light of prevailing laws.

Financial Accountability

The ULGs are answerable to the citizens as well as the Government on issues relating to financial resources and the allocation of funds for various purposes through strategic annual budget, justifying the purposes for which they are utilised. This kind of accountability enables public debate by the citizens and the elected public representatives from whom the ULGs can receive feedback for better performance in the future. ULGs should create structures that provide for 'ULG-citizen' interface in local governance. The ultimate objective of financial accountability is to improve relationship between the governing and the governed, to enable to focus on better performance, improve efficiency of the official machinery of the ULGs, and ensure that the results of performance of ULGs reach the citizens efficiently, effectively and promptly.

Accountability in respect of Urban Service Delivery

Cities in India are engulfed by a vast number of problems relating to governance in general and service delivery in particular due to quick pace of urbanisation, globalisation and liberalisation, and as the demographic transition and the forces of economic liberalisation take a grip on them. The state of urban service delivery is not commensurate with the country's income levels and is far below the established or standard norms. While the economy of India has been one of the fastest growing economies in the world and aspirations and standards are rising, the current state of urban service delivery is far below the acceptable level. This sorry state of affairs prevents urban areas from exploiting their potential for getting rapid economic growth and contributing to poverty reduction. This is, therefore, the immediate challenge for ULGs to address. Cities have, therefore, to be more competitive and their governance should be responsive to cope with fast urbanisation.

The quick pace of urbanisation owes to two factors-large scale rural population influx and a rapid growth of existing urban areas. This socio-economic change brings with it several new challenges to ULGs particularly in terms of provision and maintenance of public goods and services. In most of the urban areas the quality and quantity of public goods and services are declining as the ULGs are confronted with financial and physical resource crunch. There is, therefore, the need to generate physical, financial and man-power resources for attaining higher levels of service delivery and to fully gear them up for continuous improvement. Since urban areas are preferred locations for concentration and growth of economic activities as they are efficient and cost-effective locations for investment, provision of improved infrastructure and maintenance are vital for sound economic growth of cities to attract investments. Therefore, efficient urban management assums greater importance since a sustainable and equitable city attracts more investments that help economic development of cities.

Urban areas in India have been facing a variety of problems that need quick solutions. In democratic countries, political institutions dominate the delivery of public goods and services in many aspects. However, instead of acting in the interest of general public, the political institutions play a different role, since they are motivated by their local vested interests which hinder the delivery and distribution of public goods and services. Both bureaucracy and political institutions are often impending factors of development. This deviation of stakeholders of urban development from their assigned role results in chaos and the outcomes are haphazardous. Hence, there must a service regulatory authority in each ULG with the sole responsibility of providing better and efficient service delivery which works under the administrative control of district level authority. The other alternative institution could be public-private partnerships or some non-profit non-governmental organisations to take up the task.

The requirements and standards of urban service delivery are not the same for all cities of India, and they vary from city to city depending on the local conditions. It is, therefore, imperative for ULGs to assess the urban service needs for their respective cities although the areas of service are almost the same.

Every tax payer has a right for time-bound delivery of various services from every public establishment. Every ULG has to notify certain services for time-bound delivery and there must be a mechanism to assess the performance to ensure implementation of the enactment, thus bringing about relief at the cutting edge level in order to enlighten the citizens on their rights for demanding specific services. The implementation of the enactment must be monitored at the ground level since it is vital aspect without which there will be no built-in accountability in the ULGs. Redressal of common man's grievance is the ultimate goal and promise of the enactment.

The tradition of provision of local services has been the explicit mandate for local self-governments since 1861, when it was proposed that local services should be based on local resources. Due to massive urban growth during the last two decades, the quality of urban life has deteriorated. In view of the vital role urban India has to play in the country's economy, municipal service delivery cannot be seen in isolation. Municipal services should come together to serve the urban economy and enhance the productivity of urban centres. Urgent reforms are to be taken up to ensure that the levels of urban services will not decline further. The need for coordinated reforms in the urban sector is evident from: (1) the enhanced economic and social roles of cities; (2) the major service backlogs in most cities; and (3) the current piecemeal reforms which will not have the desired transformational effect. A new approach to urban governance and service delivery that address critical institutional roadblocks is necessary.

Defects in Service Delivery

(1) Water Supply: There are several defects in the water distribution system even in cities with adequate supply of water. Errors in metering, theft of water by industries, business houses and other establishments through political power, unbilled water consumption, wastage of water at public stand points etc. lead to high levels of non-revenue water. Poor maintenance of water supply system, poor recovery of costs are other contributory factors for inefficient water supply in urban areas. Furthermore, the ULGs will not be willing to levy adequate user charges due to public reluctance. Thus, the recovery on protected water supply is only 30–35 per cent of the actual cost of maintenance. The balance of O & M costs are met from other funds. Low cost recovery naturally leads to poor quality of service.

(2) Sewerage: The sewerage network in most of the Indian cities is very poor with the result that a large number of urbanites have to depend on public toilets. While most of the public toilets have no water supply, the outlets of most other toilets are not connected to the city's sewerage system. Thus, open defecation has been continuing in most of the urban areas in the country causing severe environmental and health implications.

(3) Solid Waste Management: The solid waste generated in the urban areas, collected and dumped in the dumping yard was a source of income to the ULGs until two decades ago when the wet organic waste was left in the compost yard, transformed into organic compost and sold to corporate clients. But the gradual increase of non-degradable waste like rubber, plastics and metals in the solid waste generated has created several problems in the disposal of solid waste. As a result, the source of income has become a matter of wasteful expenditure for ULGs for segregation of the biodegradable waste, treatment etc. If the dry organic waste is compressed into high calorific fuel fluff, it can be sold to cement and paper industries. But the segregation of biodegradable and non-biodegradable (but recyclable) waste is a herculean task due to lack of awareness on the part of residents for segregation at source and the costly process involved in segregation at the dumping yard. The ULGs have to invent efficient methods for solid waste collection, segregation and disposal through creating awareness about the process among all concerned with it.

(4) Urban Transport and Roads: The exponential growth of urban areas, the increasing concentration of economic activity and human settlements in select urban areas necessitate efficient or improved urban transport and roads in order to continue the urban economic activities. But inadequate investment on the upkeep of thoroughfares and urban transport has created several problems. Inadequate road space, the poor conditions of existing roads and the poor quality of public transport are the challenges which, if not immediately addressed, will stunt the positive contribution of urban areas to national economy. In view of the above situation, all thoroughfares in urban areas should be widened and regularly maintained by the ULGs with funds sanctioned by the Government exclusively for the purpose. The maintenance of minor roads should be the exclusive domain of the ULGs duly making a provision in the annual budget every year for their upkeep.

Measures to Improve Urban Service Delivery

The poor quality of service delivery in Indian cities is due to neglect of urban planning and infrastructure for a long period without visualising the ever-increasing needs of certain services; inadequate release of funds by the State and Central Governments for development of even basic infrastructure required for fast expanding urban areas and burgeoning urban population; total absence of institutional responsibilities at all levels of governance. Besides, inadequate investment in urban infrastructure, improper maintenance of services, inefficient administration by incompetent or unskilled official machinery, inadequate autonomy for ULGs, poor system of service delivery and lack of accountability of the ULGs to the community have contributed to the poor service delivery.

Most of urban development and urban service delivery programmes operate in a policy environment which has traditionally been characterised to a substantial degree by 'top down' planning and programming for urban service delivery. Measures to strengthen the 'bottom up' approach to urban service delivery within the framework of rules or guidelines prepared by the central government or state governments have not yielded the expected results. It, therefore, implies changing roles and responsibilities between different levels of government and devolution of adequate funds to the ULGs to meet the increasing expenditure of efficient and effective service delivery. The ULGs should be financially strengthened to play their role in the delivery strategy adequately. This requires a creative redesigning of the roles of different levels of administration in the government (central, state and local), and setting guidelines and standards for programme preparation and implementation combined with the sanction of adequate staff at service delivery point in the ULGs. "This can be achieved only if adequate incentives are provided which make local government service more attractive."[4] The ULGs have to address their financial needs through strengthening their local tax base and should consider various local surcharges on national taxes. Unless the revenues of the ULGs are substantially increased and strengthened, they cannot borrow substantially for infrastructure services. Besides achieving financial viability, decentralised and integrated programmes of urban service delivery combined with actions to strengthen local government capabilities are a more effective way of achieving improvements in coverage and quality of urban services. The ULGs should also bring about the institutional changes required to achieve tangible benefits. Emiel A. Wagelin suggests the following support actions to enhance the required institutional development and increase the understanding of the critical factors for success:

- Design and implementation of programme monitoring and evaluation studies and a frequent review of their findings;
- Regional exchange of information on features of the programmes and aspects considered relatively successful or unsuccessful, including regional review of the findings of evaluation studies. Beyond regional seminars and workshops, programmes of staff secondment also have a particular role to play;
- Institution building, technical assistance supporting the programmes, rather than attempting to radically change the course of action before a programme has had time to work itself through;
- A measured dose of capital injection by external donors carefully generated towards strengthening the incentive functions of the programmes;
- Research and pilot projects in support of attempts to overcome the programme limitations, appropriate distribution of responsibilities for urban service delivery between the various layers of government, the private sector and local communities.[5]

All Urban Local Bodies have to deal with two important issues viz., Efficient Public Management and Improved Service Delivery keeping in line with the changing needs and demands of the times. Andhra Pradesh has taken up a Public Management and Service

Delivery Improvement Programme (A.P. PMSDIP) with the principal objective of "Effective and Sustainable Poverty Reduction" in the state. This is possible through the implementation of institutional reforms, which enable improved access and quality of services for the poor. This programme is implemented through two phases.

The first phase focuses on setting up the institutional framework and building capacity within the Government of Andhra Pradesh to undertake wideranging reforms. The Centre for Good Governance (CGG) is established in Hyderabad towards achieving this goal.

The second phase supports institutional reforms that provide basic services that are central to the lives and livelihood of the poor. These reforms are to be taken up in five departments directly connected with public welfare. They are Health, School Education, Welfare, Urban and Rural Development. Besides these five departments, the General Administration Department and Finance Department provide complementary support for advancing transparency, human resource management, eradication of corruption, procurement and financial accountability and expenditure management.[6]

The ULGs can improve their performance in service delivery by breaking up bureaucratic monopolies and by allowing service providing agencies to provide services in the urban areas. The ULGs should determine their budgets in large part on the scope, coverage and quality of service they provide. The concept of encouraging the actual marketing of government services makes the preferences of actual or potential consumers of institutional service more influential in service provision. This will enable the public agencies to target different combinations of services at different levels of capital-intensity to different groups of people and communities within the urban area instead of merely extending standardised services in conventional ways throughout the urban areas. The use of performance agreement for public service delivery would enable the governments to contact private or public enterprises to provide certain services under the careful supervision of the local government technical experts duly ensuring that they meet the quantity and quality specifications prescribed by the government. The specialised private organisations can provide certain urban services like garbage collection, basic health care, fire protection and even non-formal education, duly maintaining the minimal standards.

Performance Evaluation

The performance of the ULGs in regard to efficiency in governance and service delivery can be evaluated through periodical interface with the service users or the general public. Furthermore, citizens' committees or fora should be enabled to monitor the process of various developmental works, implementation of plan schemes sanctioned by the State and Central Governments. It enables the department-wise performance and to take remedial measures for improving governance and service provision. It expresses the public perception of the ULG in respect of the discharge of its responsibilities and level of satisfaction of the public in respect of civic amenities.

References

1. Chetan Vaidya and Hitesh Vaidya, Model Municipal Law to Enable Urban Reforms, *India Infrastructure Report* 2006, Oxford University Press, New Delhi, 2006, pp. 19-20.
2. G.O.Ms.No. 158 M.A., dated April 25, 2001 of the Government of Andhra Pradesh.
3. Andhra Pradesh Act No 15 of 1996.
4. Emiel A.Wagelin, *New Approaches in Urban Services Delivery*, 1990, Butterworth-Heinemann Ltd, London, p. 255.
5. *Ibid*, p. 257.
6. APURMS Project Report, 2007, Hyderabad.

9

Urban Poverty Alleviation

The unprecedented urbanisation during the last two decades has brought with it increased urban poverty which is one of the challenges before the urban managers to tackle in a sustainable manner. While some of the programmes aimed at poverty alleviation have yielded efficacy, the urban poverty alleviation programmes are to be given further impetus to make the programme more sustainable.

It has been the Government's endeavour to eradicate poverty as an ethical, political, social and economic imperative. The Government of India have been implementing various poverty alleviation programmes to reduce the incidence of poverty during the last two/ three decades. There has been considerable progress made in the implementation of these programmes as could be seen through the socio-economic indicators. The poverty profile of India reveals that the Below Poverty Line (BPL) population was 27.20 per cent in 1987-88 which has reduced to 15.96 per cent in 1993-94 and further reduced to 15.77 per cent during 1999-2000. There is, however, much more to be done to further reduce the percentage of BPL by implementing the programmes with renewed vigour and zeal which necessitates a clear understanding the objective of the programmes and identifying the genuine beneficiaries of the scheme.

Urban poverty is assuming critical proportions due to increase of urban slum population most of who are migrants from rural areas who try to escape abject poverty in rural areas, who are faced with intense non-income poverty. Hence, ULGs are burdened with the responsibility of providing adequate access to shelter and basic amenities. Since the rural-urban migration of poor in search of livelihood cannot be prevented, adequate provision must be made in the annual budget of every ULG to provide or improve basic amenities in urban slums. In the light of the experience of last three decades of increasing urban poverty, issues of urban poverty need to be given due attention by governments at all levels and by policy-makers and urban planners in India. The success of poverty reduction programmes initiated in urban areas depend on the way the ULGs and urban planners address the broader issues of regional and local level planning, multiple vulnerabilities of the urban poor, infrastructure development, service delivery and efficient urban governance; since they are vital to face the challenges of inclusive urbanisation in India.[1] Urban informal sector is the largest provider of adequate employment to the poor. According to NSS 66th Round data, about 80 per cent of all urban workers were informally employed in construction and manufacturing activities, and wholesale and retail trade.

It is high time the importance of urban informal sector is realised. The informal sector not only provides employment to the poor and low-income groups, "it also acts as a breeding ground for enterprise and innovation. It protects and sustains local cultures and traditions. There is need for recognising, facilitating, developing, and nurturing the urban informal sector. India must realise that the urban informal economy is here to stay and is a part of the solution, not the problems."[2] It is, therefore, imperative that urban infrastructure development plan must be inclusive, providing space for the development and growth of the informal sector, since "the failure of urban planning has led to the exclusion of large sections of the urban society from the opportunities unleashed by agglomeration externalities in cities."[3]

Urban informal sector continues to attract more and more rural migrants.[4] These informal workers need shelter and minimum basic services. Urban poverty can be better addressed through labour-intensive growth in cities and towns, vocational education, and skill-development for wage earners and self-employed people, so that they can eke out livelihood on their own.

Planning

The reason for delay in total elimination of urban poverty is the fact that the economic development in the state is not benefiting all the urban poor and the poverty elimination programmes are not giving expected efficacy in reducing the gap between the rich and the poor. Provision of adequate civic services like access to safe drinking water, medical facilities and education can reduce the magnitude of poverty of the unprivileged and the under-privileged sections of the urban areas.

Strong economic development along with good governance and implementation of income-generating activities will provide opportunities to minimise, if not totally eliminate, poverty in the country. One of the Millennium Development Goals is to eradicate extreme poverty and hunger by 2015 and the Government of India is committed to achieve it by the targeted date. Hence, great emphasis is to be laid on effective implementation of the poverty reduction programmes with commitment and dedication, duly fixing targets to be achieved for each financial year.

The implementation of poverty elimination programmes during the last two decades had given satisfactory results in several urban areas while they yielded no substantive results in a few urban areas. The reasons are not far to be found.

The reasons for high success rate in certain urban areas

- Identification of local trades for which there is demand, duly scanning the local market;
- Identification of genuine beneficiaries for each economic activity;
- Formation of groups with like-minded members who have commitment and dedication to pursue the chosen trade; and
- Training the members for skill upgradation in the chosen trade for better performance of the members of the group.

Reasons for failure of the scheme in certain urban areas

- Inadequate comprehension of the objective of the scheme;
- Lack of skill in the members of the group in the economic activity chosen;

- Lack of unity of purpose among the members of the group; and
- Lack of local demand for the goods produced or the economic activity chosen.

Most of the poverty alleviation programmes initiated by governments have focused on tackling rural poverty, but urban poverty as it is prevalent today needs equal attention. The Class-I cities in India are growing faster than smaller urban areas and the highest percentage of slum dwellers is concentrated in the country's big cities. It may be construed that the growth of slums corresponds to the growth of larger urban area. Though all the BPL population of urban areas do not live in slums, slums are important places to reach the urban poor. We do not have specific knowledge of the urban poor living outside slums. Our poverty alleviation programmes are, therefore, to be concentrated on urban slum population. It, therefore, follows that our main endeavour should be to provide training to slumdwellers for skill upgradation and to provide placement for them. The growth of urban population is directly proportional to the economic output of urban areas since urban areas are not only centres of problems but also engines of growth. Urban growth and planned industrialisation have a well established relationship.[5]

The urban poor in India was estimated to be 7.5 crores which comprises 38 per cent of the total urban population in 1988, which rose to 7.63 crores in 1993-94 which comprised 32 per cent of the total urban population. The fact that an estimated 27 per cent of the urban population lives below the poverty line is the cause of concern for the government. That is why the Urban Poverty Alleviation (UPA) Initiatives of the Government have increased from year to year. The Government of India's Urban Poverty Alleviation Initiatives mainly consist of: (1) Housing, (2) Welfare, and (3) Employment.

The Planning Commission allocated a separate section to urban poverty in IX Five-year plan (1997–2002) and thus an unprecedented focus was placed on urban poverty alleviation. The principal objective of the scheme was to enable the urban poor to gain and integrate with the mainstream economic activity. The *Swarna Jayanti Shahari Rojgar Yojana* (SJSRY) scheme introduced in 1997 enabled the urban poor women, till then confined to the four walls of the kitchen and caught in a debt trap, found themselves as members of an active self-help group and could lead a life with dignity and self respect earning livelihood by taking up self-employment ventures under the scheme.

The urbanisation process is accompanied by a significant increase in the scale of poverty of urban population. The growing urban poverty in all towns and cities disproportionately affects women and children.[6] The urban dwellers are often forced into a downward spiral of marginalisation, social and economic exclusion and unhealthy living environment. Thus, urbanisation of poverty has become a serious challenge facing the urban India today. Hence, all the ULGs must address this issue in a realistic manner. There is still the need for a deeper understanding of urban poverty. Urban poverty is wrongly believed to have been caused solely by large scale migration of population from rural areas to urban areas in search of better livelihood options, though it is only one of the causes of urban poverty. Policy makers treat urban poverty as an essentially economic problem, a result of rural-urban migration. But in fact urban poverty includes destitute households, marginal income and minimal skills.

Urban Poverty Alleviation Initiatives

Even after more than six decades of Independence a large section of the Indian population continues to live a painful and miserable life under horrible conditions with extreme economic distress. Despite steep reduction in the poverty ratio, abject poverty and rising unemployment of the educated youth have aggravated social abuses and crime in the country, more particularly in larger urban areas. Thus, a sense of insecurity to life has rent the air in many larger urban areas including the nation's capital. It is, therefore, imperative that the idle human capital be deployed in income-generating activities, which is the first step in the right direction to alleviate urban poverty in the country. Far more important is the eradication of poverty. It is, therefore, a matter of serious concern to study the concept of poverty, its extent and magnitude and unemployment in the country, so as to arrive at definite programmes for implementation to alleviate poverty.

Poverty may be defined as a condition in which a person is unable to access basic needs for a minimum living standard required for his sustenance, and physical and mental development. The urban poor live in extremely deprived conditions having no access to safe drinking water, sanitation, sewerage, drainage as well as proper housing, health care, nutrition, schooling and non-formal education. According to a report of the National Commission for Enterprises in the Unorganised Sector (NCEUS) 25 per cent of Indians lived on less than Rs 20 per day with most of them working in the unorganised sector with no job or social security. The accelerated growth rate of 8.9 per cent could not integrate the excluded into the mainstream of development. The Monthly Per Capita Income of the urban poor was Rs 56.78 in 1973–76 which gradually increased to Rs 538.60 in 2004-05.

Table 9.1: Below Poverty Line Population Ratio

Poverty Line Year	*Monthly Per Capita Income (Urban)*	*BPL Population Ratio % (Urban)*
1973-1974	56.76	49.00
1977-1978	70.33	45.20
1983-1984	115.65	40.80
1987-1988	162.16	38.20
1993-1994	281.35	32.40
1999-2000	454.11	23.6
2004-2005	538.60	25.70

Source: Planning Commission, 2008.

The above figures reveal that even after five decades of implementation of a number of Poverty Alleviation Programmes in the country, India has the largest Below Poverty Level (BPL) population living in horrible conditions, despite the steep decline of Urban Poverty from 49 per cent in 1973-74 to 25.7 per cent in 2004-05. The number of poor people living in deplorable conditions is on the increase and the living conditions, particularly in slums, are awfully bad. The number of urban poor is as follows:

Table 9.2: Below Poverty Line Population of India

Year	*No. of persons Below Poverty Line in Millions*	*Percentage of BPL Population*
1973	60.0	49.0
1983	70.9	40.8
1993	76.3	32.3
2004	80.8	25.7

Source: Planning Commission, 2008.

Rising unemployment is another serious concern. A large number of talented and able urban youth are without jobs. Despite fast development of Indian economy since the period of Economic Liberalisation, it has not generated sustainable employment. Moreover, despite great potential for growth and development in urban areas, they are not able to grow due to the failure of governments to cope with the demands of industrialisation and urbanisation in adequacy. Our urban economies are not able to support employment creation in industrial and tertiary sector to absorb rural migrants. Hence, poverty alleviation through creation of enough employment opportunities is a must to cope with quick pace of urbanisation to absorb the surplus and disguisedly employed labour who migrated from rural to urban areas in search of livelihood.

Poverty Alleviation under SJSRY

The Poverty Alleviation Initiatives and Programmes have not been able to solve the chronic problem of poverty and unemployment. It is, therefore, important to promote and encourage the setting up of self-employment ventures and micro enterprises. The Government of India launched the *Swarna Jayanti Shahari Rojgar Yojana* (Golden Jubilee Urban Employment Scheme) with the principal objective of providing gainful employment to the less educated unemployed urban youth through setting up of self-employment ventures, individual as well as group activities, since micro-entrepreneurship is an effective tool to solve the problems of urban poverty and unemployment as it plays a crucial role in economic development and productive employment generation. Job creation is of paramount importance in national poverty reduction strategies. The SJSRY enables the setting up of individual self employment ventures as wells as collective entrepreneurship, i.e., group economic activities. It is the government's policy initiative to alleviate poverty and generate employment through empowering the unemployed urban youth through the setting up of micro enterprises, which trigger off the development process.

However, the scheme has yielded mixed results. The scheme has been highly successful in certain urban areas while it has not been successful in promoting sustainable self-employment ventures and micro-enterprises in other urban areas as indicated by their dismal performance. The success of the scheme was 52 per cent in 2001-02, 63 per cent in 2002-03 and 56 per cent in 2003-04.

The reasons for their poor performance in certain urban areas are:

- Reluctance of banks to sanction and release loans to applicants due to non-feasibility of the trade/economic activity chosen and poor recovery of loans;
- Reluctance of the beneficiaries to avail themselves of loan at a high rate of interest (12.14 per cent per annum) since the high cost of credit affects the profitability and sustainability of micro-enterprises;
- Beneficiaries' inadequate comprehension of the advantages of the scheme meant for their benefit. The Community Development Societies could not play any effective role in strengthening the social empowerment of the poor beneficiaries;
- Inadequate micro-entrepreneurship and lack of required skill and skill development programme;
- The ceiling of project cost to Rs 50, 000/- for individual self employment unit is too small an amount to make the venture self sustainable;
- Prescription of 9th standard as the educational qualification under the SJSRY is a barrier to self-employment programme and the setting up of micro-enterprises;
- Lack of market support for the goods produced by the micro-enterprises.[7]

Therefore certain reforms such as the following should be brought about to make the scheme sustainable.[8]

- Banks should release loans to the target groups for the Government approved projects with Government guarantee;
- The State Government should stand as surety for the timely recovery of loans from the beneficiaries through a recovery mechanism established for the purpose;

- The State Government should ensure the selection of the right beneficiaries and approval of viable projects;
- Bankers and project officers should be well trained to act as guides and advisers to counsel the beneficiaries for making the right choice of viable micro-enterprises from the point of view of marketability and quality assurance;
- Provision should be made for the rescheduling of loans in case of default;
- Cheaper credit facilities should be provided by sanctioning loans from a specially created Revolving Fund on a sharing basis between the centre and the states;
- A micro-entrepreneurship consultancy and development centre should be set up to assist the target beneficiaries in the selection of projects, project formulation, use of low cost technology, production of quality goods and provision of marketing assistance;
- A reasonable enhancement may be made of the unit cost from Rs 50, 000/- up to Rs 5.00 lakhs as per the nature of the unit, cost of materials etc.
- Government departments should purchase the products produced or supplied by the SJSRY beneficiaries and Self Help Groups as is done in Kerala;
- Local trades should be encouraged so that the beneficiaries would produce goods having local demand which helps them avoid searching for markets elsewhere; and
- District level training centres have to be established to train the beneficiaries for skill upgradation.

The spectacular progress achieved in many sectors in the country over the past five decades has not benefited the poor. Sonorous slogans like "growth with equity" and "growth with social justice" etc. have not yielded practical results. Certain specific measures will have to be taken to overcome the chronic problems of acute urban poverty.

Social and Economic Empowerment of the Urban Poor

The best solution to tackle urban poverty is through achieving a higher growth rate of the economy, which can have a tremendous impact on the quality of life of the poor, particularly the urban poor, who are the most underprivileged section of the society. The urban poor are to be empowered through strengthening their capacities and upgrading their skills to enable them to achieve a set objective.

Table 9.3: Urban Poverty Ratio

Year	*Poverty Ratio percentage*	*No. of unemployed youth (in lakhs)*
1973-74	55	—
1993-94	—	9.00
2004-05	22.27	131.00

Source: MEPMA, Hyderabad, 2008.

The above table covering three decades shows that despite steep decline in the poverty ratio, the number of unemployed or jobless urban youth has increased from year to year. The urban poor live in shanties in most horrible conditions in overcrowded slums and with inadequate social services. The majority of the urban poor work in the unorganised sector without job security or social security. This trend shows that the accelerated growth rate could not integrate the excluded section in the mainstream of development. It is, therefore, imperative for the state to intervene in the matter to improve the living conditions of the poor through the empowerment of the urban poor in order to contain the rising unemployment trends in urban areas. Empowerment of the urban poor enables them to earn adequate means of livelihood and thus lead a life of quality with dignity and self-confidence obtaining necessary facilities for their full development.

Socio-economic empowerment is an essential pre-requisite for human development and is an effective instrument for tackling poverty and to achieve sustainable development. Economic empowerment is the harbinger of social empowerment: the one cannot exist without the other. Economic empowerment can be achieved through providing credit facilities by banks for building and supporting the entrepreneurial skill of the urban poor, improving their management capabilities, training for capacity building and providing access to modern technology.

Poverty Alleviation Initiatives in Andhra Pradesh

One of the key issues before the stakeholders of urban development is provision of employment or creating income-generating schemes to tackle urban poverty. Andhra Pradesh, like some other states in the country, has witnessed a sustainable urban growth. While the urban population was 54 lakhs (17.42 per cent to total population) in the State in 1951 it went up to 205 lakhs in the year 2001, an increase of over 400 per cent. It is likely to grow further at an accelerated pace. Now that 27.08 per cent of the State's population live in urban areas, urban poverty is a matter of serious concern to the government to address. The incidence of poverty is more in urban areas than rural areas. It is estimated that 50 per cent of the poor families in Andhra Pradesh live in urban areas. This phenomenal figure is likely to increase further with each passing year owing to the accelerating rural-urban migration. The government should, therefore, explore opportunities eliminate poverty and vulnerability in a sustainable manner and improve the quality of life of the urban poor. The Government of Andhra Pradesh has introduced several income-generating schemes to achieve this objective.

In order to address this serious issue of urban poverty Government of Andhra Pradesh has conceived and adopted a path-breaking mission-mode approach called "Indira Kranthi Padham" (IKP) to enable improved quality of life for all urban poor families by accessing services from various organisations through their own strong self-reliant and self-organised institutions. This necessitates the promotion, strengthening and nurturing of self-sustainable institutions of the poor and through them addressing all poverty-related issue like access to credit, economic freedom, health, disability and vulnerability.

The SJSRY has seven components-Urban Self Employment Programme, Training in Self-employment Programme, Development of Women & Children in Urban Areas (DWCUA), Thrift & Credit societies, Urban Wage Employment Programme (UWEP), Community Structures and Infrastructure. The scheme is implemented through Self Help Groups (SHG) formed with urban poor women in a three-tier system: Neighbourhood Group (NHG), Neighbourhood Community (NHC) and Community Development Society (CDS). The scheme was implemented in all urban areas by the Urban Local Governments. The need for establishing a separate organisation to implement the entire poverty alleviation programme was keenly felt over the years. Realising this need, and in order to give a fillip to the income-generating activities and to address other poverty related issues the Government of Andhra Pradesh established the Mission for Elimination of Poverty in Municipal Areas (MEPMA) on September 1, 2007 which is the first of its kind in the country, to implement Indira Kranti Padham (Urban), an urban poverty elimination programme in all the ULBs in the state.[9] The scheme envisages: (1) Building organisations of the poor; (2) Formation and strengthening of Self-Help Groups and Federation; (3) Bank Linkage; (4) Total Financial Inclusion; (5) Placement linked skill development training programme; (6) Skill development training programme through National Academy of Construction; (7) Addressing vulnerability; (8) Development of Social Capital.[10]

1. Building Organisations of the Poor

The strategy adopted for achieving this objective is by building organisations of the poor, empowering the poor by their capacity enhancement, establishing support mechanisms, participatory monitoring and evaluation systems, creating highly trained social capital at grass-roots level to address all poverty issues like health, education, livelihood, vulnerability etc., facilitating interface between bankers and Community Based Organisations (CBOs) of the poor, promoting livelihood opportunities though skill upgradation-cum-placement assurance with market tie-up, readmission of school dropouts in the schools, improvement of infrastructure in slums, housing for the urban poor, covering all urban poor under social security measures etc.

2. Formation and Strengthening of Self-Help Groups and Federation

The urban poor women are formed into Self-Help Groups. The Self Help concept enables the creation of platform for the women to organise themselves, ventilate their felt-needs, build capacities, and thus increase their strength. The group concept provides a platform for enhanced spirit of collectivity, institutionalised mechanism for social advance and economic improvement as well as for sharing knowledge and increasing self-confidence. Since all the members of the group are united by like-mindedness in identifying their problems and a common approach in addressing their needs, group activity yields excellent results.

There are about 1.83 lakh self-help groups in all the urban areas of Andhra Pradesh covering 18.4 lakh women.

3. Bank Linkage

The urban poor are caught in the clutches of private money- lenders who lend money to them at an exorbitant rate of interest ranging from 5 per cent to 20 per cent per month based on the urgency and need. Commercial Banks meet hardly 0.8 per cent of the credit needs of the urban poor and, therefore, the bulk of their needs is met by private money-lenders. This situation makes the life of the urban poor most horrible, and some of them in a state of despair may even resort to suicide, unable to repay the debt. The Andhra Pradesh Urban Services for the Poor project which was implemented in 42 class-I towns in the state during 2000-07, with its sustained efforts, could access 10 to 15 per cent of the credit needs of the urban poor in the 42 project towns at affordable rate of interest. It could so far provide bank linkage to 71,000 self-help groups to the tune of Rs 340.97 crores. This reduced the interest burden from Rs 1644/- to Rs 137/- per annum per family. Efforts are in progress to link another 80,000 self-help groups with an amount of Rs 400.00 crores in the coming one year. While this bank linkage could reduce the debt burden of the urban poor, it has also enabled each poor family to save up to Rs 5, 000/- per year.

In order to further reduce the interest burden and to bring the poor out of the clutches of money-lenders, the Government of Andhra Pradesh has introduced "Pavala Vaddi" Scheme (25 paise interest). In this scheme loan is sanctioned to the SHGs at an interest of 3 per cent. Banks used to give loans to the self-help groups at 9 to 12 per cent interest per annum on regular repayment of loan instalments. The Government will reimburse the interest over and above 3 per cent. The scheme inculcates the habit of regular repayment of loan instalments. It also increases the habit of accessing the credit by poor. The scheme would help the poor to free themselves from the grip of the money-lenders and establish their livelihoods. The scheme would make the repayment of loan easier, and encouraging, thus making the programme sustainable. So far 21,000 self-help groups in urban areas have availed themselves of loan to the tune of Rs 4.50 crores under the novel "Pavala Vaddi" scheme. The scheme has enabled a link with banks and the urban poor can access loan on a perpetual basis; the rate of recovery of loan is enhanced, thus encouraging banks to float more loans to the urban poor and enabling the self-help groups to access more credit from banks that were earlier reluctant to sanction loans to the urban poor.

4. Total Financial Inclusion

This programme aims at clearing the existing debt of the urban poor women by providing bank linkage and enabling them to take up income generating activities to repay the loans to the bank. The incidence of their indebtedness to private money-lenders is found to be Rs 25,000/- to Rs 40,000/- per person at an exorbitant rate of interest ranging from 36 to 60 per cent per annum depending on the circumstances in which the loan is taken.

The scheme has been so far implemented in 29 poor settlements in 25 towns of Andhra Pradesh. The process involves the identification of poor settlements, assessing their debt burden and the amount required for livelihood activities, sensitising the municipal staff involved in implementing the scheme and the bankers to the modalities of the scheme, capacity building of the group members and monitoring the recovery of loan through community based recovery mechanism. The state government envisages implementing total financial inclusion with debt swapping with each bank covering at least one poor settlement in all the urban areas over a period of two years. It is expected that each family under the scheme saves Rs 25, 000/- per year and that its dependence on money-lenders would be reduced to zero.

5. Skill Development Training Programme through National Academy of Construction

Skill development through training is essential to enable the urban unemployed youth to eke out livelihood through setting up of self employment ventures taking advantage of the self-employment schemes introduced/implemented by the Government. In order to create better livelihood through skill development the Government offers the youth of the BPL category a unique opportunity to train the eligible beneficiaries in various trades of construction activity as per their native abilities duly assuring placement to all the trained beneficiaries. The National Academy of Construction offers training which meets the demands of world-class construction standards in skill, workmanship and productivity.

It is estimated that construction industry has potential for 10 lakh skilled workers. While the NAC trained about 2110 beneficiaries so far, placement was given to 1053 trained beneficiaries. It is contemplated to provide placement linked training to about 10,000 construction workers living in urban areas during the next one year.

The training programme could provide employment to highly skilled construction workers who have been positioned in urban areas, whose individual monthly income ranges from Rs 1,500/- to Rs 3, 000/-.

6. Empowerment of Physically Challenged People in Urban Areas

Gradual reduction of vulnerability of the urban poor by empowering the physically challenged persons through forming them into Self-Help Groups, building their capacities, providing bank linkages and service providers, community based rehabilitation and promotion of sustainable livelihoods, is an important objective of the income generating schemes.

The Government of Andhra Pradesh during the last one year organised 15,407 disabled persons into 2258 Self-Help Groups and provided bank linkage to 423 groups with an outlay of Rs 97 lakhs. The scheme also enabled to conduct surgical corrections to 354 persons with post-polio. Aids and appliances etc. were supplied to 1476 persons with disabilities from corporate service providers free of cost. Medical Board Certificates and other concessions and privileges were issued to 27,451 disabled persons in 18 urban areas.

It is proposed to form another 4000 groups in the next two years and link all eligible groups with Banks; to provide medical aid and rehabilitation needs. Its impact is that the disabled and vulnerable would become able and empowered.

7. Education for the Urban Poor

Major educational institutions in India meant for the poor have not concentrated much on urban areas. Even the Sarva Siksha Abhiyan (SSA) has excluded the urban poor. Neither the SSA has clear strategy for the urban schools, particularly for the slum children, nor does the JNNURM have education as a necessary component in its urban renewal mission. The urban poor do not have access to education of good quality, relevant to their needs due to the following problems:

- The large-scale rural-urban migration and cross-migration within cities create problems for children who migrate along with their parents and are not factored into planning;
- Their admission to schools is generally blocked by lack of identity proof, birth certificate, transfer certificate etc;
- The specific problems of child-workers, street children and children in famine are not factored into schematic patterns;
- The schools are either dysfunctional or poorly functioning;
- Most of the urban poor attend local non-fee charging schools which are illequipped and are without qualified teachers; and
- Local urban administration has not given education the importance it needs.

IKP (Urban) envisages addressing this problem

The Mission for Elimination of Poverty in Municipal Areas also encourages the following Social Development activities[10]:

- Livelihood programme-providing of infrastructure such as Lighting, Furniture, Stipend etc. to centres;
- Skill development training;
- Payment of interest subsidy under "Pavala Vaddi" (Rs 0.25 interest);
- Payment of subsidy under the USEP, DWCUA;
- *Anganwadi* centres;
- Medical camps for rickshaw pullers, petty vendors, sanitary health workers, children;

- Construction of Community Resource Centres;
- Purchase of tool kits;
- Providing infrastructure to Self-Help Groups;
- Providing marketing facilities to SHGs;
- Institution building of the SHGs;
- Capacity building of the SHGs;
- Preparation of plans of slum development;
- Procurement of the IEC material of social development;
- Social security pensions to the aged widows, the disabled;
- Providing water supply in slums;
- Organisation of crutch, play-schools, schools;
- Organisation of widow homes, orphanages;
- Conducting meetings of the SHGs and CBOs;
- Providing assistance to the disabled, S.C., S.T.
- Providing maternity benefit;
- Incentives for family planning;
- Providing facilities for family planning;
- Conducting house to house survey in slums;
- Beneficiary identification;
- Market scanning of opportunities for slum dwellers;
- Providing infrastructure for the CRCs and the CBOs and social development wing;
- Setting up *Seva Kendras* (service centres);
- Payment of revolving fund, CEF;
- Travelling cost of the SHG members;
- Insurance subsidy;
- Infrastructure support for income generation and other group activities;
- A & O E expenses of the ULBs;
- Training to staff on social development activities;
- Literacy programmes;
- Construction of community toilets;

- Establishment of the UPA cell; and
- Any other activity with permission of the MEPMA in the interest of poor;

All the above programmes aim at tackling urban poverty in a sustainable manner;

Poverty Elimination in APUSP Project Towns of A.P.

The **Andhra Pradesh Urban Services for the Poor (APUSP)** project was implemented in 42 class-I towns (towns with more than one lakh population) of Andhra Pradesh which was an innovative partnership programme between the Government of Andhra Pradesh and the Government of United Kingdom. In order to eliminate poverty in the project towns certain innovative measures were taken up.

Strengthening of Civil Society

If poverty and vulnerability are to be eliminated, the Civil Society should be strengthened and its role in decision-making be increased so that it plays a decisive role in achieving the objectives set forth for the project. The Civil Society was strengthened by including the B.P.L. women in Self-Help Groups so that they would become entitled to the benefits under poverty alleviation programmes.

Formation of Self-Help Groups

There are 7.99 lakhs women in all the 42 project towns out of whom 4.60 lakh women have been organised into 34,685 SHGs covering 57 per cent of the BPL Households. A special drive was been taken up in all the project towns to strengthen the SHGs. The drive includes:

- Strengthening of the existing SHGs;
- Formation of New SHGs;
- Livelihood Promotions through Self-Help Groups; and
- Increased access to bank finances.

Under the urban poverty elimination programmes Community Structures are established which would have decision-making power in the implementation of the welfare programmes like self-employment generation through skill upgradation and are under implementation through the Self-Help Groups.

Financial Assistance

Banks have financially assisted 6397 SHGs through Bank linkages with an amount of Rs 23.00 crores. The per capita availability of loan is Rs 3000/- and repayment is nearly 100 per cent. (The figures pertain to 2005-06).

UPADHI

This is an Urban Programme for Advancement of Household Income. The State Government formulated this innovative scheme with a vision to focus and provide livelihood to the poorest of the poor in slum areas. This is placement linked training. The uniqueness of the scheme is provision of 100 per cent placement after completion of training.

Target

The goal of UPADHI is to identify and make available the potential livelihood options for the youth living below the poverty line (BPL) in the age group of 18-35 in the project towns and train them in skills according to the market requirements, thereby working towards achieving the goals of self-employment and poverty reduction; and to provide young adults from the economically weaker and disadvantaged sections an opportunity to assimilate into the competitive job market and to help them acquire the required livelihoods and social skills in an environment of learning and mentoring that is responsive to the individual's emotional and development needs. It is contemplated to provide placement linked training to as many eligible youth as possible in the coming years.

The scheme is implemented by assessing the livelihood opportunities and employment potential through market scan in all urban areas of the state. After making an assessment of the available livelihood opportunities in the town or city candidates are selected under the scheme through road shows, who would be trained in their respective trades or lines of activity for three to four months which includes skill upgradation and after successful completion of training they would be given placement or placement support. The APUSP in collaboration with local charitable institutions like Dr Reddy's Foundation (DRF) and American Indian Foundation (AIF) has taken up this programme in convergence with all on-going livelihood programmes.

Achievement

The programme was first initiated in 16 project towns and was later extended to the remaining project towns. So far a total number of 32,950 candidates have been trained and placement is shown to 21,958 unemployed youth. The average per capita earnings range from Rs 1,500/- to Rs 7,000/- per month. The programme has been a remarkable success in poverty elimination. The impact of the scheme was that a large pool of employable youth was created in tune with the new economy sectors and so far a wealth of Rs 30 crore was generated against an investment of Rs 6 crore on account of monthly earnings of the trained youth.

- The Government of Andhra Pradesh decided to extend the programme to all the towns in Andhra Pradesh. Fifty eight N.G.Os have come forward to implement the programme in various towns.
- The fast growth of urban areas necessitates several supporting services which provide adequate employment opportunities to the urban poor in the unorganised sector. The contribution of the informal sector to the overall economy is estimated to be around 30 per cent of the total income generated. The programmes aimed at elimination of poverty through income generation should make a scan of the urban services needed and the candidates with native abilities in a particular trade or service for which there is demand should be trained in the particular trade or line of activity so that placement after training will be an easy process and thus poverty elimination programmes will be a tremendous success.

Poverty Eradication Activities in Kerala-Kudumbashree

Kudumbashree (Prosperity of the family) is a poverty eradication project launched under the Kerala State Poverty Eradication Mission with the principal objective of "*eradicating absolute poverty in ten years through concerted* community action under the leadership of local self governments, by facilitating organisation of the poor combining self help with demand-led convenience of available services and resources to tackle the multiple dimensions and *manifestations of poverty, holistically"*.[11] Kudumbashree is a state level nodal agency to implement the three centrally sponsored programmes viz., National Slum Development Programme (NSDP), *Swarna Jayanti Shahari Rojgar Yojana* (SJSRY) and Integrated Development of Small Medium Towns (IDSMT). Though the Kudumbashree programme is a synonym for the Development of Women and Children in Urban Areas (DWCUA) under the SJSRY, the guidelines issued for implementation of the SJSRY are slightly modified to suit the local conditions and for better performance to cover more and more eligible beneficiaries in its expanding fold. For example, the BPL family is identified based on nine indicators and if four or more indicators are positive, the family qualifies for the benefit under the scheme. The Kudumbashree programme was first launched in Alappuzhi municipality, and won laurels from the U.N. in 1995. It has been later extended to all other local bodies (rural as well as urban).

In order to implement the programme with effective convergence, a three tier Community Based Organisation (CBO) is formed which is akin to the Neighbourhood Group (NHG), Area Development Society (ADS) (which in other areas is same as Neighbourhood Committee) and Community Development Society (CDS) under the SJSRY scheme. The Neighbourhood Group undertakes various functional activities through five volunteers.

1. *President* – presides over the weekly meetings and imparts necessary leadership and guidelines to the group members;
2. *Secretary* – records the programmes of the meetings, provide motivation and team building;
3. *Community Health Volunteer* – looks after various health-related aspects of the group members including children, women and the aged. Convergence of various programmes is carried out under the leadership of the CHV;
4. *Income Generating Activity Volunteer* – looks after the activities connected with thrift mobilisation, training imparted

by NABARD for increasing their capability, maintenance of account books and registers.

5. *Infrastructure Volunteer* – tackles infrastructure backwardness of the group with the help of various ongoing Government programmes. She will liaison with the local bodies and acts as a catalyst for local development.

Activities of Kudumbashree

Besides women's empowerment through poverty eradication programmes, Kudumbashree aims at:

- Providing bank linkage for at least 20 per cent of the NHGs per annum;
- Construction of houses to all the homeless within 5 years;
- Providing safe drinking water within 300 metres of their residence in five years;
- Providing toilet facilities to all the houses in five years;
- Setting up of micro-linkage in each NHG and establishment of marketing network throughout the state; and
- Formation and implementation of special programmes necessary for the progress of the SC/CT and other backward classes.

The functioning of the self-employment units established in Kerala is found most impressive and their example should be emulated in other states.

Other Activities of Kudumbashree

AASHRAYA

The scheme provides rehabilitation to destitute families through construction of houses. Cochin International Airport Limited (CIAL) has donated Ac.0.75 cents land for this programme. The programme is under active implantation.

Health Insurance

Kerala is ahead of the other States in the country in Health Insurance Programme.

Reasons for High Success Rate in Kerala

Though Kudumbashree activities aiming at eradication of poverty are not different from SJSRY (USEP and DWCUA) activities, the reasons for the higher success rate in eradication of poverty through income-generating activities in Kerala are:

- Modification of the SJSRY guidelines to suit local conditions. The guidelines for implementing the SJSRY are not hard and fast rules but only guidelines, which can be modified to suit the requirements of local unemployed BPL youth.
- Clear understanding of the objectives of the programme and implementing them accordingly.
- Establishment of group enterprises of men also (which is not found in the SJSRY) instead of individual enterprises.
- Choosing the economic activities relevant to the native abilities of the beneficiaries.
- Total absence of political interference in the entire process right from selection of the beneficiary till grounding of the units.

References

1. Mohanty, P.K., *Cities and Public Policy*, New Delhi, 2014, p. 113.
2. *Ibid*, pp. 142-43
3. *Ibid*, p.144.
4. NSS Report No. 539, Informal Sector and Conditions of Employment in India, NSS 66th Round, January 2012.
5. B. Bhushan, *Promoting Socio-Economic Empowerment of the Poor for Grass Root Development*, Planning Commission, New Delhi, 2008, p. 6.
6. Arabi, U, *Recent Urbanisation Trends: Their Impact on the Poor in the Developing World,* Local Self Government Quarterly, Vol. LXXIX, No. 2, New Delhi, April-June, 1999, p. 6.
7. B. Bhushan, *Micro Entrepreneurship as an Effective Tool of Eradicating Urban Poverty and Unemployment*: *Lessons & Agenda for Reforms* by B. Bhushan, Planning Commission, New Delhi, 2008, p. 9.
8. Op. cited, p. 9.
9. G.O. Ms. No. 414 M.A. dated September 1, 2007 of the Government of A.P.
10. Centre for Good Governance, *Indira Kranti Padham-Urban*, A Mission to Eliminate Urban Poverty, Government of Andhra Pradesh, Hyderabad, 2007.
11. Government of Kerala, *Kudumbashree*, 2000, Trivendrum, p. 1.

10

Training for Capacity Building

Capacity building is to equip the official machinery with the knowledge, information and ability to adapt, handle and manage development; work with enthusiasm, energy and resilience; improve excellent communication, negotiating and influencing skills; adapt analytical and innovative skill in solving problems; develop sound judgement and decision-making skills; develop sound organisational skill; and draft clear and concise reports on matters relating to local governmental and inter-governmental issues. Thus, capacity building and exposure to new knowledge assume great importance in the efficient urban governance. Capacity building has to address three important dimensions: human resource development, organisational strengthening and institutional and legal framework. Equity, efficiency, transparency and accountability are accorded high priority in good urban governance. The translation of these ideals into action demand character and capacity, knowledge and intellect of the highest order for municipal functionaries. Hence, capacity enhancement is an integral part of good urban governance procedures. The ULGs must be technically empowered, financially strengthened and efficiently governed to respond to the needs of their citizens and to contribute to growth momentum.

Need for Capacity Enhancement

ULGs in India face dearth of human resources capabilities required for efficient delivery of public services. In all ULGs there is a heavy deficiency of performance management, regulatory oversight, and social accountability mechanisms for effective administration. The problems of urban management have become more complex due to the inclusion of several subjects relating to social welfare and infrastructure development in urban local administration. But the ULGs in India lack adequate administrative and technical capacity and have a weak resource base. In view of the important role the ULGs are expected to play in the light of the Constitution (74th Amendment, Act, 1992 the urgency to improve the administrative, technical and financial capabilities of the ULGs need no elaboration. But the state legislatures have not taken any steps towards this end. Thus, the ULGs have failed to perform to the best satisfaction of the urbanites.

Several evaluation committees appointed on the implementation of JNNURM Phase-I have unanimously pointed to the large capacity gap plaguing the urban local bodies and stressed the need for capacity building and recommended a strong programme of capacity creation and training for better performance of the ULBs.[1] This necessitates measures for upgrading the skills or capacity enhancement of staff performing the core functions in the ULGs.

Efficient urban governance clearly depends on a variety of factors which, *inter alia*, include political stability, social cohesion and economic self-sufficiency. Besides, the skills and motivation of the policy makers and the staff who serve in the ULGs have to build their capacities in order to achieve technical competency in the choice, design and execution of infrastructure works and their operation and maintenance, project appraisal and execution; efficiency in the use of available resources-financial, human and material-through realistic budgeting; full exploitation of the local revenue sources and sound financial management. Simultaneously, the ULGs have to improve their administrative capacity to plan, regulate, raise revenues, and implement spending decisions. Hence, local body officials are to be adequately trained and motivated to do their jobs properly so that they respond adequately to the problems facing the town or city.

The urban sector in the Indian economy is passing through major and significant structural transformation which calls for a concerted effort to strengthen the capacities of the ULGs and municipal functionaries at all levels so that ULGs will contribute to faster and more inclusive growth of urban economy and continue to play their positive role in Indian economy and help improve governance and poverty alleviation. Capacity building or enhancement is an essential pre-requisite for municipal functionaries for designing and implementing large scale urban infrastructure projects for efficient management of infrastructure assets, effective delivery of urban basic services and ameliorating the living conditions of the poor and urban slum dwellers so that the urban areas in the country provide a better quality of life through generating a growth environment and inclusive development. Politically weak and administratively cumbersome ULGs cannot implement the infrastructure projects or maintain urban basic services satisfactorily. The ULGs' governance system needs an overhaul if cities have to play a dynamic role in the economic development of India.

Need for Training

Good urban local governance needs City or Town Managers who have developed the capacity for handling down authority and men and matters directly and indirectly connected with urban administration. The stakeholders of urban management and urban development who are empowered to mange and develop should have the information, technology, skills and support to exercise their powers effectively, to perform their functions efficiently and bring about sustainable development. Urban managers need institutional and organisational support in their efforts for enforcing an efficient administration, utilising their energies and capacities efficiently and effectively.

The Urban Local Governments in India are constrained by obsolete laws, restrictive practices and outmoded equipment in delivering goods. The management role of urban managers has been hampered and traditional development is stunted by inadequacy of knowledge, information and skill of the Urban Governmental machinery. Hence, there is the need to rebuild the capacity of Urban Local Governments and their officials with the skill, knowledge and information to prepare and implement the new urban agenda keeping pace with the requirements of towns and cities. The new urban agenda includes the globalisation of urban economy; sustainability of urban environment; reduction of urban poverty; a concern for democratic, accountable, corruption-free, citizen-friendly urban governance.

Empowered and accountable urban administration with modernised service delivery mechanism and a professional municipal cadre are inevitable and essential for good urban governance. The need for organisational reforms and capacity building in urban local bodies including professionalising administration and developing municipal cadres are highlighted in various reports like Good Urban Governance Campaign and JNNURM reforms, the High Powered Expert Committee Report (2011), the McKinsey Global Institute's report (MGI, 2010), the Approach Paper to 12th Five Year Plan etc. Institutional capacity building needs clarity with regard to the functions to be performed by the ULGs and the specific services to be provided to the citizens.

Richard Batley and Nick Devas opine that massively expanded training programmes are a *sine qua non* for the upgrading of urban management to acceptable levels.[2] The Urban Local Governments have to re-energise themselves to face the ever-increasing complex urban challenges efficiently, coming out of the rigid, outdated, inflexible working cultures and deteriorating administrative standards. The impact of programmes aimed at providing infrastructure needed for expanding urban areas depends on the quality of institutions responsible for planning and implementing these programmes. It is through the urban institutional machinery that urban sector issues and priorities are articulated, projects are planned and implemented. The economic resources and human skills available in the ULGs are to be utilised for promoting urban development. It is, therefore, imperative that the capabilities of the ULGs are to be so strengthened as to meet the challenge of rapid urbanisation.

Performance, excellence, productivity and motivation for work would have to be woven around two factors, technical and human, by catering to the needs of both the sectors.[3] The staff should be trained in the right type of leadership, strengthening the communication system, promoting socially acceptable work ethos through positive policy framework, objectively formulated reward distribution system, organisational requirements etc. The apathy, indifference, withdrawal, conflict, lack of motivation, goal-response have dominated the work scene in most of the public offices. This is more in Urban Local Governments than in government departments, since the staff of local governments are recruited from local people who have more local self-interest than interest in impartial discharge of their duties. The municipal functionaries are expected to be candid in their attitude and should have a strong will to achieve the desired results out of every programme entrusted to them.

In order to improve work culture, knowledge, skills and insight among the employees, each ULG will have to publish an office manual to enable the employees to thoroughly understand the office procedures and strictly follow it. Although the District Office Manual originally was intended for District Collectorates, it is extended to all other offices. But in view of the formation of several departments in the government for different subjects in order to facilitate more specialisation in the particular fields of governmental functioning, the publication of separate departmental manuals has become absolutely necessary. The Greater Hyderabad Municipal Corporation is the first ULG in A.P. to publish such a manual for the guidance of its employees which gives a crystal clear description of the office procedures, organisational structure, work distribution, general discipline, attendance, maintenance of records etc.

Knowledge of the organisational objective to a public functionary is like the North Star to the mariner. Training helps to broaden his knowledge, information base, create deeper awareness about the urban problems and motivate the stakeholders of urban management to perform their tasks through enhanced skills and techniques.[4]

Types of Training

Training for skill upgradation is meant for organisations, systems and municipal functionaries. Realising the need for capacity enhancement of municipal functionaries, to introduce greater efficiency in municipal functioning the Centre for Good Governance (CGG), Hyderabad has undertaken a study of the Capacity Enhancement Needs Assessment (CENA) in the context of urban reforms initiated in Andhra Pradesh to improve the performance of Urban Local Governments and has prepared a detailed manual on Capacity Enhancement Needs Assessment (CENA) prescribing various kinds of training to municipal functionaries at all levels from top to bottom, which has to be implemented in toto.[5]

Capacity Enhancement Need Assessment

The study covers a number of areas directly or indirectly pertaining to the urban sector. The implementation of various reforms is expected to improve the service delivery capabilities and credit worthiness of the ULGs, enabling them access to external funding sources and domestic capital markets. The training for capacity enhancement for various functionaries and institutions is required in the following areas:

- Personality Development;
- Management of Change;
- Combating Corruption;
- Public-private Partnership for Infrastructure Development;
- Financial Budgeting and Accrual System of Accounting;
- Urban Local Governance;
- Municipal Finance: Resource Mobilisation;
- Urban Programmes and Projects;
- Urban Planning;
- Preparation of Estimates and Tender Process;
- Preparation & Implementation of Urban Projects and Appraisal;
- Office Management;
- Revenue Management in ULGs;
- Public Health & Sanitation;
- Poverty Alleviation Programmes;
- Empowerment of Self-Help Groups;
- Water Transmission and Distribution;
- Sewerage System;
- Energy Study Water Supply Schemes and Management;
- Preparation of Plans for GIS Applications;
- Development Control Regulation;
- Transport Planning, Traffic and Transportation Projects including Road Development and Widening;

- Solid Waste Management;
- Storm Water Flooding;
- Streetlights-designs and Maintenance;
- Computer Basics;
- Primary Healthcare/Preventive Healthcare;
- Disaster and Crisis Management;
- Gender Issues and Social Impact;
- Resettlement and Rehabilitation Planning.

The training for skill upgradation should aim at increasing dynamism, drive, enthusiasm, imitative and positive approach in terms of result-orientation. The prevailing conditions in the ULGs are also responsible for work apathy or lack of commitment. Staff members have no performance-orientation despite high individual skill or ability (punishments and rewards). There is no performance based reward and punishment system which makes local government service lacklustre. Added to this, there are no scientifically developed manpower norms. Where there is excess manpower there are seen excessive absenteeism, lack of discipline, inadequate linkage between productivity, wages and rewards, low commitment, demoralisation among the ministerial staff of the ULGs. Most of the ULGs, particularly in smaller urban areas, lack skilled personnel to plan and manage service delivery, especially to slum areas. The shortage of qualified technical and administrate personnel in the ULGs is often as serious a problem for ULGs as inadequate revenue. It stunts urban development and obstructs new development projects.

The organisational efficiency of the ULGs can be improved by adopting policies that encourage the use of market surrogates. This is an approach that seeks to improve performance in public sector institutions through institutional reforms, which increases incentives by enhancing competition, choice and accountability. A market surrogate society alters the competitive environment in which an organisation must operate so that there are adequate pressures to improve its service delivery and rearranges conditions within the ULGs, so that internal incentives reinforce the competitive pressures from the external environment.

Shortage of qualified and trained personnel in most of the ULGs is always a constraint on the effective provision of urban services. Personnel structures are characterised by unequal promotion opportunities to the various cadres, political interventions and favouritism in recruitment and promotion, red-tapism, rigid service conditions and personnel regulations, policy inadequacies for personal development etc. Non-recognition of performance through a system of rewards is also responsible for the growing inefficiency in municipal services. This results in poor performance and, hence, increased resistance to devolution of powers and resources needed to improve staff skills and performance. All Urban Local Governments in India have to envision a city, set their priorities, formulate strategy to achieve their statutorily set objectives, organise public consultations, promote civil society participation in civic affairs, set the norms of good urban governance, prepare budget for expenditure, raise resources, monitor works, collect revenues etc.[6] The efficient performance of these tasks is possible only when the official machinery carrying on urban administration is well-informed and well- capacitated. Each State in India has made certain efforts at toning up municipal management but they are partial and sporadic, and generally sectoral rather than holistic.

Sustainable municipal efficiency needs capacity not only for municipal functionaries (officials and elected representatives) but also for civil society stakeholders. Capacity building for good urban governance is complex because the urban scene, unlike in the past, is dynamic and capacities required vary from one ULG to another. Stakeholders of urban affairs in a smaller urban area cannot handle the affairs of a larger urban area. Capacity building should, therefore, be need-based and dynamic in its content. It should cover a wide spectrum of stakeholders and should address itself to a sufficiently large and widespread group to achieve the expected impact. In view of the limited resources of the ULGs, they should underline their optimum use through a well-designed capacity building programme.

City or Town Managers also do not have adequate opportunity of exposure to practical administration unlike their counterparts in developed countries. They have only a perspective for conceptualisation. Hence, the need arises for practical study of well-organised Urban Local Governments in India and abroad. Lack of responsiveness, commitment, awareness and accountability on the part of policy implementing agencies very often results in poor performance of their tasks. The tasks to be carried out in the process of urban development have become increasingly complex. These include: information exchange systems, urban and regional development research for policy preparation, strategic and corporate planning and progress monitoring. The effective performance of these tasks requires vocational, professional and managerial skills dealing with project development, management and evaluation. There are many stakeholders in the urban development process who have to be imparted a common training to collectively perform their tasks and to be collectively accountable for urban development.[7]

Professional training in areas such as urban planning, engineering, project preparation, financial improvement, and efficient management of urban affairs is the urgent need since most ULGs in India typically suffer from overstaffing of unskilled and incapacitated man power and inadequacy of well-trained technical staff. This expert training should be combined with exposure of the official machinery of Urban Local Governments to best practices in India in order to:

- Enable the officials entrusted with the responsibility of urban development and urban development management acquire the knowledge and skill required for formulation and implementation of various urban development projects and government sponsored schemes;
- Strengthen the role of Urban Local Governments (Municipalities as well as Municipal Corporations) in the development of infrastructure needed for urban areas, keeping pace with their needs; and
- Contrive innovative methods and emulate best examples in the fields of urban development and management of urban affairs.

Role of Training Institutions

The concern of training institutes is to identify the training needs, arrange for exposure of Urban Local Governments to new techniques in development and management, deviate from their outmoded traditions, insertion and lack of content with the real and fast changing needs and objectives of municipal government and keep pace with their new responsibilities. The training institutes have to initiate changes in their approach to urban administration and formulate strategies for urban development, help the Urban Local Governments to initiate and implement managerial and structural changes needed for their effective functioning as full-fledged local self-government units.

Training centres should cater to the multi-dimensional and inter-disciplinary challenges that urban India faces. The training centre should have a group of eminent experts who have vast experience in urban management and planning and wide knowledge of the growing urban challenges.

The training institutions should design capacity building and skill upgradation programmes for all municipal functionaries which should include creation of institutional and human resource capacity, which is essentially required for all ULGs particularly the smaller towns for accessing funds for development.

The ultimate object of capacity building is to produce efficient urban managers and regulators, city and planners-financial specialists who utilise their skills and learning for improvement of governance, enforce reforms, plan for infrastructure development and implement projects for betterment of urban life and thus transforming urban areas into the best places of living.

Areas of Training in Urban Governance

The Human Resources Development Institute of Andhra Pradesh, located in Hyderabad, has identified the training needs of various functionaries in Urban Local Governments and designed training programmes for different target groups. The important programmes needed for functionaries accountable for management of Urban Local Governments and urban developmental activities.

- Municipal Accounts and Budgeting;
- Municipal Management and Capacity Building;
- Urban Planning, Programmes and Projects;
- Poverty Alleviation Programmes;
- Public Health and Sanitation;

- Computer Applications;
- Geographical Information System (G.I.S.);
- Orientation Course for Municipal Engineers/Municipal Health Officers/Town Planning Officers; and
- Refresher Courses for various Municipal functionaries.

Capacity building has three aspects: Organisational development, Institutional development and Human resource development.

- Organisational development is the strengthening of the organisation (Urban Local Government) in attending to the public needs, in making itself accountable to Central Government, State Government and Civil Society and to fulfil its obligations to the public. It deals with rules and regulations, job descriptions and allocation of work, establishment of hierarchy, management practices and procedures. ULGs need to provide for a more flexible and responsive management style for improvement and management of urban areas. It envisages new organisational structure in the Urban Local Governments besides team-work, shared goals, objectives, values among the different organisations which have a role in the management of urban development, besides a common vision.
- Institutional development envisages legal and regulatory changes in the local governance structures in order to enable different institutions, organisations and agencies having a common vision and common goal enhance their capacities.
- Human resource development is to train the policy implementing machinery with the required understanding and skill, with the information and knowledge so as to enable them to perform their task effectively with increased efficiency. Incentives and rewards for meritorious services, better career opportunities for the skilled officials and competitive pay scales will go a long way in improving human resource development. A dynamic and responsive organisational environment is required to achieve this objective.

The official machinery involved in the management of urban development who have to deal with different fields of activity need to develop administrative skills which enable them to distinguish the important from the unimportant, the more important from the less important aspects of various issues of urban governance, application of modern knowledge to current problems etc. In particular situations certain issues in Urban Local Governments take precedence over others in their need for attention and for resources. The next important aspect is the complete restructuring of local authorities, enterprises and citizens' organisations in order to bring about a new style of functioning of the ULGs. This includes decentralisation of powers, functions and responsibilities, devolution of finances; privatisation of the delivery and maintenance of urban services; formation of new partnerships for the supply and management of public services and amenities; empowering the communities in the effective management of their localities. Yet another important aspect is the creation of work environment and career structure in every Urban Local Government so as to attract and motivate the best talent-professionals, technicians and managers.

The Community-based organisations and Non-Governmental organisations, which function as parallel institutions to local self-governing units and guards the interests of the citizens, play a decisive role as a new tier in urban governance. The competitive ability of these units has to be encouraged through legislative deregulation and incentives to enable them to play a better role in urban local governance.

Training Institutes for Capacity Building

There are many stakeholders in urban development and urban development management whose capacity building should be a continuous, flexible, need-based process. There are institutions which are specialised in providing capacity building services. These institutions play an important role in human resource development. They include the Indian Institute of Public Administration, and Human Settlement Management Institution, New Delhi; All India Institute of Local Self-Government, Mumbai; Regional Centres for Urban and Environmental Studies located at Hyderabad, Lucknow and Mumbai; Administrative Staff College of India, Hyderabad, Engineering Staff

College of India, Hyderabad; Human Resource Development Institute of Andhra Pradesh, Hyderabad etc. The training centres have to be centres of excellence in all issues relating to urban governance such as urban protected water supply, sanitation, traffic management, good urban governance, municipal finance, urban housing, infrastructure development etc. The centres should function as urban planning habitats wherein experts in different branches of urban administration can experiment with new layouts, building materials, landscaping, heritage preservation etc.

Urban India seeks to sustain its economic growth in the years to come. There is a need to foster innovation and link education to global issues and leading fields of development so that the well-trained urban managers put their best efforts towards urban development in such a way that urban India continues its positive contribution to national GDP. The early and mid-career municipal functionaries should be exposed to multi-perspective issues, challenging their thinking and encouraging new practices that result in superior future leadership.

In respect of training in Public-Private partnership, practical examples of success stories of PPP should be included in the study material for training of early and mid-career professionals, to provide quick outline of the PPP framework and to equip the participants with the requisite knowledge to understand and appreciate the urban sector better and make informed decisions on PPP bids. The workshop should serve as a platform for information exchange to elicit innovative ideas and solutions for urban issues from participants across the country. This particular aspect is very important in view of the fact that urban India emerges within an increasingly global world and the idea of the 'world-class cities' has captured the imagination of policy makers *et. al.* The principal objective of advanced training and information exchange is to re-examine the urban visions and the critical questions of urban growth and development that underpin the urban issues.

Training institutions play a better role in imparting expert training to municipal functionaries by keeping pace with the prevailing conditions of radical and rapid changes taking place in urban areas. The Governments at all levels must make the best use of the institutions, for otherwise their role will be stymied.

Training Methods for Urban Managers for Skill Upgradation

Training the municipal functionaries involved in grievance redressal and service delivery is a prerequisite particularly in these days of deteriorating administrative standards and the inadequate comprehension of the stakeholders of urban management about their role in enforcing citizen-friendly urban local governance. Specialisation in a particular line of activity improves the efficiency of the trained officials to perform their task better. Training should be imparted in the following directions:

- There should be a closer link between training and operational programmes and projects in order to offer field experience to trainees. The trainees should be enabled to undertake particular tasks within their work organisation;
- Training programmes should be geared to whole institutions, instead of training isolated individuals. The training modules should be so designed as to aim at transforming the overall competence and style of organisations;
- Training should aim at analytical and problem-skills rather than concentrating on professionally-oriented standards and techniques;
- Training should reorient professionals to a management role in plan implementation rather than mere plan preparation;
- Training implications in the development of new approaches to management should be concerned more with enabling rather than with direct provision which implies the need for new skills in communication, response to and support for community and individual initiatives. Training is also required in new skills in revaluation, monitoring, quality assurances etc; and
- Training should aim at the output value of training programme. This implies the need for training programme to be tailored precisely to the specific needs of a particular situation; this involves a great deal of preparation, research and material gathering. There is a need for rigorous selection of trainees according to suitability and relevance to the course, and participants must be given adequate time to prepare for training.

To sum up, the capacities of both institutions and municipal functionaries have to be improved through education, research, training, hand-holding, and policy support to ULGs. The absence of professional institutions of excellence to perform the above task is a key issue in urban management. The High Powered Expert Committee recommended the establishment of five centres of Indian Institutes of Urban Management, which should be institutions of excellence that should be used for upgrading the skills of existing personnel in all branches of urban governance. The Committee recommends the creation of a Reform and Performance Management Cell (RPMC) which will be supported by the Centres of Excellence/Innovation.[8] The NIUM, established as per the suggestion of High Powered Expert Committee, aims at filling this gap. The NIUM is entrusted with the responsibility to train both municipal functionaries and public representatives in activities relating to administration, finance, accounts and audit, public health engineering, public works, maintenance of civic services, social development, e-governance etc.

References

1. JNNURM Toolkit for Comprehensive Capacity Building Programme, *MoUD, GoI*, April, 2013, p. 2.
2. Richard Batley and Nick Devas, *The Management of Urban Development*, Birmingham, U.K., 1988 p. 110
3. Baba K. Dey, Work Culture in India-Achievements and Failures, *The Indian Journal of Public Administration*, April-June, 1989, Vol. XXXV, No. 2. p. 168.
4. G.Palnithurai (ed) *Dynamics of New Panchayat Raj System in India*, Vol.VI, Capacity Building, Concept Publishing Company, New Delhi, 2009, quoted in Book Reviews, Local Government Quarterly, Vol. LXXIX, No.2, April-June, 2009, p. 112.
5. Centre for Good Governance, *Urban Reforms and Municipal Services in Andhra Pradesh*, Capacity Enhancement Needs Assessment Study, Hyderabad 2003, p. 6.
6. G. Sai Prasad, *Accountability of Urban Local Governments in India*, Atlantic Publishers, New Delhi, 2007.
7. G. Sai Prasad, *op. cited*.
8. HPEC *Report on India Urban Infrastructure and Services*, New Delhi, 2100, p. 108-09.

11

Summary and Conclusion

In the foregoing chapters of this thesis an attempt is made to indicate the objectives of the study, to analyse the structure, functions, duties and powers of the ULGs in India vis-à-vis their role in the changing urban scenario, their relation with the central and the state government, to examine the problems of providing infrastructure in urban areas and the management of urban development, to dwell on the problems of urban finance, to discuss the poverty initiatives in the country. The present chapter sets forth a summary of what is presented in the preceding chapters and puts forth concluding observations.

Urban development in India is stunted since urban areas have received scant attention of governments regarding their problems and solutions. It could not evolve a policy to match the increasing complexities posing a serious threat to stakeholders of urban development and management. The multi-dimensional decline of the Urban Local Governments necessitates the urgency of reforms. The official machinery of the ULGs and the political organs are to be so restructured as to function as active partners in development of the towns and cities. This requires a major policy decision on the part of the government and political will for its fulfilment. Efficient urban local governance implies higher performance not only in managing local services that best satisfy the tax payers but also in enabling local communities solve their problems and to create a better future for their stakeholders.

The Constitution (74th Amendment) Act, 1992 infused new blood into city governance in the country but the efficacy has not been achieved owing to various factors like inadequacy of urban administrative machinery and lack of a state-wide broad-based urban cadre, both administrative and technical. The Municipal Directorate (or the Commissionerate as called in certain states) is to be strengthened to function not only as a vital channel of communication but also as a staff agency to provide managerial and technical service.

Urban administration must be reorganised to suit the fast changing urban scenario. It is impossible to prevent rural push and urban pull in the coming years since urban areas only have the facilities for training professionals as a result of which the children of the migrants to urban areas will enjoy the advantages of educational and employment opportunities. Instead of taking up measures for prevention of urbanisation, Government must make efforts to improve the quality of urban life by large scale investment for provision and maintenance of urban infrastructure to keep pace with rapid urbanisation so that urban life can be sustained. Such investment can be financed by loans and grants from central and state governments. The financial resources of the ULGs are not sufficient to finance urban infrastructure and its maintenance. If cities have to continue to function as the political, commercial, financial and industrial centres the Governments have to provide the needed financial investment without hesitation.

The rapid deterioration of urban environment caused by acute shortage of housing, pressure on infrastructure and service facilities is a matter of serious concern. Added to it are proliferation of slums and rapidly increasing air pollution which are visible symptoms of the urban malaise. The central and state governments have to assess the magnitude and severity of the urban problems and the urgency of alleviating it in the interests of both welfare and economic growth so that the process of change can start.

It is obvious from the analysis presented in the preceding chapter that urban administration needs a special attention in view of the Challenges that urbanisation creates. The Governments, have to take special measures to sustain urban life in order to get the maximum benefit of urbanisation. The policy makers, planners and administrators have to keep these factors in view in preparing plan outlay every year and in policy formulation so that the lakhs of people attracted into the expanding folds of cities and towns feel at home in urban areas of the country. The translation of this ideal into action demands a policy framework in which urban development finds its firm place. Besides the above, Urban Local Bodies should create local administrative machinery, quite different from the existing self-seeking, aggrandised, corrupt system, to move forward with dedication and commitment to civic welfare which responds to public expectation promptly and without any hope of reward, and which establishes a lasting partnership with the citizens in their endeavour to provide a citizen-friendly administration.To achieve this objective:

1. A public information system has to be established to enlighten the citizens about the services rendered by the Urban Local Government and the procedure prescribed to avail themselves of those services.
2. Citizens have to be sensitised about their duties and responsibilities towards local government so that they play their role effectively and efficiently to help Urban Local Government serve them to their best satisfaction. The ULGs should create public consciousness about the programmes and decisions of the ULGs affecting public interest so that citizens' feedback improves the performance of the ULG.
3. A public grievance redressal system has to be set up to redress public grievances within a prescribed time frame.

After examining the various aspects of Urban Local Governments, it is appropriate to incorporate the various suggestions received from the public and officials of the municipal corporation and academicians who responded to the questionnaires administered to them to make this study more practical:

- A planned urban development process is essential for balancing the imbalances in the growth of urban areas which calls for capacity building at the local level and the creation of an appropriate institution at the regional level to attend to the task of planning of city development;
- The ULGs in India suffer from excessive administrative and financial control of the State Governments which prevents

them from functioning independently in decision-making. Despite democratic decentralisation over the decades, it is only on paper but not in practice and administration has been moving towards more and more centralisation. The ULGs in India have a long history as service delivery vehicles but not vehicles for local level accountability. As a result the ULGs are not accountable to the people. Urban areas are governed by a plethora of agencies with weak coordination and very weak accountability. Decentralisation of powers and responsibilities should be accompanied by devolution of adequate funds;

- In regard to devolution of funds it is suggested that there should be uniform laws for the governance of the ULGs all over the country so that all ULGs are covered whenever a policy decision is taken by governments. Transfer of functions and devolution of funds to ULGs from year to year shall be governed by a policy framework both at the centre and the states duly defining the criteria;
- In regard to urban finance, ULGs should achieve financial self-sufficiency through raising their internal resources so as to meet the expenditure on maintenance of urban infrastructure required for expanding urban areas. At the same time it is necessary that urban dwellers must be relieved of the heavy burden of direct taxes and instead user charges should be introduced in place of taxes and the deficit between requirement and local revenue must be filled through central and state government grants. Some of the respondents are of the staunch opinion that rural areas contiguous with towns and cities are enjoying the infrastructure created by the ULGs but they are paying taxes to the *gram panchayats*. Hence, all the rural areas contiguous with well developed urban areas should be merged with the adjoining towns or cities and should be brought under the administrative control of the adjoining Urban Local Governments for mutual advantage. It is significant that certain state governments have decided to constitute all villages with more than 40,000 population as

municipalities and to merge the rural areas with urban characteristics and contiguous with towns or cities into the nearby towns or cities so that the benefits of urbanisation can be extended to the rural areas contiguous with urban areas;

- In regard to administrative reforms in the ULGs for improved service delivery and ensuring accountability, changes are required in the administrative system for transforming the grassroots level bureaucracy, who are the real service providers to the people. There is the need to have legal, regulatory and participatory measures through which accountability of ULG staff can be enhanced. The local political and social process should be so organised that they would not hinder the effectiveness of the accountability of the ULGs. Besides, there has to be an intensive campaign carried out to disseminate information on the developments in the ULGs and inviting the cooperation of citizens wherever and whenever required;
- The local administration should fix priorities for providing services on the basis of their necessity. For example, providing adequate safe drinking water is a top priority item, followed by sanitation, health facilities, street lighting etc. The decentralisation measures should continue since this process helps the urbanites avail themselves of the services to the full extent and file legal complaints and reach consumer courts in case of dissatisfaction. Administration at grassroots level should be made responsible to people's needs duly upgrading human resources quality and insisting on result-consciousness and time-frame with delegation and accountability built into the system by gearing the official machinery to show its excellence in the performance of their functions through incentives and reward for better performance and punishments for poor performance. This needs organisation of the working conditions, work systems, methods of work disposal, skill utilisation in the ULGs such that the marked employees' dissatisfaction is removed and that their performance will improve. Besides, diligent employees should be given adequate opportunities for personal development in their service or

organisation duly making the best use of their knowledge and skills. There has to be unity of command-every employee should receive order, direction or command from his immediate superior officer only so that the confusion due to multiplicity of directions or instructions will not affect the efficiency and quality of his work or the result of his functions. The service conditions of the Local Government employees must be improved from its present lacklustre state so as to attract real talent into local government service who would perform their tasks with vision, foresight, commitment and dedication. To further ensure the accountability of the municipal functionaries it is suggested that performance audit of the ULGs should not be conducted by the government staff since it will reduce the scope for independent functioning. Instead, performance audit should be conducted by independent organisations without government control so that performance audit serves as a corrective mechanism. It is also necessary to create new structures of accountability through facilitating a greater role for citizens in urban governance and enhancing the answerability of the official machinery and the elected representatives. Citizens' involvement and participation in governance enhances the accountability of the ULG staff since this enables the citizens of what is legitimately due to them from local self-governments;

- In regard to the accountability of public representatives it must be noted that at present public representatives are not answerable to anyone and will not own any responsibility for their failures or offences or incapacity or irresponsibility. Hence the principle of accountability must be included in the functions of the elected public representatives to ensure that they act in a manner that is above reproach and disqualification of elected members for failure of accountability to the public must be introduced so that the local government representatives become aware of their functions and duties and perform them with care and a sense of responsibility. Transparency in urban governance enables urban dwellers a better understanding of the functioning of the ULG that ultimately leads to its effective accountability to urbanites;

- In regard to private sector participation in the development and maintenance of civic infrastructure, it should be encouraged through implementing innovative reforms in municipal tax structure, levy and collection of user charges and exploitation of other income generating sources so that private sector can be assured of the cost-effectiveness of the infrastructure it has created. In the absence of this assurance the private sector will not come forward to actively participate in the development of civic infrastructure; and
- In regard to the functioning of the citizen charter it is necessary to improve the system further. An institution like the Ombudsman (as in Sweden) should be created in every ULG to receive grievances from the public on any issues relating to planning and implementation of development programmes or civic affairs with short redressal time to have positive impact and which should be empowered to order corrective measures.

It shall be ultimately concluded that a local self government institution functions efficiently only when the citizens play their role efficiently. It is not enough if the people make themselves the local sovereign but they should, at the same time, make themselves intelligent.

Bibliography

1. Amareswar Mishra, *Urban Government and Administration in India* Anu Books, Meerut, India, 1986.
2. Bhushan, B., *Micro Entrepreneurship as an Effective Tool of Eradicating Urban Poverty and Unemployment: Lessons & Agenda for Reforms,* Planning Commission, New Delhi, 2008.
3. Bhushan, B., *Promoting Socio-Economic Empowerment of the Poor for Grass Root Development,* Planning Commission, New Delhi, 2008.
4. Centre for Good Governance, *Urban reforms and Municipal Services in Andhra Pradesh, Capacity Enhancement Needs Assessment Study,* Hyderabad, 2003.
5. Chahar, S.S. (Ed), *Governance at Grassroots Level in India.*
6. Darshini Mahadevia (ed), *Inside the Transforming Urban Asia, Process, Policies and Public Actions,* Concept Publishing Company, New Delhi, 2008.
7. Darshini Mahadevia, *Sustainable Urban Development in India: An Inclusive Perspective,* UNRISD, Geneva, 2002.
8. David Stterthwaite (Ed), *Sustainable Cities,* Earthscan Publications Limited, London, 1999.
9. Dennis A. Rondinelli, *Extending Urban Basic Services in Developing Countries: Policy Options and Organisational Choices*, Syracuse, New York, U.S.A., 1986.
10. Department of Municipal Administration, Government of A.P, *Urban Sector Profile of A.P.* Hyderabad, 2008.
11. Emiel A.Wagelin, *New Approaches in Urban Service Delivery,* Cities, U.K., August, 1990.
12. Gwendyn Hallsmith, *The Key to Sustainable Cities.*
13. Dr. Isher Judge Ahluwalia, *Report on Indian Urban Infrastructure and Services, March 2011.*
14. http://urbanisation.nic.in.

15. Jagannadham, V. and N.S. Bakshi, *Property Tax Administration,* Indian Institute of Public Administration, I.P. Estate, New Delhi-1, 1971.
16. Lakshmi Narayana, M., *Sustainable Development of Cities.*
17. Meshram, D.S. and M.L.Chotani. *Urban Infrastructure Development: Issues and Options,* in *Urban Infrastructure Development* released by 47th National Town & Country Planners Congress, Bhuvaneswar, December, 1998.
18. Ministry of Housing & Urban Poverty Alleviation, *Toolkit on Comprehensive Capacity Building Programme for Improved Urban Governance & Poverty Reduction* issued JNNURM Mission Directorate, 2009.
19. Mohanty, P.K., *Urban Sector Reform Agenda: Financing Civic Services and Development*, Centre for Good Governance, Hyderabad, 2005.
20. Mohanty, P.K., *Cities and Public Policy*, SAGE, New Delhi, 2014.
21. Mohanty, P.K. (Ed.), *Urbanisation in India*, SAGE, New Delhi, 2014.
22. Muttalib, M.A. and Mohd. Akbar Ali Khan, *Restructuring of Property Tax Administration* RCUES, Hyderabad and Sterling Publishers Private Limited, New Delhi, 1985.
23. Muttalib, M.A. and N.Umapathy, *Urban Government and Administration,* 1980, Regional Centre for Urban and Environmental Studies, Osmania University, Hyderabad.
24. Nadkarni, D.V. *Manual of Meetings*, Local Self-Government Institute, 11, Elphinstone Circle, Fort, Bombay-1, 1950.
25. Niraja Gopal Jayal *(Ed) Local Governance in India, Decentralisation and Beyond*, Oxford University Press, New Delhi, 2006.
26. Peter Roberts and Huge Sykes, *Urban Regeneration.*
27. Pranati Datta, *Urbanisation in India,* Kolkata, June 2006.
28. Prasad, R.N., *Urban Local Self Government in India*, Mittal Publications, New Delhi, 2008.
29. Richard Batley and Nick Devas, *The Management of Urban Development*, Birmingham, U.K., 1988.
30. Shabbir Cheema, G., *Strengthening of Urban Institutional Capabilities: Issues and Responses,* UNCRD, Nagoya, Japan, 1990.
31. Singh, U.B., *Urban Administration in India,* Serials Publications, New Delhi, 2008.
32. Singh, U.B., *Urban Local Government,* Rawat Publications, Jaipur, 1997.
33. Singh, U.B., Ed. *Ethics and Social Accountability in Urban Governance*, New Delhi, 2014.

34. Sujatha Srikumar, *Urban Infrastructure Development in India* 2008, IL & FS Infrastructure Development Corporation Ltd.
35. Sundaram, P.S.A., *Maintenance of Urban Infrastructure in India: Certain Management and Financial Issues*, Chennai, 2008.
36. Thomas L. Blair *(Ed.) Urban Innovation Abroad: Problem Cities in Search of Solutions*, Plenum Press, New York, 1984.
37. UN-HABITAT Paper on *"Urban Policies and the Right to the City, Towards Good Governance and Local Democracy"* UNESCO, March, 2005.
38. UN-HABITAT www.unhabitat.org/www.unesco.org/shs/urban/rtte
39. Urban Poverty Report 2009, World Bank, Oxford University Press, New Delhi, 2009.

Articles

1. Centre for Good Governance, *Indira Kranti Padham-Urban,* Municipal Administration & Urban Development Department, Government of Andhra Pradesh, A.C. Guards, Hyderabad, 500004, 2007.
2. Dr A. Gunasekharan, *Good Governance in Reduction of Poverty.*
3. C.Nagaraja Rao, *Kudumbashree* (case studies) 2006.
4. Sriram Maheshwari, *Accountability in Public Administration: Towards a Conceptual Framework* paper submitted to the Seminar-cum-Workshop on Developments in Public Administration, April 18-20, 1991, IIPA, New Delhi.
5. Greater Municipal Corporation of Hyderabad, *Official Manual, Greater Hyderabad Municipal Corporation,* Hyderabad, 2008.
6. Arabi, U, *"Recent Urbanisation Trends : Their Impact on the Poor in the Developing World,* Local Government Quarterly, April-June, 2009, Vol. LXXIX, No. 2, All India Institute of Local Self-Government, Mumbai.
7. *Urban Finance* by Om Prakash Mathur in India Infrastructure Report 2006, Oxford University Press, New Delhi, 2006.

Acts

1. A.P. Municipalities Act, 1965.
2. Greater Hyderabad Municipal Corporation Act, 1955.
3. A.P. Municipal Corporations Act, 1994.
4. M. Satyanarayanamurty Naidu, *Municipal Office Manual*, Triveni Publishers, Machilipatnam, A. P., India, 1979.
5. District Office Manual, Government of Andhra Pradesh, Hyderabad, 1959. Various Orders of the Government of Andhra Pradesh.

Index